Energy Law and the Sustainable Company

T0358475

What kind of decision making should multinationals engage in to create a sustainable company? There is substantial debate over why CEOs, senior management and boards of directors make the wrong decisions by not asking the right questions, with the result that not only is the company itself damaged, but all of the stakeholders find themselves at a detriment.

Focusing on innovation, technology transfer and the use of intangible assets, *Energy Law and the Sustainable Company* features case studies from the oil and gas sector, to illustrate how to develop a sustainable business. Considering corporate social responsibility from the perspective of international and national law, the book demonstrates how companies can be both profitable and ethical using the influences of psychology to encourage senior decision makers to make the right decisions. It is revealed that reputation is the main principle influencing decision making. The book also discusses how companies have reported on their sustainability strategy and considers how technology transfer and intangible assets may play a part in addressing global sustainability.

This book should be invaluable reading to students and scholars of Sustainable Business, Business Law, Corporate Social Responsibility, Environmental and Energy Law as well as Environmental and Energy Management.

Patricia Park is a visiting expert at Cass Business School, City University London, UK.

Duncan M. Park is a Director and intellectual property consultant at Leogriff AS, Norway.

Routledge Research in Sustainability and Business

Energy Law and the Sustainable Company

Innovation and corporate social responsibility

Patricia Park and Duncan M. Park

Routledge
Taylor & Francis Group

LONDON AND NEW YORK

First published 2016
by Routledge

2 Park Square, Milton Park, Abingdon, Oxfordshire OX14 4RN
711 Third Avenue, New York, NY 10017

Routledge is an imprint of the Taylor & Francis Group, an informa business

Firstissuedinpaperback2017

British Library Cataloguing in Publication Data
A catalogue record for this book is available from the British Library

Library of Congress Cataloging in Publication Data
Park, Patricia D., author.
Energy law and the sustainable company : innovation and corporate social
responsibility / Patricia Park and Duncan Park.
pages cm
ISBN 978-1-138-78594-6 (hb) -- ISBN 978-1-315-76578-5 (e-book)
1. Energy industries--Law and legislation. 2. Corporate governance--Law
and legislation. 3. Social responsibility of business. 4. Sustainable
development--Law and legislation. I. Park, Duncan, author. II. Title.
K3981.P369 2016
333.79068'4--dc23
2015020494

ISBN: 978-1-138-78594-6 (hbk)
ISBN: 978-0-8153-6444-3 (pbk)

Typeset in Times New Roman
by Taylor & Francis Books

Contents

Preface

This book evolved as part of over 25 years of research and teaching corporate social responsibility to MBA students, philosophy in research to Ph.D. candidates, and international law specialising in the environmental and energy sector of one author; in addition to over 20 years of experience as an intellectual property professional both as an internal corporate advisor and consultant, and in private practice of the other author.

We have worked together for a number of years and had many conversations on how to influence both the decision makers of tomorrow, that is the post graduate students, on the one hand, and current decision makers, that is the senior managers in the energy sector, on the other. We were greatly influenced by the publications of a number of Nobel Laureates including James M. Buchanan, whose seminal work *Liberty, Market and State* introduced the thought that you cannot change people; they are as they are and you must take them as such. Colin Mayer's book, *Firm Commitment*, confirmed our line of thinking. But if you take Buchanan's thesis, how can anything be changed for the better?

We then started to discuss our thoughts with psychologists who introduced us to the concept of 'nudge theory'. This opened up a new line of research and so, based on nudge theory, we set up a number of interviews with high level decision makers. As our specialisation is in the energy sector, and we have high level contacts in major multinational oil and gas companies, we used these to interview and define what the most important factors were with regard to decision making. These interviews were used to inform the study, and the main point to come out of them was that reputation was of paramount importance with regard to the sustainability of the company.

Given that this was the strongest point to come from the interviews we used reputation as one of the main themes within the book. As the law is the basis of company sustainability, we considered both hard law and soft law in respect of whether the law should be changed. How state law is enforceable within the state and sometimes beyond; how soft law, in the form of guidelines and norms, can be enforceable. This includes intangible assets such as intellectual property and how these should be included in any strategic plan for a sustainable company.

The law can be interpreted in a number of different ways and sometimes people will interpret the law to their own advantage rather than that of the company or civil society. Firstly we considered Hofstede's research on cultural differences to decide if different cultures had different approaches to society, employment and decision making. With respect to differing interpretation of the law, at this point we brought in behavioural economics and here we are indebted to Fiona Butcher who gave unstintingly of her time and extensive knowledge and advice. We didn't realise that the psychology of law and decision making could be such fun.

We present our thoughts and findings as part of the discourse on the sustainability of multinational companies, particularly in the energy sector but these findings can be transferred to any multinational which may have an effect on sustainability and climate change in general.

Patricia Park
Cass Business School
City University
London

Duncan Park
Leogriff
Oslo

May 2015

1 Energy law and the sustainable company

Introduction

This book will be part of the current discussion on why Chief Executive Officers (CEOs), senior management and boards of directors make the wrong decisions by not asking the right questions, with the result that not only is the company itself damaged, sometimes beyond repair, but all of the stakeholders find themselves at a detriment. Just as people will always be imaginative in creating new ways of making money legally, so others will devote their talent to doing so illegally. As Professor James M. Buchanan described in his seminal work, *Liberty, Markets and State*, people are as they are and we can only accept them as such. So how does society encourage them to make the right decisions in favour of both making the company sustainable and to the benefit of society? Alternatively, how can society make sure that the right questions are asked and the right checks and balances are in place to make sure that the answers reflect best practice for the creation of long term sustainable value? If that structure is subverted, it becomes too easy for the senior decision maker to succumb to the temptation of self-dealing.[1]

It was Adam Smith who pointed out in *The Wealth of Nations* that: 'It is not from the benevolence of the butcher, the brewer, or the baker, that we expect our dinner, but from their regard to their own interest. We address ourselves not to their humanity but their self love.'[2]

We must remember that Adam Smith was not an economist as many people describe him, but a social philosopher, and his argument that the existence of selfish (or at least self interest) propensities suggests that those facets of human nature which incline man to the social state cannot of themselves be sufficient to sustain it in any degree of harmony or order. In other words, certain sources of control are required over the self-regarding activities of individual men/women; sources of control such as rules of justice and morality which must be known and observed by the members of any social group. This observation has been developed by others since Smith, but it is this fundamental discussion of the necessity and origin of those general rules that guide the activities of men which is of great importance, not least because it exposes one of the most characteristic features of his thought.

Smith's argument, therefore, suggests that social order becomes possible by virtue of the restraints which individuals impose upon themselves[3] and, if not, then by society.

The MacKinsey Global Survey July 2014, states: 'Executives at all levels see an important business role for sustainability. But when it comes to mastering the reputation, execution, and accountability of their sustainability programs, many companies have far to go.' Many other examples were identified by Monks and Minow in the fourth edition of their book *Corporate Governance,* including:

> After working as a very successful CEO for three years without a written contract, the CEO asked the Board to provide him with one. This would not be considered unusual as about one third of Fortune 5000 CEOs had written contracts outlining the negotiated terms leading to their employment. What was unusual was that the CEO required an unprecedented clause in the contract which stated that a conviction of a felony was not grounds for the termination of the contract, unless the felony was directly and materially injurious to the corporation. Did any member of the Board ask "what was the need for such a clause and why now after three years of employment?" No, the Board of Tyco signed the contract.
>
> Another very successful company was presented with the concept of a "special purpose entity" that would allow the company to move some of its debt off the balance sheet. However, this would be a violation of the company's conflict of interest rules. Again did the Board ask any questions? No, the Board of Enron agreed to the waiver on three separate occasions.[4]

They ask the question 'What is wrong here?'

Globalisation

The globalisation of business means that companies must improve their awareness of the effects of their increasingly complex and diverse operations in a wide variety of geographical regions and cultures, some of which may be unfamiliar to management until recently. There are many books on Corporate Social Responsibility (CSR) but none consider the subject within the context of law and regulation. Also there is no published work on the use of intangible assets to develop a sustainable company and yet Intellectual Property Rights (IPR) and knowledge transfer are becoming more important under international treaties.

The purpose of this book is to develop ideas based on current legal requirements, both at international and state level. We will lay out a strong argument to identify how companies can be both ethical and profitable by encouraging CEOs to behave ethically in the interests of making a sustainable company. The starting point of the book is the development of corporate social responsibility and the modern version as a more systematic and integrated programme; we then go on to assess the environmental and social impact of business and how to manage it in a strategic and sustainable manner.

Many international treaties require technology and knowledge transfer which introduces the concept of how a company may develop technology and knowledge transfer to the benefit and sustainability of a multinational company. Multinationals must comply with not only the jurisdiction within which they operate but also public international law, which may impose more onerous standards than do local laws. The understanding of legal concepts, rules and process are essential to businesses which have limited liability, lender responsibility, and shareholder rights. Additionally the responsibilities of the parent company for subsidiaries are all central to understanding a company's responsibilities and liabilities.

Business activities are described, facilitated and confined by the law, and a fundamental of sound corporate governance policy is legal compliance with international minimum standards. Understanding the nature and impact of legal obligations on the business is a basic precondition to designing not only a workable but also a sustainable business strategy.

However, the proposed solutions to such problems are not always in the form of law. The threats to order and justice that emerge over time can give rise to a number of responses, of which legal regulation has become perhaps the most prevalent in the twentieth century. Laws reflect current needs and are inevitably responsive. For example, society demanded guarantees of a right to privacy only when technology threatened that privacy, and government intrusion necessitated a response. In the international arena, law is not the only form of social control or normative claim. Other forms of requirements of behaviour emerge from morality, courtesy, and social custom.[5] Compliance with such norms is expected and violations can be sanctioned. Like legal norms, they grow out of the understanding and values of society. The role of non-binding norms in the international legal system, UN Norms and Guidelines, and the commercial codes of the International Chamber of Commerce and International Accountancy and Sustainability Reporting all go to reputational value.

No challenge derails managers from the goal of sustainability more than understanding what it means for an organisation to really be sustainable. Some people think sustainability is all about environmental issues. Others see it in terms of the bottom line. And then, of course, there are people who use the term synonymously with corporate social responsibility and shared value.

A good example of sustainability is the investment approach taken by Norwegian sovereign wealth funds, which put aside royalties from natural resources for future generations and deploy the interest to meet current needs. Unfortunately, most countries, including Canada and the United Kingdom (UK), spend royalties as they accrue, exploiting the wealth in the ground, leaving little for future generations.

The corporate social responsibility camp focuses on balancing current stakeholder interests. A socially responsible oil company would build local schools and hospitals to compensate communities for their resource extraction. But such measures do not always acknowledge the long-term impact on the communities. Keep in mind that schools and hospitals require staff and ongoing servicing. So CSR measures can actually impose long-term liabilities on affected communities, making good-intentioned actions unsustainable. So the question to be considered is: Should CSR remain a voluntary principle or should aspects of it be legislated for on a mandatory basis? Much of the accepted CSR agenda is already a requirement under both international and some national legislation. However, if there was legislation covering the full extent of CSR, business could grind to a halt simply by attempting to be in compliance with legislation on every statute book.

The book will argue that there should be sufficient legislation to create a level playing field which must apply to all corporations wherever they may be located. The main problem, however, would be one of enforcement. If it remains voluntary, as supported by the International Chamber of Commerce (ICC), how would CEOs and senior managers be persuaded to comply? This is the essence of the book and will be discussed within the context of the theories of James M. Buchanan and Colin Mayer's theories on trust to change senior managers' behaviour to create a sustainable company. The book concludes that the most effective and sustainable changes in behaviour will come from the successful integration of cultural, regulatory and individual change.

Imperatives of international law and norms

In his book *Globalization: A Very Short Introduction,* Steger states that: 'At its core...globalization is about shifting forms of human contact.'[6] However, Muchlinski[7] states that globalisation is in itself an ideologically contested concept. Nevertheless, these two approaches have influenced the developing concept of 'global consumerism' as discussed from the international corporate social responsibility perspective in Chapter 6.

Both scholars and judicial decision makers have characterised the international legal system as a system of equal and sovereign nation states whose actions are limited only by rules freely accepted as legally binding.

> International law governs relations between independent states. The rules of law binding upon States therefore emanate from their own free will as expressed in conventions or by usages generally accepted as expressing principles of law and established in order to regulate the relations between these coexisting independent communities or with a view to the achievement of common aims.[8]

Brierly defines international law as 'the body of rules and principles of action which are binding upon civilised states in their relations with one another'.[9] Originally this state-centred system excluded any role for non-state actors and was based upon a belief in the factual as well as the legal independence of states.

Obligations were largely bilateral between two or more states and enforced by self-help with the subject matter of international legal regulation limited largely to diplomatic relation, the maritime sector, trade and extradition. Shelton notes that the international legal system has undergone tremendous changes recently inasmuch as historically being dominated by western states there are now more than four times as many states than existed at the beginning of the twentieth century. Additionally other communities have emerged, who now play an important role in the international arena. Intergovernmental organisations, non-governmental organisations, professional associations, transnational corporations, and mixed entities all contribute to the making of international norms. What is more, they are increasingly bound by these norms.

Subjects once deemed as private have now passed into the public sector and from there into issues of transnational concern.[10] The expanding management of the international commons is now regulated through complex multilateral agreements with supervisory organs established to implement, monitor, and enforce compliance. Technological change has also made possible communications and travel, which places new problems on the global agenda, such as human rights, where the duty is owed to those within the state rather than the state itself. The needs and approaches of international environmental law and the notion of the protection of the 'commons' requires state reporting as a supervisory mechanism and has become widespread in international instruments concerning environmental protection.

Hard law and soft law

The lines between law and non-law may seem blurred, and even more so the need for compliance. This is part of an increasingly complex international system which includes a varying form of instruments with a common purpose of regulating behaviour within a legal framework. Frequently hard law instruments can be identified by the internal provisions and final clauses, but these are becoming increasingly difficult to identify. For example the Commission on Sustainable Development supervises the implementation of Agenda 21. Whereas in other instances, states have been asked to submit reports on implementation of, and compliance with, declarations and programmes of action in a manner that almost duplicates the mechanisms utilised in treaties.

Many scholars have distinguished hard law by claiming that any breach will give rise to legal consequences; whereas the breach of a soft law norm gives rise to political consequences. However, the breach of a soft law norm will also go to due diligence. This may result in an unfavourable outcome if the breach becomes the subject of litigation. It seems that more often compliance with soft law cannot be separated from the issue of more active participation of non-state actors, such as the International Chamber of Commerce. Public participation is not only a goal but a reality in the development and implementation of international norms, and so soft law permits non-state actors a role that is rarely included in the more traditional hard law making process.

International law in relation to multinational enterprises

The role of multinationals as special interest groups that seek to influence the development of the law in a manner conducive to the furtherance of their interests cannot be ignored. There is little doubt that multinationals lobby governments and international governmental organisations to ensure that normative development is business friendly.[11] They may not always be successful, as their failure in the Multilateral Agreements on Investment (MAI) or the adoption of investment rules by the World Trade Organization (WTO) may suggest. However, their influence on domestic legal developments may be considered to be more successful.[12] Another significant group of non-actors who influence the development of rules and procedures in the wider area of international business regulation are the non-governmental organisations (NGOs). Not only are they active in the area of human rights protection but NGOs have been increasingly active in the field of foreign investment, purporting to represent the voice of 'civil society' or public participation. It is together that multinationals and civil society groups may be seen as the informal initiators of regulatory actions while seeking to further their respective policy interests.

Much of the earlier legal literature on multinational enterprises and their investment in foreign countries has concentrated on the host state country along with the international relations literature.[13] However, more recently, this concentration on the host state has been questioned.[14] The bulk of international obligations have previously fallen to the host nations whilst the multinational investor companies and their home states have few. However, increasingly, attention is being paid to the duties of the multinational companies towards the countries in which they invest under the guise of 'international corporate social responsibility'. Additionally it is required that the home states undertake certain responsibilities. Given that the majority of the multinationals' home states are developed, whilst the host states are frequently underdeveloped or developing, it is becoming more relevant to impose certain duties on home states to provide incentives for technology transfer. It is the home state's legal and regulatory system which may be used to ensure that multinationals based there conform to certain standards of good corporate citizenship through sanctions within the home country legislation providing redress for claimants from outside the home country who are in dispute with the parent company for the acts of its overseas subsidiaries.[15] This discussion brings us on to considering areas of jurisdiction with regard to both the home and the host states.

Jurisdictional limits of regulation

The principal jurisdictional level for the regulation of multinational companies remains at the nation state. However, this creates a problem of extra-territoriality due to the international nature of organisation and management within the multinational company structure. We therefore need to consider the rules of public international law concerning state jurisdiction and state practice. In particular how the various bases of extraterritorial jurisdiction have been used in the fields of prescriptive, personal, and enforcement jurisdiction.

The legal regulation of state jurisdiction is covered by rules of public international law, which are based on the exclusive sovereignty of each state over the territory it controls. As all states are equal in the eyes of international law, this power is enjoyed by states without let or hindrance from any other sovereign state. Consequently each state has a reserved domain of domestic jurisdiction. However, this has as its corollary a duty of non-intervention on the part of other states.[16]

The idea that this principle of state jurisdiction be observed to the letter, however, would severely restrict any assertion of extraterritorial jurisdiction by a state's legitimate interest in the effective enforcement of its laws against multinational organisations. This would then raise the question of whether the territorial principle can be modified to justify a measure of extraterritorial jurisdiction. According to Brownlie,[17] international law is developing in the light of the need to modify the territorial principle. Therefore, alternative bases of jurisdiction (subject to the reservation that these must preserve a substantial and genuine connection between the subject matter of jurisdiction and the territorial base, and reasonable interests) are being sought by the state seeking to exercise jurisdiction.[18] Various exceptions have been put forward but three are of particular relevance to the regulation of multinationals: the principles of nationality, protective jurisdiction, and objective territorial jurisdiction.[19]

Nationality

It is accepted that in certain cases a state can assert jurisdiction over its nationals abroad.[20] According to this principle, the home state of a multinational could seek to justify jurisdiction over activities of an overseas subsidiary in a number of situations. For example, the managers of an overseas subsidiary, by reason of their home country nationality, could be subjected to home country legal requirements. Should there be no home nationals on the board of the subsidiary, or they are in the minority, then the home state could require the parent company to order its overseas subsidiaries to act in compliance with home country laws by reason of the nationality of the parent company as the principle shareholder in the foreign subsidiary. This will have the effect of disregarding the foreign nationality of incorporation of the subsidiary.[21] Alternatively, where the parent company operates abroad through unincorporated branches, these will retain the nationality of the parent and could be subject to the direct jurisdiction of the home country by reason of their corporate nationality.[22]

Protective jurisdiction

Almost all states accept the right of a state to exercise extraterritorial jurisdiction over acts done abroad which adversely affect the vital interests of the regulating state.[23] Under the 1982 United Nations Convention on the Law of the Sea a coastal state has the authority to create regulations over not only its territorial waters but also the extended economic zone up to 200 nautical miles. This is not only to protect the security of its coastline but also in order to protect the ecosystems therein, including fish stocks and, in addition, mineral wealth. Carrying this forward it is arguable that the exercise of this extra-territorial jurisdiction extends to multinational companies in areas of public governmental regulation. An example of this would be the control of tax avoidance by the parent company through the use of transfer price manipulation between itself and its foreign subsidiaries. However, this could only be argued in the genuine public interests of the regulating state and those designed to favour its commercial interests at the expense of other states.

Objective territorial jurisdiction

The modification of the strict territorial jurisdiction arises where the elements of a criminal offence are commenced in one state and are completed in another. This has given effect to the assertion by states of an objective territorial jur-isdiction over offences initiated abroad and completed within the jurisdiction.[24] The Permanent Court of International Justice (PCIJ) accepted this 'objective' principle as a valid basis for the exercise of state jurisdiction in criminal matters in the case of *The Lotus*.[25] The Turkish courts had convicted, on a charge of involuntary manslaughter, the officer of the watch on a French ship that had collided with a Turkish vessel on the high seas, causing the death of a number of Turkish nationals on board the Turkish ship. The PCIJ held that Turkey was entitled to exercise its criminal jurisdiction on the basis that the effects of the offence were produced on the Turkish vessel. Under maritime law the Turkish vessel could be regarded as a place assimilated to Turkish territory, and that, therefore, the offence was committed within Turkish territory, even though the perpetrator was, at the time, aboard the French ship. The PCIJ held that states retained a wide measure of discretion in respect of the application of their laws and the jurisdiction of their courts to persons, property, and acts outside their territory.

Although the PCIJ did not clarify the limits of this discretion, later decisions of the International Court of Justice (ICJ) have stressed the need for a genuine connection between the subject matter of the claimed jurisdiction and the territory of the state seeking to exercise its jurisdiction.[26] However, the applica-tion of the objective principle gives rise to two main areas of dispute. Firstly, the activity involved may be criminal in the state where it is completed but not in the state where it was initiated.[27] Secondly, there is the problem of establishing a sufficient causal link or nexus between the initiation and completion of the crime to justify applying the objective principle.

Having considered these developments to the strict extraterritoriality principle in international law we will turn to consider how state practice has evolved in relation to the extraterritorial regulation of multinational companies.

Although there is a general presumption against the extraterritorial application of legislation, claims have also arisen in the context of economic issues when some states, and in particular the United States of America, have sought to apply their laws outside their territory, in a manner which may precipitate conflicts with other states.[28] When claims are founded upon the territorial and nationality doctrine of jurisdiction, problems do not often arise, but claims made upon the basis of the 'effects' doctrine have provoked considerable controversy. This goes beyond the objective territorial principle to a situation where the state assumes jurisdiction on the grounds that the behaviour of a party is producing 'effects' within its territory. This is claimed even though all of the behaviour complained of is taking place within another state.[29] For example, the US regards subsidiaries of US companies abroad as of US nationality even where such companies have been incorporated abroad, while the state of incorporation has regarded them as of its nationality and thus subject not to US law but to its national law.[30] The US has vigorously maintained the 'effects' doctrine particularly in the area of antitrust regulation.[31] In the case of *US v Aluminum Co. of America,* the court declared that

> Any state may impose liabilities, even upon persons not within its allegiance, for conduct outside its borders that has consequences within its borders which the state reprehends.

This approach was reaffirmed by a series of later cases but was, to some extent, modified by the requirement of intention and the view that the effect should be substantial. Nevertheless, the wide-ranging nature of the approach aroused considerable opposition outside the US, as did American attempts to take evidence abroad under very broad pre-trial discovery provisions in US law and the possibility of treble damage awards.[32] In view of this considerable opposition by foreign states, the US courts modified their approach in the *Timberlane Lumber Co. v Bank of America*[33] and *Mannington Mills v Congoleum Corporation*[34] cases. In these cases the courts held that not only did the courts have to consider the effects test, but also a balancing test of 'a jurisdictional rule of reason'. This involved a consideration of other nations' interests and the full nature of the relationship between the actors concerned and the US. In the Supreme Court case of *Hartford Fire Insurance Co v California*[35] the majority judgment claimed that it was well established that the relevant Sherman Act 'applies to foreign conduct that was meant to produce and did in fact produce some substantial effect in the United States', but a dissenting opinion took the view that such exercise of extraterrestrial jurisdiction was subject to the test of reasonableness, with which the majority did not agree.

The *Hartford Insurance* case gave rise to considerable criticism as it was considered that the court was reviving the 'pure effects' approach to extraterritorial jurisdiction that effectively diminished the comity based balancing process developed in earlier cases. It was considered that this could only harm US economic relations with major trading partners and allow for an exercise of US jurisdiction in all but the clearest cases of conflict. Nevertheless this approach was endorsed by the US Department of Justice Antitrust Enforcement Guidelines for International Operations in 1995. Additionally, more recent cases have extended the operation of the *Hartford* approach from private party civil cases to criminal suits brought by the US Government.[36] Latterly there have been few major disputes over extraterritorial application of US antitrust law due to the adoption by the US of bilateral antitrust cooperation agreements with major trading partners.

That the US has been the most assertive in claiming jurisdiction over subsidiaries of a multinational company is perhaps not surprising. Not only is it the most dominant political power in the international economy, but it also has a legal experience based upon the creation of a unified transcontinental economy that has influenced its legislators, administrators and judges towards an acceptance of extraterritorial jurisdiction in most forms. However, this has led to conflicts generated by the US assertions of extraterritorial jurisdiction and given rise to numerous attempts to minimise it. The effects of trying to minimise conflicting requirements being placed upon multinational companies is still open to question.

Corporate governance and disclosure

Governance and disclosure has become a highly important issue in the wake of recent corporate scandals involving multinational companies including both the energy and financial sectors. Additionally there are a number of non-governmental stakeholders,[37] notably investors, creditors, employees, and consumers, who need information from the company about matters of direct concern to their interests; this results in demand for increased disclosure which has given rise to significant developments in national and regional disclosure laws and has stimulated new policy proposals. This in turn has given rise to calls for the enhancement of a multinational company's accountability through changes in the international structure of the corporation.

Reasons for enhanced accountability and disclosure

Apart from the traditional recipients of corporate information such as shareholders, bankers, lenders, and creditors, those interested in disclosure and accountability now include employees, trade unions, consumers, governments, and the general public. This has resulted in calls for a wider conception of disclosure than that needed by the financiers of the company.[38] In response the Organisation for Economic Co-operation and Development (OECD) has produced a guideline on disclosure.[39] The guideline also offers a summary of responses to the various concerns underlying international corporation disclosure. The guidelines should also be read in conjunction with the OECD *Principles of Corporate Governance* which offer more detailed analysis of the terms used in the disclosure guideline.[40] The basic starting point for disclosure in the *Principles of Corporate Governance* is that 'the corporate governance framework should ensure that timely and accurate disclosure is made on all material matters regarding the corporation, including the financial situation, performance, ownership and governance of the company'. This is deemed central to shareholders' ability to exercise their ownership rights on an informed basis and thus to allow capital markets to operate efficiently. Apart from shareholder interests, the disclosure guidelines and the corporate governance principles both stress the need for a broad disclosure of company objectives, which cover not only commercial objectives but also policies relating to business ethics, the environment and other policy commitments, with the aim of better evaluating the relationship between companies and the communities in which they operate and steps taken to implement their objectives. Importantly, the information on key board members and their remuneration will assist in identifying conflicts of interest and monitoring the effects of remuneration schemes, such as stock options, and their relationship to company performance.

Under the corporate governance principles the issue of 'related party transactions' are described in more detail rather than the basic requirements of the disclosure guideline. Full disclosure of such transactions is necessary to ensure that the company is being run with due regard to the interests of all its investors. This should be done on an individual basis indicating whether the transactions in question have been made at arm's length and on normal market terms.

It is clear from the OECD approach to disclosure that it seeks to encourage greater openness and transparency by multinational companies for public policy purposes in addition to their existing national disclosure requirements, as a means of creating a more informed environment for policy responses to be formulated. The OECD, therefore, goes beyond disclosure aimed at mere investor protection. However, the OECD *Guidelines* and *Principles* are considered to be 'soft law' as the ultimate arbiter of disclosure requirements still remains the country in which the company operates.

The creation of soft law norms in international law

There is a strong link between the method of creating soft law norms and the identification of soft law authors. States may choose to create legal norms in binding or non-binding form, whereas non-state actors, including most international institutions, cannot choose the form or instruments they adopt because their legal status allows them to adopt only non-binding rules.

Creation of non-binding norms by states

The drafting of non-binding norms by states meeting in conferences is particularly important in the field of environmental protection. First, global conferences like the 1972 Stockholm Conference on Human Environment followed by the 1992 Rio de Janeiro Conference on Environment and Development

(UNCED) adopted declarations that articulated new values emerging from growing environmental awareness. In addition, when states' parties to international treaties meet in the conferences of the parties, they will often be required to develop further norms to provide guidance for compliance with the obligations contained in the treaties. Generally, these norms have a non-binding character, because conferences of the parties are not vested with the power to impose hard obligations on the contracting parties. However, provisions of legally non-binding instruments can be formulated in mandatory terms, as illustrated by certain memorandum of understanding concluded pursuant to the Convention on the Conservation of Migratory Species of Wild Animals.

Conferences may stimulate joint action by states outside a formal framework. For example, the 1979 Montreal Protocol on Substances that Deplete the Ozone Layer provided for chlorofluorocarbon (CFC) reductions of 50 per cent by 1999,[41] the March 1989 London Conference provided that the European Community pledged a reduction of 85 per cent as soon as possible and 100 per cent by the year 2000. This eventually led to the Helsinki Declaration in May 1989 with 82 countries calling for a complete CFC phase-out by the end of that century. This demonstrates the interaction between hard law instruments and soft law and from there the way to new hard law standards.

Creation of soft law by international institutions

Soft law development by international institutions, both global and regional, is important both qualitatively and quantitatively. The constituting instruments of international organisations generally do not confer on those organisations the power to impose binding obligations on member states, except in respect to internal organisational matters. Most recommendations, however, do not concern internal matters, but are intended to address the conduct of states, and sometimes non-state actors. The content of normative resolutions can either call on member states to order their conduct in a specific manner or can declare principles of a general scope.

The elaboration of soft law is an important method by which the United Nations Environmental Programme (UNEP) Governing Council has contributed to the development of international environmental law. Since 1978, UNEP has drafted a series of guidelines and principles. Once adopted by *ad hoc* groups of experts nominated by governments, these provisions normally are approved by the UNEP Governing Council for submission to the UN General Assembly, which either incorporates them in a resolution or recommends them to states for use in the formulation of international agreements or national legislation.[42] The Food and Agriculture Organization/UNEP legally non-binding instruments on pesticides and chemicals show the possibility of cooperation between different institutions in the creation and the management of such instruments. Indeed, under the leadership of UNEP, non-binding regimes in several fields have evolved into binding treaties, reflecting a belief that legal form does make a difference and that non-binding instruments can facilitate the achievement of consensus on content for hard law.[43]

Specialised intergovernmental bodies also frequently elaborate technical standards that generally function satisfactorily without being obligatory. The Statute of the International Atomic Energy Agency specifically charges the Agency, which has no legal powers, to establish standards of safety for the protection of health and minimisation of danger to life and property. Its safety standards thus constitute recommendations only; there is no statutory obligation to take these standards into account or to report on compliance with them.

Texts elaborated by non-state actors

Non-state actors also produce soft normative instruments. Declarations by non-governmental expert groups may well attain reference status, even without approval by governments. The Helsinki Rules on the use of the waters of international rivers, drafted in 1966 by the International Law Association,[44] have been referred to as guidelines for state practice.[45]

Non-governmental industrial, environmental, and consumer protection associations can also conclude agreements considered as international soft law. A number of worldwide technical standards related to the environment have been adopted and updated by the International Organization for Standardization (ISO). Similarly, industry associations, such as the Chemical Manufacturers Association (CMA) and the American Petroleum Institute (API), have developed codes of conduct which international companies and other business entities must accept as a condition of membership.

The adoption of non-binding normative instruments by international organisations and non-state actors reflects the growing complexity of the international legal system, in which states no longer have an exclusive role, but have yet to relinquish full law-making functions to other entities. The result is a normative content in non-binding form. This may well be a point of transition, leading to the eventual conferring of legislative powers on international organisations and other non-state actors, or it may be a long-term method of managing the line between binding obligations states are willing to accept and non-binding exhortations they agree are useful and to which they politically commit.[46]

Compliance at the international level

State compliance with soft law instruments can consist in agreeing to be guided by soft law rules in international relations. In addition, non-binding norms can also be applied internationally after their domestic adoption by a state. In this respect Japan applies the OECD principles related to environmental impact assessment to its major overseas development projects. The Japan International Co-operation Agency and the Overseas Economic Co-operation Fund formulated internal guidelines for Japanese development assistance projects and strengthened the systematic assessment of their environmental effects.[47]

Although soft norms may not be binding *per se,* they can indicate the likely direction in which formally binding legal obligations will develop. Compliance can lead to the formation of hard law rules through the inclusion of soft law rules in binding international texts, or through the creation of customary international law on the basis of soft law norms.

Compliance with norms created by non-state actors

Under the memorandum of understanding relating to Port State Control, maritime authorities have undertaken to ensure that ships entering their ports comply with standards laid down in international instruments related to safety at sea, living and working conditions, and pollution prevention. They inspect ships, irrespective of whether the flag states are party to the relevant instrument. The 1982 Paris memorandum of understanding requires inspections of at least 25 per cent of ships entering port for compliance with international treaties related to marine pollution control. In recent years, Norwegian authorities controlled some 33 per cent of ships in national ports,[48] the Netherlands more than 25 per cent,[49] and the British 30 per cent. Altogether, 85 per cent of ships operating in European waters were inspected by European authorities in at least one port.[50] The rate of compliance with the 1994 memorandum of understanding on Port State Control was also high in the Asia Pacific Region.

Compliance with ISO 14001 standards is monitored at the corporate and the facility level by corporate self-audits. However, ISO displays two serious deficiencies at the compliance oversight stage. ISO standards have considerable influence, although their legal implications vary from country to country. In the US, Federal officials are encouraged to participate in establishing voluntary consensus standards, which may then become binding regulatory requirements.

Policy guidance and compliance: the World Bank operational standards

Although these non-binding norms appear to be quasi-administrative in nature for internal use by the World Bank to guide its staff in their activities, they are also applied in the framework of financing development projects through loan and credit agreements negotiated between the World Bank and borrowing countries. As such, they gain an external dimension, potentially affecting the behaviour of the borrower.[51]

The World Bank does not operate in isolation, however, and its environmental and social operational policies and procedures reflect concerns related to the promotion of sustainable development as expressed in many other fora. Operational standards are in fact vehicles for achieving this objective, although they are not necessarily exhaustive in covering the issues. The relationship between these policies and international law standards highlights their mutually reinforcing contribution to the promotion of sustainable development and the rule of law. In particular, the policies' references to international law promote respect for best practices. Although some policy statements make precise reference to various international treaties, they do not exclude the possibility of taking into account treaties not explicitly mentioned. Operational policies and procedures also refer to soft law instruments, and in so doing promote respect for them. Both types of instruments are taken into account because they are intrinsically linked to the World Bank's activities.

The policies on environmental assessment, indigenous populations, and involuntary resettlement require that World Bank-financed projects take into account the domestic legal order of the borrowing country. The World Bank should exercise due diligence and good faith in assessing the legal situation prevailing in a borrowing country, including the international commitments the country has undertaken. Clearly, various means exist for integrating international commitments into domestic legal orders, including enabling legislation, direct incorporation, or executive order. Such requirements then may be taken into consideration when implementing the relevant operational standards. While the World Bank's standards normally will correspond to the domestic legal order, in some cases its mandatory policy standards may call for the application of higher standards than those contained in national law.

As a general requirement, first stated in a policy adopted in 1984,[52] the World Bank has committed itself not to finance projects that contravene international environmental agreements to which the concerned member country is a party. This commitment was reiterated in the Operational Policy (OP) on forestry[53] and in the OP on environment assessment.[54] It not only shapes the conduct of the World Bank with respect to international environmental agreements, but also increases the awareness of borrowing countries of the need to implement and comply with international environmental law.

Operational policies and procedures also may expressly refer to international principles and rules as a means of identifying the good and best practices to be followed, helping identify the minimum standards applicable to a World Bank project. The binding nature of these international instruments may vary, but the main reason for referring to them is their wide acceptance and usefulness for development activities. The OP on 'Management of cultural property in Bank-financed projects', for example, makes explicit reference to country obligations under international treaties concerning cultural property, such as the 1972 Convention Concerning the Protection of the World Cultural and Natural Heritage.[55] These are but a few of the operational policies that refer to international treaties, and the interaction between these international instruments and the operational standards and policies underline the pragmatic nature of such standards and policies, which aim to identify and implement the best practices to promote sustainable development. They also highlight the flexibility of international law in general, allowing for practices to be codified in both hard law and soft law instruments. The general recognition of such practices in appropriate international fora serves as a useful tool for promoting sustainable development.

Operational policies and procedures constitute a means by which new patterns of behaviour are encouraged in borrowing countries. As such, they favour the emergence or consolidation of international practices which may acquire the status of customary norms. This has been the case notably with the Environmental Assessment policy. Since it was first introduced in 1989, it has served as a model for the legislation of many countries and for multilateral development banks, including the Inter-American Development Bank, the Asian Development Bank, and the European Bank for Reconstruction and Development, for bilateral donors and for the private sector in providing assistance and investment activities.[56] In addition, it helped pave the way for inclusion in the Rio Declaration on Environment and Development of an 'Environment Impact Assessment' requirement as a national instrument.[57]

Such cross-fertilisation also can be seen in respect of the requirement that riparian countries of an international watercourse be notified in cases of planned measures or projects financed by the World Bank. The application of the World Bank policy on international waterways[58] has contributed significantly to the recognition of this procedural requirement in general international law and its codification in the UN Convention on the Law of the Non-Navigational Uses of International Watercourses.[59] Such a practice highlights the composite nature of the norm-creating process whereby non-legally binding instruments and policy instruments, such as the World Bank operational standards, play a role in the formation and development of an international customary norm, enabling *lex ferenda* to become *lex lata*.

While operational policies and procedures promote respect for progressive and process-oriented standards, their application on the ground may face resistance or there may be uncertainty about how to soundly implement them.[60] The requirement of public participation and/or meaningful consultation provides a good example of the challenges and difficulties. It is one thing to establish the sequencing of actions to be conducted and the timing of public participation, but quite another to put in place a real and meaningful participation process. Cultural traditions, the need for public space for debate, the existence or lack thereof of an institutional framework, the rate of literacy, etc., all play a significant role in implementing the principle and have to be taken into account within the flexibility provided by the relevant operational policies and procedures. The borrowing country is required to expend its best efforts to take the appropriate measures for implementing the policy requirements,[61] while the World Bank should exercise due diligence during the preparation and the implementation of the project to make sure that the borrower complies with the policy requirements. The emergence of patterns of behaviour for promoting public participation takes place in a rather experimental context whereby the World Bank and borrowers engage in a dialogue on how best to implement public participation requirements and both share responsibility in shaping such practices.[62]

The fact that the international instruments to which a borrowing country has committed itself should be taken into consideration or should be considered as reflecting agreed international good and best practices, shows the close relationship of the operational standards with international law principles and standards in areas covered by them. It also demonstrates the virtues of operational policies and procedures in promoting the implementation of international law instruments, be they of a binding or non-binding normative or technical nature. Another important compliance feature is the role played by operational standards in contributing to the development of new international practices. They create normative expectations and pave the way for the con-solidation of patterns of behaviour. In addition, they lead to the emergence of principles and rules and may contribute to their recognition as *lex lata* under international law.

A few paradoxical comments by Laurence Boisson de Chazournes[63] help to underline the hybrid but nonetheless rich nature of the World Bank operational standards. These standards were originally designed to provide guidance for the staff of the World Bank in its operational work; however, that role has evolved over time, as they have been increasingly perceived as quality assessment tools in its operations as well as means for ensuring transparency and accountability. This has contributed to focusing attention on the need to strengthen the means for ensuring compliance. A wide array of mechanisms and procedures has been established, strengthened, or revitalised so as to meet this objective. Checks and balances of an operational nature have been created to ensure that operational standards are complied with during the entire cycle of a project from inception to completion. Increased attention is put on the role of the Operations Evaluation Department (OED) to identify non-compliance problems in its post-project evaluations and for drawing lessons. Legal tools have been attracting increasing attention, with a view to ensuring that when policy terms are transformed into legal terms through their incorporation in loan or credit agreements, they acquire a more established status under international law, and they therefore benefit from the legal remedies that can be taken in the event of a breach. In addition, the need was felt to institutionalise compliance concerns in establishing an independent and permanent organ within the World Bank's structure which investigates complaints brought by groups of individuals whose rights or interests would have been adversely affected by the Bank's failure to comply with operational standards in the context of a project. The establishment of the Inspection Panel also contributed to increasing the World Bank management's accountability towards the board with respect to the implementation of operational standards.

The operational standards are the product of the particular institutional setting of the World Bank and are designed for internal purposes. They nevertheless entertain multiple relationships with the international legal system, whether through their elaboration or their implementation. External actors, such as NGOs, play a role in their elaboration. Local NGOs are involved in the design and implementation of projects, as they are granted a voice through participation and consultation processes. Furthermore, environmental and social operational standards take account of international good practices as reflected in other international instruments. A process of cross-fertilisation is noticeable, which can lead to the emergence of principles and norms of general international law. All these elements reveal the composite nature of the law-making process in the international legal system. Policy instruments and attention given to their compliance contribute in many ways to this process. They reveal that porosity and interactions are core aspects of the contemporary legal system, where a plurality of actors is engaged in activities at the local, national, and international levels. Although states retain a pre-eminent role in the making and implementation of international law, international organisations, NGOs, and individuals play an increasingly important role in shaping new practices and ensuring their respect.

Notes

1 Monks, R. and N. Minow (2008) *Corporate Governance*, 4th edn, Chichester: Wiley, p. 1.
2 Smith, Adam (1776) *The Wealth of Nations*, Penguin Books, bk 1, ch. 2, p. 10.
3 Smith, Adam (1759) *The Theory of Moral Sentiments*, Penguin Books.
4 Monks and Minow (2008), p. 1.
5 Shelton, D. (ed.) (2007) *Commitment and Compliance*, Oxford: Oxford University Press, p. 228.
6 Steger, M. (2013) *Globalization: A Very Short Introduction*, Oxford: Oxford University Press, p. 65.
7 Muchlinski, P. (2007) *Multinational Enterprises and the Law*, 2nd edn, The Oxford International Law Library, Oxford: Oxford University Press, p. 81.
8 *Case of the SS Lotus* (1927) Permanent Court of International Justice (PCIJ), Ser. A, No. 10, p.18. http://www.icj-cij.org/pcii/serie_A/A_10/30_Lotus_Arret.pdf.
9 Brierly, J.L. (1963) *The Law of Nations*, Waldock. Oxford: Clarendon Press, p. 60.
10 Shelton, D. (ed.) (2007) *Commitment and Compliance*, Oxford: Oxford University Press, p. 228.
11 Rowlands, I.H. (2001) 'Transnational Corporations and Global Environmental Politics', in D. Josselin and W. Wallace (eds), *Non-State Actors in World Politics*, Basingstoke: Palgrave Publishers, p. 133.
12 Muchlinski, P. (1997) '"Global Bukowina" Examined: Viewing the Multinational Enterprise as a Transnational Law Making Community', in G. Tuebner (ed.), *Global Law without a State*, Aldershot: Dartmouth Publishing, p. 79.
13 Wallace, Cynthia Day (1983) *Legal Control of the Multinational Enterprise*, The Hague: Martinus Nijhoff Publishers.
14 UNCTAD *World Investment Reports 2003–2014*, New York and Geneva: United Nations.
15 Muchlinski, P. (2001) 'Corporations in International Litigation: Problems of Jurisdiction and the UK Asbestos Case', 50 *International and Comparative Law Quarterly* 1; Kammings, M.T. and S. Zia-Zarifi (eds) (2001) *Liability of Multinational Corporations under International Law*, The Hague: Kluwer Law International.
16 Shaw, M. (2008) *International Law*, 6th edn, Cambridge: Cambridge University Press, p. 169.
17 Brownlie, Ian (2003) *Principles of Public International Law*, 6th edn, Oxford: Oxford University Press, chs 14 & 15.

18 Ibid.
19 The principle of universal jurisdiction may also be relevant in civil as well as criminal cases in respect of the violation of human rights arising outside of the forum jurisdiction.
20 Under English law a British subject can be prosecuted in the English courts for a number of offences committed abroad. *R v Casement* [1917] 1 KB 98 (treason); Offences Against the Person Act 1861 s 9 (murder).
21 However, this does have difficulties in practice.
22 This has been a matter of significance in the extraterritorial regulation of the overseas branches of US banks.
23 *DPP v Joyce* [1946] AC 347 (acts of treason are within the jurisdiction of the English courts).
24 *Harvard Research Draft Convention on Jurisdiction with Respect to Crime*. 1935; 29 *American Journal of International Law*. Supp. 443 at 484–487.
25 *The Lotus* (1927) PCIJ, Ser. A, No. 10, 23.
26 *Fisheries Case* (United Kingdom v Norway), ICJ Reports (1951) at 116: 'jurisdiction to delimit territorial sea must be exercised in the light of a genuine connection between the land domain and the sea.' However, there is no definition as to what constitutes a 'genuine connection'. http://www.icj-cij.org/docket/files/5/1809.pdf.
27 See the case of the 'Nat-West Three'; where the activity objected to was not unlawful in the UK, but was contrary to the banking regulations in the USA. Eventually the three UK top banking officials were extradited to the USA and pleaded guilty under a plea bargain.
28 The UK government has stated that it opposes all assertions of extraterritorial jurisdiction by other states on UK individuals and/or companies. Ministerial Statement, House of Lords Debates, vol. 673, 21 July 2005.
29 In many cases the disputes have centred upon nationality questions.
30 Higgins, R. (1998) *Problems and Process: International Law and How We Use It*, Oxford: Oxford University Press, p. 73.
31 See the US Sherman Antitrust Act 1896, 155 USC, paras 1ff; The Export Administration Act 1981; Bridge, J.W. (1984) 'The Law and Politics of United States Foreign Policy Export Controls', 4 *Legal Studies* 2.
32 Shaw, M. (2008) *International Law*, Cambridge, UK: Cambridge University Press, p. 669.
33 549 F. 2d 597 (1979); 66 *International Law Review*, 270.
34 595 F. 2d 1287 (1979); 66 *International Law Review*, 487. It was in this case that the court put forward a series of factors which should be considered in the process of balancing each nation's interests, at p. 487.
35 *Hartford Fire Insurance Co. v California*.113 S. Ct 2891 (1993). 88 *American Journal of International Law*.
36 *United States of America v Nippon Paper Industries Co.* (US CA 1st Cir decision of 17 March 1997).
37 Stakeholders may be defined as any identifiable groups or individuals who can affect the achievement of the corporation's objectives or who are affected by such achievements.
38 Radebaugh, L.H., S.J. Gray and E.L. Black (2006) *International Accounting and Multinational Enterprises*, New York: Wiley, pp. 22–23.
39 OECD (2000) *The Guidelines for Multinational Enterprises*. These Guidelines have now been updated on a number of occasions with the latest version being in 2011. http://www.oecd.org/corporate/mne/oecdguidelinesformultinationalenterprises.htm.
40 OECD (2004) *Principles of Corporate Governance*. Paris. http://www.oecd-ilibrary. org/industry-and-services/oecd-principles-of-corporate-governance-2004_9789264015999-en.

41 Opened for signature 16 September 1987 (1987) 26 *International Legal Materials* 1550, Art 2 para 4.
42 Conclusions of the Study of Legal Aspects Concerning the Environment Related to Offshore Mining and Drilling within the limits of National Jurisdiction (1982), UNGA Res. 37/217.
43 Kiss, Alexandra (2007) 'Commentary and Conclusions', in D. Shelton (ed.), *Commitment and Compliance*, Oxford: Oxford University Press, p. 225.
44 Report of the 52nd Conference in Helsinki (August 1966) at p. 484.
45 Kiss (2007), p. 226.
46 Ibid., p. 228.
47 Japan, OECD, Environmental Performance in OECD Countries. OECD Series of Environmental Performance Reviews. http://www.oecd.org/environment.
48 OECD Reports, Norway. OECD Environmental Performance in OECD Countries series. http://www.oecd.org/norway/.
49 OECD Reports, The Netherlands. http://www.oecd.org/netherlands/.
50 OECD Reports, United Kingdom. http://www.oecd.org/unitedkingdom/.
51 Boisson de Chazournes, Laurence (2007) 'Policy Guidance and Compliance: The World Bank Operational Standards', in D. Shelton (ed.), *Commitment and Compliance*, Oxford: Oxford University Press.
52 See (1984) Operational Manual Statement (OMS) 2.36 on Environmental Aspects of Bank Work. The provision reads 'the Bank will not finance projects that contravene any international environmental agreement to which the member country concerned is a party'.
53 Operational Policy (OP) 4.36 on Forestry. Provision reads 'governments must also commit to adhere to their obligations as set forth in relevant international instruments to which they are party'.
54 OP 4.01 on Environmental Assessment reads 'EA...takes into account the obligations of the country, pertaining to project activities under relevant international treaties and agreements. The Bank does not finance project activities that would contravene such country obligations, as identified during the EA.'
55 The 1972 Convention Concerning the Protection of the World Cultural and Natural Heritage is given as a reference for defining the notion of cultural property. OP 4.11, para 2(a).
56 Nolkaemper, A. (1995) 'Marine Pollution', 6 *Yearbook of International Environmental Law*, 225–244.
57 Principle 17 of the Rio Declaration on Environment and Development reads 'environmental impact assessment, as a national instrument, shall be undertaken for proposed activities that are likely to have a significant adverse impact on the environment and are subject to a decision of a competent national authority'.
58 OP 7.50 International Waterways (October 1994).
59 Boisson de Chazournes (2007).
60 Ibid.
61 See Art. 2, para 1. of the International Covenant on Economic, Social and Cultural Rights, Compilation of General Comments and General Recommendations adopted by Human Rights Treaty Bodies HRI/GEN/1/Rev. 3, paras 1–14.
62 Boisson de Chazournes (2007).
63 Ibid.

2 Human rights in binding and non-binding law

Introduction

To date human rights norms have been used by corporations to protect their vital interest against what they may view as acts of excessive state regulation. This has led to the gradual development of a practice of protection of corporate vital interests against what companies may view as acts of excessive state regulation. Increased concerns in this area may be attributed to a number of factors, including increased unease at the seemingly unaccountable operations of private capital in a globalising economy; the perception that the ability of the nation state to act in the public interest has been weakened by the effects of economic globalisation, and as a result of the greater ease of communicating cases of corporate misconduct through the media. In addition, the increased vigilance of NGOs that are concerned with such misconduct has led to greater awareness of this issue.[1]

The right of natural persons to be protected against the human rights abuses of a state actor is at the heart of human rights law. The observance of fundamental human rights can also be said to lie at the heart of ethical business practice. However, in relation to business ethics, the use of human rights standards is replete with conceptual difficulties. Indeed, others have put forward a number of strong arguments against such an extension of human rights responsibilities to multinational companies.[2] It is, therefore, predictable that not all states and companies will take care to observe fundamental human rights.

However, it should be noted that multinational companies have been expected to observe socially responsible standards of behaviour for a long time.[3] This expectation has been expressed in national and regional laws and in numerous codes of conduct drawn up by intergovernmental organisations. Indeed, multinationals appear to be rejecting a purely non-social role for themselves through the adoption of corporate and industry based codes of conduct. Also, the observance of human rights is increasingly being seen as 'Good Business'. It is argued that business cannot flourish in an environment where fundamental human rights are not respected – what firm would be happy with the disappearance or imprisonment without trial of employees for their political opinions thereby being deprived of their labour? In addition, businesses themselves may justify the adoption of human rights policies by reference to good reputation.[4] The benefit to be reaped from espousing a pro-human rights stance is seen as outweighing any 'free rider' problem, which may be in any case exaggerated.[5]

Andrew Clapham has forcefully argued that changes in the nature and location of power in the contemporary international system, including an increase in the power of private non-state actors such as multinational corporations (which may allow them to bypass traditional state-centred systems of governance), have forced a reconsideration of the boundaries between the private and the public spheres. This, in turn, has brought into question the traditional notion of the corporation as a private entity with no social or public obligations, with the consequence that such actors, including multinational corporations, may in principle be subjected to human rights obligations.[6] This position coincides with the fear that these powerful entities may disregard human rights and, thereby, violate human dignity. It follows that corporations, including international companies, should be subjected to human rights responsibilities, notwithstanding their status as creatures of private law, because human dignity must be protected in every circumstance.[7] Furthermore, in response to the view that multinational companies cannot be subjected to human rights responsibilities because they are incapable of observing human rights designed to direct state action, it may be said that, to the contrary, multinationals can affect the economic welfare of the communities in which they operate and, given the indivisibility of human rights, this means that they have a direct impact on the extent that economic and social rights, especially labour rights in the workplace, can be enjoyed. Although it is true that multinationals may not have direct control over matters arising outside the workplace they may nonetheless exercise important influence in this respect. Thus, multinationals may seek to defend the human rights of their employees outside the workplace, to set standards for their sub-contractors and to refuse to accept the benefits of governmental measures that seek to improve the business climate at the expense of fundamental human rights. Equally, where firms operate in unstable environments they should ensure that their security arrangements comply with fundamental human rights standards.[8] Moreover, where companies have no direct means of influence they should avoid making statements or engaging in actions that appear to condone human rights violations.

Despite this strong theoretical and moral case for extending responsibility for human rights violations to international companies, the legal responsibility for human rights violations remains uncertain. Thus, much of the literature on this issue suggests ways to reform and develop the law towards full legal responsibility, rather than documenting actual juridical findings of human rights violations by multinationals, or indeed, non-state actors.[9]

Substantive human rights obligations of multinational corporations

The precise content of the human rights obligations of multinational corporations is open to considerable speculation; however, it is clear that corporate actors will not carry the same responsibilities as states. Some state responsibilities are simply impossible for multinationals and other business enterprises to carry out, such as protecting rights of asylum, the right to take part in government, rights to nationality, and provision of rights to due process. Equally states, as public actors, do not themselves enjoy human rights protection, whilst multinationals, as private actors, can possess rights that may need to be balanced against those of other non-state actors.

Historically, the observance of human rights standards has been an obligation of the state alone. Accordingly, a link must be made between the obligations of states, and non-state actors, to promote universal respect for, and observance of, human rights and fundamental freedoms. An express reference to such a link is found in the Universal Declaration of Human Rights (UDHR). This instrument is addressed both to governments and to 'other organs of society'. Following this provision, the third recital of the preamble to the UN Norms recognises that 'even though States have the primary responsibility to promote, secure the fulfilment of, respect, ensure respect of and protect human rights, transnational corporations and other business enterprises, as organs of society, are also responsible for promoting and securing the human rights set forth in the Universal Declaration of Human Rights'. This is clear acceptance of the view that corporate entities do have human rights responsibilities on the basis of their social existence. However, the legal status of the UDHR remains that of a non-binding declaration, and so this reference to the UDHR wording in the UN Norms may be no more than a statement of an ethical duty at best, reinforced by the fact that the UN Commission on Human Rights regards the UN Norms as a draft proposal.

Although the first concern of the UN Norms is to address the obligations of transnational corporations (TNCs) and other business enterprises in respect of human rights, this instrument continues to address the obligations of governments as well. However, the USA opposed the resolution of 20 April *inter alia* on the grounds that 'human rights obligations apply to states, not non-state actors, and it is incumbent on states when they deem necessary to adopt national laws that address the obligations of private actors'.[10]

Paragraph 1 of the UN Norms describes the obligations thus:

> States have the primary responsibility to promote; secure the fulfillment of, respect, ensure respect of and protect human rights recognized in international as well as national law, including ensuring that transnational corporations and other business enterprises respect human rights. Within their respective spheres of activity and influence, transnational corporations and other business enterprises have the obligation to promote, secure the fulfilment of, respect, ensure respect of and protect

human rights recognized in international as well as national law, including the rights of indigenous peoples and other vulnerable groups.

Although this provision places states over TNCs and other business enterprises as the principal regulators of human rights observance, it also recognises that states and businesses operate in different fields and so each has a specific set of responsibilities in their particular field of operations, thereby obviating the possibility that business enterprises could supplant the state in its obligations to uphold and observe human rights, or that the state could use the Norms as an excuse for not taking action to protect human rights.[11]

The key to extending any human rights responsibilities to multinationals is how to ensure that any emergent substantive human rights obligations of such entities are actually upheld. This would inevitably involve a mix of informal self-regulation by firms and formal regulation by way of national and international legal approaches. Corporate self regulation on human rights issues is far from developed, as compared with environmental self regulation, which is discussed later. Whether firms can, or should, engage in such activity generates some controversy. Some business voices feel that this is a step too far, requiring firms to become quasi-governmental organisations that would engage in political decisions far beyond the limits of their capabilities. In fact, any human rights activism by multinationals may undermine their position as providers of beneficial foreign investment to less developed countries that may object to such interference in their internal political affairs.[12] Alternatively, it can be said that human rights concerns may be of such a fundamentally different magnitude, as compared with other corporate social responsibility issues, such as environmental protection or day-to-day employment and health and safety matters, that they should never be entrusted to self regulatory responses. However, in practice, some multinationals have found themselves caught in situations where human rights abuses have arisen and their responses have left much to be desired. For an example see the experience of Shell with the Ogoni people's rights, that founds the basis of the claim brought against the company by the relatives of the human rights activist Ken SaroWiwa. Accordingly multinationals may have little choice but to address human rights concerns as part of their business management strategy, particularly where they invest in conflict zones, politically authoritarian and/or corrupt states, or less developed countries. Indeed, the UN Norms expect TNCs and other business enterprises to develop a human rights policy and appropriate internal monitoring systems. Thus, the trend towards developing clear internal management responses may be inevitable. However, self-regulation, of the kind seen in relation to environmental matters, may well be inappropriate in the case of human rights issues, as the state remains the prime protector of such rights and it would be politically illegitimate to hand this responsibility over exclusively to the corporation.

Turning to formal legal regulation at the national level, both standard setting through new laws and regulations, and public interest litigation, taken against firms alleged to have broken their human rights obligations, may be used. However, at the international level there arises the possibility that intergovernmental organisations have a monitoring role that can supplement such national initiatives, in particular, by requiring states to comply with certain obligations to ensure that their domestic regulatory structures adequately reflect the emerging norms in this area and by providing adequate and effective remedies for those who allege to have been harmed by the failure of firms to observe fundamental international human rights.[13]

At the national level, there has been little progress on standard setting through new laws or regulations embodying human rights standards under the UN Norms which state: 'States should establish and reinforce the necessary legal and administrative framework for ensuring that the Norms and other relevant national and international laws are implemented by transnational corporations and other business enterprises.'[14] The most significant examples are the US and EU initiatives to link labour rights protection to the extension of trade preferences, or the UK Ethical Trading Initiative.

In US national law a degree of direct responsibility for human rights violations on the part of multinationals is being recognised through litigation brought by private claimants against the parent companies of affiliates operating in the claimants' countries. In the United States District Court case of *Doe v Unocal*[15] it was held, for the first time, that multinationals could, in principle, be directly liable for gross violations of human rights under the US Alien Tort Claims Act (ATCA).[16] However, the key difficulty here was to show that the company was in some way implicated in human rights violations. This raises the question whether there has to be evidence of direct involvement or whether some lesser degree of involvement is sufficient.

Turning to intergovernmental organisations in monitoring and enforcement, two sets of issues arise. Firstly, what should the legal status of any standard setting instruments be and, secondly, what kinds of procedures for monitoring and enforcement could be put in place. The discussions over the UN Norms are instructive as these very questions have had to be faced by the participants. It is clear that the legal status of the UN Norms is yet to be settled and for the time being they should be regarded as non-binding. However, Weissbrodt and Kruger argue that the UN Norms are 'non-voluntary' and derive a degree of legal authority from the numerous implementation provisions they contain and from the binding sources from which they are derived.[17]

The main advantage of a voluntary instrument is that it could be used in conjunction with existing voluntary corporate codes of conduct to develop a more comprehensive system of internal values to be observed by the company. This would need to be supplemented by an effective system of accountability within the company.[18] However, the discussions on the UN Norms have tended to favour a binding instrument, bearing in mind the past history of non-binding codes, the fact that many non-binding guidelines already exist and also the need for developing practical methods for enforcing human rights standards against TNCs, especially where states might not do so, given their need to focus on attracting inward investment.[19] In response, the introduction to the second draft of the UN Norms offers a middle way. It asserts that 'it would be unrealistic to suggest that human rights standards with regard to companies should immediately become the subject of treaty obligations', given that only some of the standards contained in the UN Norms are binding treaty-based norms, and that the precise legal status, in the international legal order, of companies and other non-state actors remains uncertain. Indeed, even 'if the Working Group wishes to pursue a legally binding instrument or even a treaty, it would ordinarily start with some form of "soft law" exercise'.[20] This has been the normal pattern of operation in relation to the adoption of other binding human rights instruments. Hence in the absence of state opinion to the contrary some transition from 'soft' to 'hard' law is more likely to occur.

Connected to this issue is the question of how to make the UN Norms effective through implementation and monitoring procedures. In this regard the UN Norms require TNCs and other business enterprises to adopt, disseminate, and implement internal rules of operation in compliance with the Norms. In addition, they must incorporate the principles contained in the UN Norms in their contracts or other arrangements and dealings with contractors, sub-contractors, suppliers, and licensees in order to ensure their implementation and respect. The UN Norms also require that TNCs and other business enterprises shall monitor and verify their compliance in an independent and transparent manner that includes input from relevant stakeholders.[21]

The draft presented to the 54th Session of the UN Sub-Commission on Human Rights in 2002 introduced, for the first time, a provision requiring TNCs and other business enterprises to provide compensation for violation of the UN Norms with the final version reading thus:

> Transnational corporations and other business enterprises shall provide prompt, effective and adequate reparation to those persons, entities, and communities that have been adversely affected by failures to comply with these Norms through, *inter alia,* reparations, restitution, compensation and rehabilitation for any damage done or property taken.[22]

The UN Norms have also introduced some clarification of where such reparation is to be determined. Paragraph 18 states: 'In connection with determining damages, in regard to criminal sanctions, and in all other respects, these Norms shall be applied by national courts and/or international tribunals, pursuant to national and international law.'

By taking this approach, the UN Norms envisage a binding enforcement mechanism, centred on national courts and/or international tribunals, which offers directly effective rights of reparation for the individuals or groups affected as a consequence of a violation of the instrument. This presupposes a legally binding document that is effective within the national laws of the UN member states that adopt it.[23] A further issue concerns the identification of the precise forum before which any claim for reparation under paragraph 18 can be brought. As it stands paragraph 18 is silent on this matter, although it could be presumed that the question of forum remains to be determined by the national laws of the jurisdictions in which a claim is brought, or by reference to an international tribunal.

Given the above discussion, the prospects for human rights based approaches to corporate liability remain rather restricted. International business will not readily accept an analogy between private corporations and the state in terms of human rights responsibilities, the actual legal issues raised by such claims are still to be properly developed, and it is not clear that using human rights arguments is necessarily better than focusing on regulation and liability under established heads of law.

Labour relations

The international protection of human rights, elaborated in agreements and non-binding texts, is largely a development of the second half of the twentieth century, although the International Labour Organization (ILO) took up human rights issues long before the United Nations was created and continues to do so. When considering transnational companies, the development of specialised standards for the conduct of labour relations are contained primarily in the OECD Guideline on Employment and Industrial Relations (the OECD Guideline),[24] and in the International Labour Organization's Tripartite Declaration of Principles on Multinationals and Social Policy (the ILO Declaration) as supplemented by the ILO Declaration on Fundamental Principles and Rights at Work (the 1998 Declaration).[25] 'Both of these codes are based on a consensus between governments, industry, and trade union representatives and, as such, represent "corporatist" policy responses.'[26] Despite considerable changes in political thinking since that time, both codes remain in effect.

The ILO and OECD codes

The ILO became involved in the formulation of a code of conduct in response to demands from labour representatives and developing countries that had been made since the 1960s. In the early 1970s the developing countries pressed for an ILO conference which could adopt a binding international code for multinationals. This was resisted by the employers' representatives who favoured the adoption of a voluntary code, but in 1972 the negotiating process started with the first 'Tripartite Meeting on the Relationship between Multinational Enterprises and Social Policy'. The ILO Declaration was finally adopted on 16 November 1977.

The OECD Guideline on Employment and Industrial Relations is part of the more general OECD Guidelines for Multinational Enterprises, and is therefore less detailed than the ILO Declaration.

General policies of the codes and their relationship to national laws

The principle difference in the general approach of each code concerns which group they address. The OECD Guideline is jointly addressed by the Member Countries to multinational enterprises (MNEs) operating in their territories, whereas the ILO Declaration is addressed to governments, the employers' and workers' organisations in both home and host countries, and the MNEs themselves.[27] They aim to reflect good practice for all, without discrimination as to nationality, and both codes envisage the primacy of national law, thus the ILO Declaration states: 'All parties concerned by this Declaration should respect the sovereign rights of States, obey the national laws and regulations, give due consideration to local practices and respect relevant international standards.'[28]

The primacy of national law is reinforced by the requirement that the disputes procedure cannot be used to determine issues arising out of national law. Similarly, the OECD Employment Guideline begins by stating that enterprises should respect the standards it contains, 'within the framework of applicable law, regulations and prevailing labour relations and employment practices' in each of the countries in which they operate.

This reference to the primacy of national law tends to weaken the effectiveness of both codes which preserve the rights of each state to determine the nature, scope and effect of its national labour laws. Consequently, despite the exhortations to the contrary, the codes can do little to prevent competition between states over the reduction of labour standards as a means of reducing the cost of investment in their respective territories. In this regard the ILO Declaration contains certain additional provisions of a general nature, not found in the OECD Guideline. Thus, governments which have not yet done so are urged to ratify the core ILO Conventions as listed in paragraph 9 of the ILO Declaration. Furthermore, multinationals are expected to take full account of the general policy objectives of the countries in which they operate, especially the development priorities and social aims and structures of these countries. Moreover, governments of home countries are urged to promote good social practice in accordance with the ILO Declaration having regard to the social and labour law, regulations, and practices in host countries as well as to relevant international standards. This provision urges home states to ensure that home based corporations observe good practice in their overseas operations. This suggests that bilateral arrangements may offer a way forward in ensuring the observance of higher standards throughout the network of countries in which a multinational operates.

The relative weakness of the ILO Declaration may be contrasted with the approach of the 1998 ILO Declaration on Fundamental Principles and Rights at Work. This provides what can be termed an international base of fundamental labour rights in Article 2, which states:

> all Members, even if they have not ratified the Convention in question, have an obligation arising from the very fact of their membership of the

ILO, to respect, to promote and to realize, in good faith and in accordance with the Constitution, the principles concerning the fundamental rights which are the subject of those Conventions, namely:

a Freedom of association and the effective recognition of the right to collective bargaining;
b The elimination of all forms of forced or compulsory labour;
c The effective abolition of child labour; and
d The elimination of discrimination in respect of employment and occupation.[29]

This provision raises the question whether an ILO member can now deviate from these standards in its national laws, notwithstanding the primacy of national law under the ILO Declaration. The wording of Article 2 asserts an obligation to observe the fundamental rights listed therein. However, there is no apparent sanction. Thus the ILO process remains one based on good faith and best efforts, even in relation to norms that can be regarded as binding principles of international human rights law.

Finally, the codes do not address the problem of conflicting labour standards that may arise as a result of the international operations of multinationals. For example, where the firm employs a national of the home state in the host state, it may wish that person's employment contract to be governed by the law of the home state. Where home state law sanctions terms and conditions that are contrary to host state law, the contract may be unlawful in the host state. Indeed, many states may have mandatory rules of employment law that cannot be avoided through the choice of a foreign law as the proper law of the contract of employment. The territorial principle of jurisdiction still prevails in the field of labour law, making for considerable differences in the content of laws that will govern employment issues within the international corporation.

This territorial basis of labour law creates particular problems where employees are 'peripatetic', when they are based in one country but frequently assigned to another to carry out work there; also if they are 'expatriate' when they are based permanently abroad though working for a home country firm. In 2006 the UK House of Lords considered a case of *Lawson v Serco Ltd, Botham v Ministry of Defence*,[30] relating to unfair dismissal. The question arose whether UK laws relating to unfair dismissal could apply to such classes of employees. Their Lordships held that although the territorial principle applied in the standard case, in that such laws extended only to employees who were working in the UK, in the case of 'peripatetic' employees UK unfair dismissal law could apply if the employee was in fact based in the UK but ordinarily worked outside the UK, regardless of the formal place of work specified in the contract. With regard to 'expatriate' employees UK law would not normally apply unless the employee was working as an employee of a UK-based employer and he or she was working as a representative of a business conducted at home in the UK or was operating within an extraterritorial British social or political enclave in a foreign country, such as a British military base.

Employment issues

The ILO Declaration deals with promotion, equality of opportunity, and treatment and security of employment under this heading; whereas the OECD Employment Guideline contains standards concerning equality of opportunity, and security of employment. However, paragraph 4 of the General Policies Guideline in the OECD code asserts that enterprises should 'encourage human capital formation, in particular by creating employment opportunities and facilitating training opportunities for employees'.

(a) Employment promotion

The ILO Declaration asserts that governments should 'declare and pursue, as a major goal, an active policy designed to promote full, productive and freely chosen employment', and that multinationals, 'particularly when operating in developing countries, should endeavour to increase employment opportunities and standards, taking into account the employment policies and objectives of the governments, as well as security of employment and the long term development of the enterprise'.

These aspects of the Declaration now seem rather dated in the wake of the global recession, and it is doubtful if multinationals make much difference in the creation of employment opportunities as they suffered the same employment constraints as other firms operating in the throes of a recession. Thus, although it contains a sentiment that is no doubt generally accepted, the practical utility of its exhortations may be doubted. Full employment in a global high-technology economy is becoming harder to envisage, as the demand for unskilled and semi-skilled labour decreases and automation reduces the total number of jobs required for profitable operation. Nevertheless, it is undeniable that multinationals have a capacity to generate new employment both directly and indirectly through new investments which, in turn, may encourage other foreign investments linked to the original project. In addition, while the quantity of employment so generated is important, the quality of the resulting jobs must also be considered. Ideally foreign investment will allow for a rise in the technical quality of the work offered as a spur to economic growth. In this regard training and technology transfer is of central importance which is discussed in more detail in Chapter 5.

(b) Equality of opportunity and treatment

The ILO Declaration provides that both governments and multinationals should pursue policies designed to promote equality of opportunity and treatment in employment. They should aim to eliminate discrimination based on race, colour, sex, religion, political opinion, national extraction or social origin. However, note should be taken by multinationals of host governmental policies and consideration of preferential treatment for host company employees or to governmental policies designed to correct historical patterns of discrimination.[31] The OECD Employment Guideline echoes the ILO Declaration by recommending that enterprises should:

> not discriminate against their employees with respect to employment or occupation on such grounds as race, colour, sex, religion, political opinion, national extraction or social origin unless selectivity concerning employee characteristics furthers established governmental policies which specifically promote greater equality of employment opportunity or relates to the inherent requirements of the job.[32]

Therefore, both codes accept positive discrimination, or 'affirmative action', on the basis of governmental policies. However, the ILO Declaration goes further and accepts the legitimacy of preferential treatment for host state employees. This has been generally accepted as neither code has raised significant issues of interpretation in this area. Multinationals, therefore, are subject to the same requirements as national enterprises, but much depends on the internal management culture, and whether, regardless of legal rules, a moral principle of non-discrimination is observed.

In this context multinational operations should apply this principle extraterritorially and so ensure that the same legal protection applies to all employees wherever they work. This issue has arisen in relation to the application of US non-discrimination laws to US employees working in the foreign subsidiaries of US corporations. In 1991 the US Supreme Court held that Title VII of the Civil Rights Act 1964, which prohibits discrimination in employment on the basis of race, religion or national origin, did not have extraterritorial reach so as to protect a US citizen working abroad in a US controlled company.[33] This ruling was reversed by the Civil Rights Act of 1991 ensuring that US citizens working abroad in US controlled foreign corporations did not lose the protection of Title VII. Equally, Title VII applies to the US based subsidiaries of foreign corporations despite the protection of the right of free management of foreign companies in the US under US Friendship Commerce and Navigation treaties, which includes the right to hire executive and other specialised employees of the foreign firm's choice.[34]

In addition, when employees of a multinational company are sent on a short-term posting to another state it is arguable that they should be entitled to benefit from the protection of host state labour rights even though their contract of employment with the multinational may be governed by the law of another state. In order that this protection exist the EU has adopted legislation on the protection of posted workers in the service sector which seeks to ensure that certain employment laws generally applicable to the Member State to which the worker is posted apply to him even though the contract of employment is governed by the law of another Member State.[35]

(c) Security of employment

Multinational and national enterprises should, through active manpower planning, 'endeavor to provide stable employment for their employees and should observe freely negotiated obligations concerning employment stability and social security'.[36]

Both the ILO Declaration and the OECD Employment Guideline accept that multinationals are free to change their operations, even if this results in major employment effects, as in the case of the closure of an entity involving collective lay-offs or dismissals. In the *Batco* case, the OECD Committee on Multinational Enterprises held that the Employment Guideline cannot be interpreted as prohibiting the closure of even a profitable subsidiary, as this remained a prerogative of management. All that the company had to do was to follow the requirements of national law regarding the effects of the closure and to provide reasonable notice to the host government and cooperate in the mitigation of any adverse effects. In the *Badger* case, where a US parent company closed down its Belgian subsidiary, the OECD Committee on International Investment and Multinational Enterprises stated that this obligation included assistance to the subsidiary so as to enable the payment of termination claims to be made in accordance with the national law of the host state. However, in the *Philips* case the OECD Committee noted that 'once multinational enterprises have made a decision to terminate branch activities, the Guidelines do not require them to solve or improve resulting regional development problems of the host countries'.[37]

Significant advances have been made within the EU for the protection of employment rights that are of direct relevance to the operations of multinationals. Collective redundancies and employees' rights on the transfer of undertakings have been the subject of harmonisation measures in the form of directives. These directives must be incorporated into national laws of all Member States, and failure to do so may result in an enforceable right to damages against the defaulting Member State.[38]

With regard to collective redundancies, Council Directive 98/59/EC was passed to ensure that existing workers' rights to information and consultation in cases of collective redundancies could not be undermined where such redundancies were caused by decisions of undertakings, other than the immediate employer, located in another Member State. The Group as a whole must ensure conformity with the terms of the directive.

When considering EU provisions relating to employees' rights on the transfer of undertakings, Directive 2001/23/EC serves to protect the rights of an employee of an undertaking that is transferred or merged.[39] The directive does not apply to a transfer on insolvency, or where an employment relationship does not actually exist at the date of transfer.

Training of workers

In a world economy characterised by increasing industrial restructuring, training issues acquire an importance far greater than before. National training schemes will apply to multinationals as well as national enterprises without distinction. However, multinationals may offer special skills based on their international experience. Thus they may be expected to provide greater assistance, particularly in developing countries. Equally as skill levels of employees become increasingly important in information based industries, firms may need to engage in active training to remain competitive.

Conditions of work and life

The ILO Declaration divides such issues between wages, benefits, and conditions of work, minimum age and safety, and health matters. Whereas the OECD Employment Guideline says little on the first set of issues but simply asserts that multinationals should observe standards of employment not less favourable than those observed by comparable employers in the host country.[40] The second set of issues is referred to in paragraph 1(b) of the guidelines which asserts that enterprises should 'contribute to the effective abolition of child labour'. Safety and health issues are covered in the OECD Environmental Guideline, which is discussed in the next chapter.

Wages, benefits, and conditions of work

Both the OECD Guideline and the ILO Declaration apply the national treatment standard to these matters by stating: 'Wages, benefits and conditions of work offered by multinational enterprises should be not less favourable to the workers than those offered by comparable employers in the country concerned.'[41]

In the *Warner Lambert* case, the OECD Committee on Multinational Enterprises held that the national standard did not exclude the possibility that, temporarily and under exceptional circumstances, agreement may be reached on wages less favourable than those observed by comparable employers in host countries. The multinational concerned should in good faith aim at restoring wages to the national standard as soon as the specific circumstances which gave rise to such agreement no longer persist.[42]

When operating in developing countries, where comparable employers may not exist, multinationals should provide the 'best possible wages, benefits and conditions of work, within the framework of government policies';[43] thus, the declaration does not prevent multinationals from moving their operations to lower wage areas if they choose, all that is required is that the firm does not fall below the national treatment standard in the host state.

Minimum age

It was not until the 2000 revision of the ILO Declaration that this section was inserted in order to incorporate ILO Conventions No. 138 on Minimum Age and No. 182, the Convention on the Prohibition and Immediate Elimination of the Worst Forms of Child Labour.[44] The ILO asserts that 'multinational enterprises, as well as national enterprises, should respect the minimum age for admission to employment or work in order to secure the effective abolition of child labour'.[45]

This wording only refers to 'child labour' while the Convention 182 deals only with the 'worst forms of child labour' as follows:

a   all forms of slavery or practices similar to slavery, such as the sale and trafficking of children, debt bondage and serfdom and forced or compulsory labour, including forced or compulsory recruitment of children for use in armed conflict;
b   the use, procuring or offering of a child for prostitution, for the production of pornography or for pornographic performances;
c   the use, procuring or offering of a child for illicit activities, in particular for the production and trafficking of drugs as defined in the relevant international treaties;
d   work which, by its nature or the circumstances in which it is carried out, is likely to harm the health, safety or morals of children.[46]

Although this list includes types of work that multinationals would not expect children to perform, it is not impossible that some of their subcontractors might, for example, employ debt bonded child labourers. Clause (d) on health and safety, however, may be of direct relevance to multinationals.

It would appear that the ILO Declaration, if read literally, means that multinationals must abolish *all* labour of persons under the legal minimum age for work in the host country. Whereas the OECD Guideline merely urges enterprises to contribute to the effective abolition of child labour. Multinationals can nevertheless contribute to this goal through the creation of well paid jobs, and raising the standards of education of children living in host countries.

In conclusion, international human rights law has utilised a combination of binding and non-binding instruments to set forth human rights guarantees and obligations of states in regard to them. The United Nations Charter contains references to human rights, including the obligation of member states to take joint and separate action in cooperation with the organisation to achieve universal respect for, and observance of, human rights and fundamental freedoms. The first instrument adopted by the member states to define the rights referred to in the Charter was the 1948 Universal Declaration of Human Rights (UDHR), a non-binding resolution of the UN General Assembly. From the beginning, however, the drafters of the Charter intended that it be the first step to 'a common standard of achievement' that would lead to a binding agreement on the subject. The 1996 Covenants on Civil and Political Rights and on Economic, Social and Cultural Rights fulfilled the drafter's expectations by incorporating the UDHR rights in binding international agreements. The UDHR remains, however, and many assert that its norms have become legally binding on all members of the United Nations as an authoritative interpretation of member states' human rights obligations, or that the UDHR is binding on all states as customary international law through state practice and *opinion juris*.

It is unusual to find human rights norms that exist only in soft law form, given the complex interweaving of treaty and non-binding instruments, global and regional texts. Human rights law is also complicated by the existence of judicial and quasi-judicial bodies that decide cases and build a jurisprudence that itself is a combination of hard and soft law. A decision of the European Court of Human Rights or the Inter-American Court of Human Rights, for example, is legally binding on the state party to the case, but is not binding on other parties to the treaty. In the field of human rights, therefore, it may be useful to attempt to categorise non-binding norms, as follows:

Primary soft law can be considered as those normative texts not adopted in treaty form that are addressed to the international community as a whole or to the entire membership of the adopting institution or organisation. Such an instrument may declare new norms, often as an intended precursor to adoption of a later treaty, or it may reaffirm or further elaborate norms previously set forth in binding or non-binding texts. In many instances, primary soft law elaborates previously accepted general or vague norms found in binding agreements or non-binding instruments. The Universal Declaration of Human Rights defines the term human rights as it is used in the United Nations Charter. The UN Declaration on the Rights of the Child in turn calls the Universal Declaration of Human Rights the 'basis' for its adoption. The UN Declaration on the Rights of Persons Belonging to National or Ethnic, Religious and Linguistic Minorities is comprehensive in its references.

Secondary soft law includes the recommendations and general comments of international human rights supervisory organs, the jurisprudence of courts and commissions, decisions of special rapporteurs and other *ad hoc* bodies, and the resolutions of political organs of international organisations applying primary norms. Most of this secondary soft law is pronounced by institutions whose existence and jurisdiction are derived from a treaty and who apply norms contained in the same treaty. Such secondary soft law derives from the increasingly important work of specially appointed individuals or working groups.[47]

Soft law is used regularly for international human rights norm-setting, either as an ultimate or an intermediate expression of international consensus. In developing human rights treaties, it is now common to pass through a soft law, declarative stage. Probably even more common is the 'secondary' soft law that is not preliminary or declaratory in nature, but is intended to be the ultimate and authoritative determination of a legal question. In this regard, hard law and soft law interact to shape the content of international obligations. Soft law formulates and reformulates the hard law of human rights treaties in the application of this law to specific states and cases. Paradoxically, this secondary soft law may be harder than the primary soft law declaring new standards.

Soft law is clearly useful in enunciating broad principles in new areas of law-making, where details of obligation remain to be elaborated. In addition, soft law can be seen as a necessary mechanism related to the traditional consensual nature of international law formulation, which allows hard law to be made and imposed only on those who agree. Even where there is no over-whelming consensus on the need for action and on the negative impact that inaction will have on all states, norms cannot be imposed on objectors. Soft law can express standards and broad international consensus when unanimity is lacking in state practice and thus the will to establish hard law is absent. Ultimately, as compliance increases soft law may serve to pressure the few non-consenting states to comply with the majority views.

Whether the norms are binding or non-binding, compliance seems most directly linked to the existence of effective monitoring and independent supervision. The role of non-governmental organisations has been crucial, but without a forum to which to take the results of their investigations and the evidence they gather, they are limited in their effectiveness.[48] In short, it is the synergy between human rights bodies created by intergovernmental organisa-tions and non-governmental organisations that leads to greater compliance by states. The existence of non-binding norms and the consensus that emerges as states begin to comply with them also appears to stimulate the development of legally binding norms.

The influence of international trade unionism

Trade union activity has historically been focused at local site or country level but the emergence of organised and internationalised Global Union Federations over the last decade means multinationals now face more co-ordinated and concerted pressure from trade unions across national borders.

Whilst their roots trace back over many decades, Global Union Federations (GUFs) have only existed in their current form since 2002. There are currently nine GUFs, following the merger of three unions in June 2012 to create a super federation for the industrial and manufacturing sector.

GUFs bring together individual trade unions from around the world and are funded by subscriptions from member unions. Their objective is to increase international cooperation, joint action and global solidarity among trade unions in different countries that share common employers and secure enforce-able bargaining, consultation and co-determination rights at the transnational level. Long term, their goal is to raise employment standards in all countries to the level of the best and beyond.

Nicholas Squire[49] says that companies still tend to view industrial relations as a localised issue, but the rise of increasingly organised and powerful Global Union Federations means multinationals now face a greater strain on their employee relations across national borders. Their ability to deal with trade unions needs to be global.

Because unions are broadening their focus beyond domestic concerns to a company's international workforce and global operations, they are exerting pressure on shareholders, suppliers and other stakeholders to sanction employers who do not meet the necessary standards. By using social media global unions can raise awareness of a labour relations issue around the world, and give the impression of a large and well resourced campaign that may in reality only be very small scale. By elevating local issues to the global level, multinationals face the risk of severe reputational damage in markets far removed from the source of the issue.

There are a number of tools used by global trade unions to pursue their strategies at the international level, but the primary tool is the International Framework Agreement (IFA).[50] These are essentially voluntary agreements, without legal underpinning, between a company and trade unions. Both sides make commitments to each other in areas of common interest.

Over 95 multinational companies have signed such agreements with GUFs, with unions seeking to strengthen the agreements by adding concrete dispute resolution and implementation mechanisms to hasten progress towards a more mature form of international industrial relations.

Conclusion

There is a growing number of examples of an increasingly international approach to industrial relations, with multinational companies capitulating to trade union demands often after long running campaigns.

Soft laws, as outlined above, are proving to be an impressive leverage tool for the trade unions. In 2010, the UK National Contact Point ruled that a Malaysian subsidiary of British American Tobacco had failed to comply with OECD guidelines for operating overseas. The Malaysian Trades Union Congress brought the complaint against the UK registered multinational for failing to consult an in-house trade union before a major workforce restructuring. As a result, the subsidiary agreed to formalise its communications guidelines and committed to hold face to face meetings with employees or trade unions. Even if industrial action is not available under local laws, one of the biggest threats facing multinationals is reputational damage.

Notes

1 Muchlinski, P. (2001) 'Human Rights and Multinationals – Is there a Problem?' 77 *International Affairs* 31, 33–35.
2 Ratner, S.R. (2001) 'Corporations and Human Rights: A Theory of Legal Responsibility', 111 *Yale Law Journal* 443; Clapham, Andrew (2006) *Human Rights Obligations of Non-State Actors*, ch. 6, Oxford: Oxford University Press.

3   UNCTAD (1999) *The Social Responsibility of Transnational Corporations*, United Nations, New York and Geneva; UNCTAD (1999) *World Investment Report*, United Nations, New York and Geneva.
4   Williams, J.R. (1999) 'How Principles Benefit the Bottom Line: The Experience of the Co-Operative Bank', in M.K. Addo (ed.), *Human Rights Standards and the Responsibility of Transnational Corporations*, The Hague: Kluwer Law International.
5   Muchlinski (2001).
6   Clapham, A. (1993) *Human Rights in the Private Sphere*, Oxford: Clarendon Press.
7   Ibid.
8   Amnesty International (1998) *Human Rights Guidelines for Companies*, London: Amnesty International, pp. 8–11.
9   Baxi, U. (2002) *The Future of Human Rights*, New Dehli: Oxford University Press.
10   United States Statement on Item 17 of the Sixty-First Session of the UN Human Rights Commission, 20 April 2005. http://www.business-humanrights.org.
11   Muchlinski, P. (2007) *Multinational Enterprises and the Law*, Oxford: Oxford University Press.
12   Likosky, M.B. (2005) *The Silicon Empire: Law Culture and Commerce*, Aldershot: Ashgate.
13   Muchlinski (2007).
14   UN Norms, Section H, para 17.
15   963 F Supp 880 US Dist Ct, CD Cal, 25 March 1997.
16   The Act states that 'The district courts shall have original jurisdiction of any civil action by an alien for a tort only, committed in violation of the law of nations or a treaty of the United States.'
17   Weissbrodt, D. and M. Kruger (2003) 'Norms on the Responsibilities of Transnational Corporations and Other Business Enterprises with regard to Human Rights', 97 *American Journal of International Law* 901.
18   Muchlinski (2007).
19   Muchlinski, P. (1999) 'A Brief History of Regulation', in S. Picciotto and R. Mayne (eds), *Regulating International Business: Beyond Liberalization*, London: MacMillan Press.
20   Introduction (2001) UN Doc E/CN.4/Sub.2/2001/WG.2/WP.1 at 12 para 36.
21   (2001) UN Doc E/CN.4/Sub.2/2001/WP.1/Add 1 Sec H para 17. Commentary at (c).
22   UN Norms, Section H, para 18.
23   Muchlinski (2007).
24   OECD (2000)*OECD Guidelines for Multinational Enterprises*, OECD, Paris, pp. 21–22.
25   The revised version of this was adopted 28 March 2006. http://www.ilo.org/public/english/employment/multi/download/english.pdf.
26   Muchlinski (2007), p. 473.
27   ILO Declaration, para 4.
28   ILO Declaration, para 8.
29   ILO Constitution, Art 19 (5)(e). http://www.ilo.org/public/english/about/iloconst.htm#a3p5.
30   *Lawson v Serco Ltd, Botham v Ministry of Defence, Crofts and others v Veta Ltd and Others* [2006] UKHL 3, [2006] 1 All ER 823 (HL).
31   ILO Declaration, para 22.
32   OECD Guidelines, para 1.
33   *EEOC/Boureslan v ARAMCO* 113 Sup Ct 274 (1991).
34   *Sumitomo Shoji America v Avagliano* 457 US 176 (US Sup Ct 1982).
35   Council Directive 96/71/EC OJ [1997] L 18/1.
36   ILO Declaration, para 24.
37   For all these cases see Blanpain, R. (1977) *The Badger Case and the OECD Guidelines for Multinational Enterprises*, The Hague: Kluwer International Publishing.

38 *Francovich v Italy* (1993) 2 CMLR 66.
39 OJ [2001] L82/16.
40 OECD Employment Guideline, para 4(a).
41 ILO Declaration, para 33.
42 Blanpain (1977).
43 ILO Declaration, para 34 and Recommendation No. 116 concerning Reduction of Hours of Work.
44 ILO Convention Concerning the Prohibition and Immediate Elimination of the Worst Forms of Child Labour. 17 June 1999; 38 ILM 1207 (1999).
45 ILO Declaration, para 36.
46 ILO Declaration, para 1(b) and the Commentary, para 22.
47 Shelton, D. (2007) *Commitment and Compliance: The Role of non-binding Norms in the International Legal System*, Oxford: Oxford University Press, p. 452.
48 Ibid., p. 462.
49 Nicholas Squire, Partner in Freshfield Bruckhouse Deringer's employment practice.
50 See http://www.ilo.org/wcmsp5/groups/public/@ed_emp/documents/publication/wcms_122176.pdf and http://www.global-unions.org/+-framework-agreements-+.html.

3   Environmental accountability

Introduction

Adam Smith, in his book *Wealth of Nations*,[1] stated: 'Every injudicious and unsuccessful project in agriculture, mines, fisheries, trade or manufactures, tends … to diminish the funds destined for the maintenance of productive labour'.

Conflicts between, and the limitations in, relevant parts of municipal and international law are at the basis of the concept of corporate accountability within international environmental law. The control over multinationals at the national level, that is the legal control over a subsidiary of a multinational company by the host state, and the legal control over a multinational parent company by the home state, is increasingly showing its inefficacy. Ensuring the environmentally sound conduct of business under the international law on state responsibility, or civil and criminal liability in international environmental law, is also affected by significant limits.

International environmental law can be seen as calling upon states to regulate the behaviour of non-state actors that are the source of harm to the environment,[2] while at the same time it hardly ever mentions expressly non-state actors, in particular business corporations.[3]

The implementation of international environmental provisions does not envisage a special role for private companies, but rather provides for states to enact the necessary legislation to direct and control the conduct of these actors in their territory and under their jurisdiction.[4] The International Court of Justice (ICJ) referred to safeguarding the earth's ecological balance as an essential interest of all states to protect the international community as a whole,[5] thus most of international environmental law can be seen as obligations *erga omens*.[6] What each state does to protect the environment from non-state actors' activities under its jurisdiction is, therefore, at least in some instances, of a 'common concern' to the whole of the international community, that is the common interest of all states in certain forms of ecological protection.

The role of soft law with regard to the environment

International environmental law itself has been developed to a significant extent on the basis of soft law, which is so carefully negotiated and drafted that is can be argued that there is at least an element of good faith commitment by states and an element of influence on the development of state practice and international law. Although the support of state members of the international organisations under the aegis of which these instruments of soft law have been adopted do not express an *opinion juris* (the conviction to the effect that the conduct at stake is required or permitted as a matter of law), but rather a political commitment, states are no longer in a position to raise objections against the general orientation indicated in these documents.[7]

As soft law can address not only states, but also other members of the international community such as individuals and corporations, in identifying emerging international standards for corporate environmental accountability soft law instruments are drawn upon, such as declarations of international conferences, guidelines and instruments proposed by NGOs, and/or adopted voluntarily by business associations. The flexibility of soft law ensures the continuous adaptation to the changing conditions in which private companies operate and enables a follow-up process to monitor state practice, and identify an evolving system of law on multinationals.[8] Many soft law initiatives in the field of corporate accountability have been developed by international organisations, NGOs, and the private sector, often in the absence of intergovernmental approval. These types of initiatives are a reflection of the lack of formal international law-making capacity of such non-state actors, their impact ultimately depending upon the political and economic interests of relevant players.[9] Nonetheless, these soft law instruments still constitute a significant contribution at the international level.[10]

When comparing earlier and recent activities on corporate accountability within the UN with the related activities in the OECD, one should bear in mind that the membership of the OECD is significantly more limited than that of the UN. The OECD was created in 1961 as an organisation of countries 'sharing a commitment to democratic government and market economy',[11] thus grouping major capital-exporting states. The OECD first approved its Guidelines for Multinational Enterprises in 1976, as part of the Declaration on International Investment and Multinational Enterprises, which was designed to improve the international investment climate and to strengthen the basis for mutual confidence between enterprises and the society in which they operate. Some viewed the birth of the OECD Guidelines as the developed countries' strategy to create their own framework for the activities of multinationals in order to reinforce their negotiating position at the multilateral level, in particular in the negotiations for the UN Code.[12] Others went further to identify a desire of OECD countries to pre-empt stricter regulations under the UN Code. What is certain is that the success of the parallel OECD initiative was due to the smaller number of like-minded states involved in the negotiations, and the extensive involvement of business and labour organisations in drafting and reviewing the Guidelines, through the Advisory Committees of Business and of Labour Federations. This participating process contributed to 'prevent misunderstandings and build an atmosphere of confidence and predictability between business, labour and governments' within the OECD.[13] This understanding was based on the traditional view that governments were more powerful than multinational companies; however, developing countries were voicing concerns about the growing power of multinationals, which was considered as almost overwhelming the host countries' capacity for control.

The Guidelines were significantly revised in 2000 and now expressly state their applicability to the operations of multinationals and all their entities,[14] in adhering countries and abroad. They also stress that all business entities, not just multinationals, are subject to the same expectations of good corporate conduct. The environmental provisions within the Guidelines were significantly strengthened in order to reflect the Rio Declaration on Environment and Development and Agenda 21 and to respond to the calls for the improvement of internal Environmental Management Systems (EMS) and for greater disclosure of environmental information. The objective of sustainable development was also introduced in the Guidelines at this time.

Both the 2000 review and the discussions on corporate accountability at the 2002 World Summit on Sustainable Development (WSSD) revived the interest within environmental NGOs of the OECD Guidelines and so the Guidelines have accordingly been defined as the only multilaterally endorsed code that has comprehensive subject matter and whose promotion is supported by an explicit government commitment to ensure acceptable corporate conduct.[15] As a document with intergovernmental consensus, but lacking legally binding force, the OECD Guidelines have been praised by some scholars for contributing to providing a common frame of reference for multinationals to ensure that their operations are compatible with expectations by host countries and for legitimising the social sanctions performed by non-state actors against irresponsible companies, such as boycotts.[16] The Guidelines can also be seen as a tool for interpreting the meaning and guiding the application of other international instruments and domestic laws.

The convergence of environmental standards

The UN Draft Code of Conduct devoted three paragraphs to the protection of the environment which prescribes that multinationals should carry out their activities in accordance with national laws, regulations, administrative practices, and policies, but also with 'due regard to relevant international standards'. Additionally, corporations were expected to take steps to protect the environment and, where damaged, to restore it.[17] Shelton, however, identifies an inherent problem in the attempt within the Draft Code to reconcile the requirement of non-interference with the internal affairs of the host state, with that for corporations to adhere to international environmental standards even when the host states have not done so.[18] In addition, the Draft Code in paragraph 42 required the multinationals to supply to the competent authorities of the host countries all relevant information concerning products, processes, and services. The detailed list of information is considered as one of the main contributions of the Draft Code to the definition of corporate environmental accountability.[19] Finally the Draft Code expects transnational companies to cooperate not only with national governments, but also with international organisations, for the protection of the environment.[20] The Code envisaged that the environmental provisions of the Draft Code were drafted in a sufficiently flexible manner, thus permitting the adoption of different national implementing measures.[21]

The UN Global Compact encourages businesses to undertake initiatives to promote greater environmental responsibility, whereas the Guide elaborates on environmentally sound business practices encompassing resource productivity, cleaner production, corporate governance, and multi-stakeholder dialogue.[22] Finally the Global Compact expects adhering companies to encourage the development and diffusion of environmentally friendly technologies.[23] These are defined in the Guide to the UN Global Compact by express reference to Agenda 21, thus including technologies that allow for limited pollution, protection of the environment, sustainable use of natural resources, and the reduction or re-use of waste.[24]

The Sub-Commission's Norms provide the most detailed provisions on corporate environmental accountability with the imprimatur of the UN, with the Preamble highlighting the obligation for multinationals and other business enterprises to respect 'generally recognised responsibility and norms contained in UN treaties and other international instruments'. Among these, reference was made, even in the earlier drafts, to the Convention on Civil Liability for Oil Pollution Damage and the Convention on Civil Liability for Damage Resulting from Activities Dangerous to the Environment,[25] which are two examples in International Environmental Law (IEL) of civil liability of private business entities. The 2003 version of the documents also includes reference to the Biodiversity Conventions, the Rio Declaration, the WSSD Plan of Implementation, and the Millennium Declaration. The operational section on environmental protection[26] of the Norms is framed in obligatory terms and requires 'accordance with national laws, regulations, administrative practices and policies of the countries in which multinationals operate'.

The Commentary to the Norms greatly expands on Section G, inasmuch as it calls for the respect of the rights to a clean and healthy environment, respect of concern for intergenerational equity, and respect of 'internationally recognised standards' on air, water pollution, land use, biodiversity, and hazardous waste.[27] Additionally, the Commentary expects companies to be responsible for the environmental and human health impacts of all their activities. Finally, business enterprises are to assess the environmental impacts of their activities on a periodic basis in order to ensure that the burden of the negative environmental consequences does not fall on vulnerable racial, ethnic, and socio-economic groups.

Emerging international standards

The three UN documents acknowledge the necessary observance on the part of, and the direct applicability to, businesses of international standards for the protection of the environment. This is done either by directly specifying such a requirement, as in the case of the UN Draft Code and of the Norms, or by implying it, as in the case of the sources of the environmental principles of the UN Global Compact, which is based on the Rio Declaration. In this respect, it is interesting to note that all three initiatives are built upon pre-existing international documents on the environment, which had been developed within the UN system, and approved at governmental level. The debates on the environmental regulation of the multinationals have flourished from the merger of the discussions within the UN on the role of multinationals in the global economy and those on international environmental protection.[28]

Both the UN Draft Code and the Norms place great emphasis on the provision of information on the environmental impacts of business enterprises, with the UN Global Compact pointing to multi-stakeholder consultation as part of its encouragement to undertake initiatives promoting greater environmental responsibility. The Norms go beyond the detailed prescription of the Draft Code, by expressly indicating that information is to be provided not only to the government of the state in which its activities are taking place, which may already be requested by national legislation, but that information is also to be provided by the state of incorporation, to relevant international organisations and to the public at large.

Both the UN Global Compact and the Norms intend to apply the precautionary principle/approach to business enterprises. Notwithstanding the uncertainty as to the precise legal meaning of precaution, this development seems particularly significant, especially in consideration of the commitment of thousands of companies participating in the UN Global Compact. Whilst the UN Norms do not attempt to translate the precautionary principle in a standard for corporate accountability, the Guide to the UN Global Compact suggests a proactive approach based on 'the most cost-effective early action to prevent irreversible environmental harm'.

The 1990s were characterised by a series of factors that changed considerably the attitude of the international community towards multinational corporations and business in general. Firstly, nationalisation of foreign enterprises and direct state control over the utilisation of natural resources were no longer considered by a large number of countries as the principle road to economic development. Secondly, due to the development aid crisis, the debt crisis, and the shortfall in investment towards developing countries, a re-evaluation of benefits of multinationals took place. This was accompanied by increasing privatisation, a growing number of bilateral investment agreements, and international action aiming at the establishment of new structures for investors' protection through the World Bank and the World Trade Organization (WTO). Thirdly, a changed system of international governance increasingly involved non-state actors, both the private sector, and the NGO community, in the shaping and implementation of international law.[29]

In consideration of all these new circumstances, a more detached and analytical approach with regard to corporate accountability was developed within the UN system. In the late 1990s, the UN aimed at ensuring further understanding of multinationals' activities and their impacts on development, in order to facilitate access of developing countries to foreign direct investment.

Standards on corporate accountability in International Environmental Law

The above international instruments aiming at identifying minimum standards on corporate environmental accountability within the framework of the UN, and the OECD in varying forms, have consistently referred to international standards based on sustainable development, disclosure and information, environmental impact assessment and precaution. These have directly translated into international environmental law principles, objectives and basic obligations for states which become normative benchmarks. These are then directly applicable to international companies. These various documents and initiatives on corporate accountability have converged to produce certain standards for the protection of the environment which include self assessment of environmental impacts; environmental management; prevention; precaution; disclosure of environmental information; consultations with the public; sustainable use of natural resources; and respect for internationally protected sites. Considering the activities of NGOs, the commitments voluntarily undertaken by private companies at the international level, and recent developments in international environmental law assist in better defining these standards.

One of the principles to protect the environment which is considered to be an essential element of sustainable development is that of integration.[30] This implies that countries and international organisations commit to integrate environmental considerations into economic development, and take into account the needs of economic and social development in drafting, applying, and interpreting environmental obligations.[31] Although initially the principle of environmental integration was conceived with regard to national development planning, it is now the very basis of the concept of corporate environmental accountability. It translates directly into the general expectation that business enterprises take into account environmental concerns within their corporate decision making process.

With regard to companies, this standard implies the explicit consideration of environmental impacts of corporate activities at the boardroom level, so that any negative impact would need to be identified, rectified and prevented from recurring.[32] Private companies are clearly bound by national environmental laws to this effect in the case of major developments. However, they may also be reasonably expected to go beyond the specific legal requirements of the host state on the basis of the specific implementation and enforcement capacity in such a state, to pursue at the very least minimum environmental integration as a precondition for all their operations on an ongoing basis. Therefore, if a private company plans and/or undertakes activities in complete disregard of possible environmental consequences, it would be against minimum international environmental standards.

Tools have been identified for implementing the integration standard by private companies, which are *inter alia*: self assessment of environmental impacts, and the adoption of an Environmental Management System (EMS). These tools are considered to be an integral part of the integration system and are highlighted by the UN Norms, the OECD Guidelines, and the International Finance Corporation (IFC).

Self assessment of environmental impacts

Environmental Impact Assessments (EIAs) have been well established since the 1970s, both at international and national level, as a technique for states to integrate environmental concerns into socio-economic development and decision making.[33] Notwithstanding that the procedures and methodology have not been standardised at the international level, it is clear that EIA implies the need for scientific evidence, effective consideration of possible impacts on the environment, and communication to authorities of the findings.[34]

Should a state not require foreign and national enterprises to undertake EIAs, a corporate accountability standard still applies. These are usually confined to major developments that are likely to have negative impacts on the environment and, therefore, national legislation typically sets thresholds below which an EIA is not required. An international standard of corporate environmental accountability based on the integration principle may entail that the private sector assesses the possible impacts on the environment of all its activities, on the basis of scientific evidence and communication with likely affected communities. Further, it requires companies to take such an assessment into account in deciding whether to carry out such activities or not. An international requirement for EIA for companies can compel private companies' management to pay greater attention to environmental performance and contribute to the transfer of valuable information on environmental control technology and costs.

A human rights approach to the EIA standard is found in the UN Norms on the Responsibility of Transnational Corporations, according to which business enterprises are to assess the environmental impacts of their activities on a periodic basis, in order to ensure that the burden of the negative environmental consequences does not fall on vulnerable racial, ethnic and socio-economic groups.[35] The OECD Guidelines also stress the need for a lifecycle assessment of impacts.[36]

To better define this standard, the Convention on Biological Diversity (CBD) Guidelines on Biodiversity and Tourism Development call upon the proponent of tourism developments to undertake the following steps:

1   Identify the various stakeholders involved in or potentially affected by the proposed project.
2   Assess the potential impacts of the proposals.
3   Provide information on these potential impacts through a notification process.
4   Undertake and fund necessary studies.
5   Involve indigenous and local communities in the assessment.

In addition the CBD Addis Ababa Principles also suggest that, where possible, companies should consider the aggregate and cumulative impacts of activities on the target species and ecosystems in management decisions to that species or ecosystems.[37] Notably, the international standard on environmental integration calls not only for an assessment of environmental impacts by the private company before commencing a new project or development, but also as an ongoing process throughout the life of the project.[38]

Environmental Management Systems

As self assessment of environmental impact is necessary. It is also a precondition for companies to set in place an Environmental Management System. This is another practical means to implement the integration standard. In fact an EMS is a necessary follow on from an impact assessment; otherwise the assessment would be merely a procedural exercise devoid of any practical implication.[39] EMSs may serve to control both direct and indirect environmental impacts of enterprise activities over the long term, and involve both pollution control and resource management elements.[40] The OECD identifies this as the first tool to provide the internal framework necessary to control a company's environmental impacts and integrate environmental considerations into business operations.

Such systems provide for companies to engage in a process of continual improvement of their environmental performance,[41] through the collection and evaluation of information and monitoring of measurable environmental objectives and targets, without setting absolute performance standards.[42] These systems also provide a practical way for companies to assess whether they are employing the 'best practical means' or the 'best available technology' with regard to their environmental performance. A further important feature of the EMS is the disclosure of information and community engagement. It should also be understood that the standard on self assessment of environmental impacts and environmental management is tightly intertwined with that on disclosure of information and public participation.

The preventive principle

The preventive principle calls for states' due diligence to avoid conducts harmful to the environment, by reducing, limiting, or controlling activities that may cause or constitute a risk of environmental damage.[43] This identifies the obligation for states to prevent damage to the environment within their own jurisdiction, normally by means of regulatory, administrative and other measures.[44] In other words this means that states should take action at an early stage before any damage has been caused by prohibiting activities that cause or may cause damage to the environment in violation of standards which have been established under international law.

The practical translation of the prevention principle into a corporate accountability standard operated by the OECD Guidelines implies that companies should put in place contingency plans for preventing, mitigating, and controlling serious environmental and health damage from their operations, including accidents and emergencies, as well as mechanisms for immediate reporting to competent authorities.[45] An enterprise that is the user of a hazardous industrial process, or the disseminator of a harmful product or waste, has a responsibility to ensure that the process, product or waste, as the case may be, does no harm. The preventive principle is enacted in numerous national environmental protection laws and in Principle 11 of the 1992 Rio Declaration, which requires states to enact 'effective environmental legislation'.[46] The principle ensures that companies themselves become the first line of defence against environmental harm by seeking to prevent such harm from arising by reason of their adopting effective environmental management practices and technologies. Thus the preventive principle forms the basis of self regulation as well as external regulation.

The most prominent rule of international environmental law is the prohibition on causing trans-boundary environmental harm, which is a customary international rule and applies to all states, and the whole of the international community.[47] As an interstate obligation, it implies that states have to ensure that activities within their jurisdiction or control do not cause damage to the natural systems located outside of their territory. This obligation also entails notification of imminent harm, assistance in emergencies, advance notification and consultation, and equal access to administrative or judicial procedures.

The precautionary principle

The concept of the precautionary principle was first pioneered in the domestic law of West Germany, and was subsequently accepted in other national laws and thus in the Rio Declaration.[48] The principle stresses that where there exists a real risk of serious and irreversible environmental damage, it is incumbent upon the regulator to act and to prevent that damage from arising even where there is lack of full scientific certainty as to the threat in question. The major difficulty lies in determining when there does exist a sufficiently serious risk and, if such a determination is made, what action should be taken to mitigate the risk. This could have serious commercial implications for enterprises subjected to such regulation. It could lead to an overprotective approach that stifles corporate freedom to exploit potentially hazardous forms of trade or investment that may otherwise be economically and socially useful. In this regard, it may be claimed that a regulatory taking could take place. That is when an unreasonable and inflexible application of the precautionary principle by a governmental authority could lead to the effective neutralisation of the economic value of an investment. On the other hand, the fear of such litigation may itself be counterproductive, in that it may lead to so called 'regulatory chill' whereby the risk of such litigation will, by itself, lead to less than optimal regulation on the part of the host country, in the belief that fully effective regulation might be challenged as a regulatory taking.[49]

Under the Rio Declaration formulation, precaution implies that states should not use the lack of scientific certainty as a reason for postponing cost effective measures to prevent environmental degradation where there are threats of serious or irreversible damage.[50] Accordingly, it was the basis of international action for the protection of the ozone layer,[51] tackling climate change[52] and ensuring biodiversity.[53]

However, several intergovernmental organisations and environmental NGOs have relied on the precautionary principle approach to define the concept of corporate environmental accountability.[54]

In general terms, a precautionary standard may require companies to act carefully and with foresight when taking decisions concerning activities that may have adverse impacts on the environment. More specifically, it may prevent companies from using a certain level of scientific certainty as an excuse for carrying out activities potentially dangerous for the environment. In all these instances it will depend on a case by case determination of the cost effective measures that a company can take, and the level of scientific uncertainty and of environmental threat or likely harm at stake.

Primarily, the importance of a precautionary standard for private companies and multinationals is supported by almost all recent international initiatives aimed at defining corporate accountability, namely the UN Global Compact,[55] the OECD Guidelines for Multinational Enterprises[56] and the UN Norms.[57] The Guide to the UN Global Compact emphasises that the principle entails that businesses should take the most *cost effective, early* action to prevent the occurrence of *irreversible* environmental damage, and to this end, companies are expected to carry out assessments of their environmental impacts and environmental risks, invest in sustainable production methods, and research and develop environmentally friendly products.[58] However, the OECD Guidelines intend to use the precautionary approach to prevent multinationals from delaying action to prevent or minimise *serious* environmental damage in the absence of full scientific certainty, as long as such action entails *cost effective* measures.

Whereas the UN Global Compact emphasises the role of private companies in taking action, the OECD Guidelines express in negative terms that companies should not delay precautionary action. Both refer to cost effective measures, but the UN Global Compact links the standard to irreversible environmental damage, while the OECD Guidelines set a lower threshold by referring to serious harm, and the UN Norms avoid defining the way in which precaution applies to companies altogether.

Sustainable development

The legal regulation of the environmental activities of multinational corporations is, therefore, based on a number of core concepts. However, the most fundamental of them is that of 'sustainable development'. Sustainable development was fully endorsed at, and informed much of, the Rio Declaration, as well as the Convention on Climate Change and Biological Diversity. It is also central to the elaboration of global environmental responsibility by these and other instruments.[59] Agenda 21 also refers in its preamble to the need for a 'global partnership for sustainable development', and most of its provisions are intended to promote the concept, whose implementation is monitored by the Commission on Sustainable Development.[60] With the adoption of the Rio instruments, sustainable development became and has so far remained the leading concept of international environmental policy. The Brundtland Report characterised sustainable development as a process that 'meets the needs of the present without compromising the ability of future generations to meet their own needs'.[61] United Nations Environmental Programme's Governing Council later added that this 'does not imply in any way encroachment upon national sovereignty'.[62]

Although 'sustainable development' is used throughout the Rio Declaration, it was not until the 2002 World Summit on Sustainable Development that anything approaching a definition of the concept could be attempted by the UN as three 'interdependent and mutually reinforcing pillars of sustainable development'. These were identified in the Johannesburg Declaration as economic development, social development, and environmental protection.[63]

Since Rio numerous governments at both national and regional levels have adopted sustainable development as a policy. It has influenced the application and the development of law and policy by various international organisations, including Food and Agriculture Organization, International Maritime Organization, the World Bank, the World Trade Organization, and United Nations Development Programme, as well as treaty bodies such as the International Tropical Timber Organization and the European Energy Charter.[64] Principle 27 of the Rio Declaration and Chapter 39 of Agenda 21 call specifically for further development of international law 'in the field of sustainable development'.[65] However, although it is possible to identify the main elements of the concept of sustainable development it is far from certain what their specific normative implications are, or indeed how they relate to one another.

Legal status of sustainable development

Given the breadth of international endorsement for the concept of sustainable development, few states would quarrel with the proposition that development should, in principle, be sustainable and that all natural resources should be managed in this way. However, what is lacking is any consensus on the meaning of sustainable development, or on how to give it effect in individual cases.

This means that states retain substantial discretion in interpreting and giving effect to the principle. Given the social, political and economic value judgements involved in deciding on what is sustainable, and the necessity of weighing conflicting factors, it is difficult to see an international court reviewing national actions and concluding that they fall short of a standard of 'sustainable development', save in the most extreme case.[66] However, courts could review the sustainability of economic development by reference to detriment to human rights, including the right to life, private life or property, or economic, social and cultural rights. Take for example the *Ogoniland* case, after noting 'the destructive and selfish role played by oil development in Ogoniland, closely tied with repressive tactics of the Nigerian Government, and the lack of material benefits accruing to the local population', the African Commission on Human and Peoples' Rights (ACHPR) found, *inter alia*, that the right of peoples to dispose freely of their own natural resources had been violated as well as their right to 'ecologically sustainable development'.[67] Any challenge to the sustainability of economic development would be most effective if it were focused on the long-term impact on the environment on which those most affected depended for their livelihood.

Additionally, although international law does not require all development to be sustainable, it does require the decisions to be the outcome of a process which promotes sustainable development specifically if states do not carry out environmental impact assessments, or they refuse to cooperate in the management of global and trans-boundary risks. Should states fail to integrate development and environmental considerations in their decision making, or if they do not take account of the needs of intra- and inter-generational equity, they will have failed to implement the main tools employed by the Rio Declaration and other international instruments for the purpose of facilitating sustainable development.[68]

An interpretation which makes the process of decision making the key legal test of sustainable development, rather than the nature of the development, is implicitly supported by the *Gabcíkovo-Nagymaros* case. In this case, although the ICJ did not question whether a project conceived in 1997 was sustainable, the court required the parties in the interest of sustainable development to 'look afresh' at the environmental consequences and to carry out monitoring and abatement measures to contemporary standards set by international law.[69] Such arguments, then, focus on the components of sustainable development, rather than on the concept itself. In other words, even if there is no obligation to develop sustainably, there may nevertheless be law 'in the field of sustainable development'.[70]

Corporate accountability for sustainable development

The emphasis of sustainable development then is on human needs rather than wants, and on inter- and intra-generational equity. The accommodation is between economic growth, environmental concerns, and the wider social effects of economic activity. Economic growth is seen as a necessary prerequisite for environmentally sound development, but the methods and processes of economic growth must ensure the survival of a sustainable ecosystem that can last for generations. Equally, the social effects of environmental protection, or damage, as the case may be, need to be taken into account as part of the complex range of interactions that characterise the concept of sustainable development. It is in this regard that sustainable development may be seen as an aspect of human dignity, and hence of human rights in general.

Key to the pursuit of sustainable development is determining how far the operation of the modern global economy threatens the ecosystem. Depending on how that question is answered, resulting policy responses may be very restrictive of international trade and investment or very permissive.[71] Even within the environmentalist camp there are deep differences of opinion. Those who support the concept of sustainable development are dismissed by 'deep ecologists' for failing to appreciate that there can be no sustainable development so long as the present economic system, based on competition in deregulated markets and ever increasing consumerism, is allowed to function. For 'deep ecologists' this very system must be stopped if the ecosystem is to survive. Supporters of sustainable development are criticised by 'deep ecologists' as doing no more than legitimising the economic project of globalisation.[72] Nevertheless, the concept of sustainable development may be sufficient to include issues of development in less developed countries.

The concept should also permit some accommodation between free traders and environmentalists in that it sees economic growth, to be achieved through liberalised trade and investment, as a desired goal. It does not reject market-based techniques for ensuring more environmentally sensitive business and regulatory behaviour. However, the concept demands recognition of the fact that unregulated industrialisation and growth will create environmentally unacceptable consequences. In particular the environmental effects of domestic and foreign investment alike will be considered. Therefore, a degree of control over the environmental effects of domestic and foreign investment alike will be required.[73]

Disclosure of environmental information

The international obligations to collect and disclose environmental information by states on the state of the environment and activities with potential adverse effects is now a well established requirement. This is a prerequisite for effective national and international environmental management, protection and cooperation, as well as for allowing preventive and mitigation measures and ensuring public participation.[74]

For the private sector, disclosure of environmental information is also the basis of its cooperation with local and other authorities, in particular for compliance with the prevention standard. In 1989 UN reports were prioritising corporate environmental information disclosure as an 'essential element for the implementation of "sustainable development".[75] Here it was recommended developing an internationally accepted list of basic environmental data items that should be disclosed on a regular basis by individual firms. Concurrently commentators drew attention to the growing body of policy recommendations on transnational disclosure of information on hazardous products and processes.[76] Several cases of environmental damage led to aggravated consequences because of the lack of timely disclosure of information to public authorities and affected communities.[77] In the Bhopal disaster, for example, the private company did not send out an immediate alarm when the gas escaped; it did not take any steps in communicating to the local authorities or the local communities information about the consequences of exposure to leaked gas produced, nor did it give information on the medical steps to be taken in the aftermath of the disaster.[78] Also the late disclosure of information by the company significantly worsened the consequences of the Seveso dioxin release.[79]

The fundamental character of the standard on disclosure of information for the concept of corporate accountability was evident in the 1990 UN Draft Code of Conduct.[80] Also the UN Global Compact considers disclosure of information a necessary component of companies' multi-stakeholder dialogue.[81] The UN Norms, the OECD Guidelines, and the IFC Performance Standard all link the environmental integration standard with disclosure of information.[82]

Recent developments related to access to environmental information show an initial shift from standards to actual legal rules. The Arhus Convention on environmental information is directly relevant to the private sector inasmuch as the adoption of the Protocol on Pollutant Release and Transfer Register (PRTR Protocol) is the first legally binding instrument in international environmental law in this area.[83] The Protocol is open to all countries, even if they have not ratified the Aarhus Convention or are not members of the UN Economic Commission for Europe (UNECE).[84] The objective of the Protocol is to enhance public access to information through the establishment of coherent, integrated, nationwide pollution release and transfer registers (PRTRs), to facilitate public participation in environmental decision making, and to contribute to the prevention, and reduction of pollution in the environment.[85]

PRTRs are required to operate as a cost effective tool for encouraging improvements in environmental performance, and for providing public access to information on pollutants released and transferred by the private sector. Governments may use them for tracking trends and monitoring compliance with certain international agreements; also setting priorities and evaluating progress achieved through environmental policies and programmes.[86]

The Protocol covers releases and transfers of more than 80 pollutants listed in its Annex II, including greenhouse gases, acid rain pollutants, ozone depleting substances, heavy metals, and certain carcinogens, such as dioxins. PRTRs cover releases and transfers from certain types of major point sources of pollution, such as thermal power stations, waste and waste water treatment plants, and paper and timber industries, as well as available data on releases from diffuse sources such as transport and agriculture. Through the international harmonisation of the requirements for disclosure of environmental information by private companies, the Protocol represents an important precedent as a legally binding international instrument on corporate environmental accountability, providing substantive obligations on environmental information for the private sector, with a view to applying the precautionary approach.[87] A further relevant application can be found in the guidance to contractors for the assessment of possible environmental impacts arising from the exploration for polymetallic nodules in the sea bed 'Area',[88] which comes under the jurisdiction of the Seabed Authority,[89] which is the first international organisation with direct and immediate competence over private operators.

The international standard for disclosure of environmental information applies to companies not only before a certain project or activity is commenced, but also throughout the life of such projects in the case of EIA.

Public consultation

International standards make reference to the need for the private sector to facilitate participation of affected communities, in particular indigenous ones, in relation to the EIA and EMSs. Both the UN Norms and the OECD Guidelines identified a role for the private sector in ensuring participation of affected individuals. It would appear that community involvement should be ensured by the private sector, in particular in cases where it is expected that likely environmental impacts may hinder the enjoyment of local and indigenous communities' rights to their traditional lifestyle. Many international organisations also point to the fact that involvement of these communities in the EIA and management of private sector projects can contribute to the quality of the assessments and better decision making.[90]

Conclusions

Both at national and international level complaints have been made concerning environmental harm caused by substandard corporate conduct. The most recent standard setting initiative by an international organisation is the Performance Standards on Social and Environmental Sustainability.[91] This was launched by the International Finance Corporation (see Chapter 4) in 2006 in an unprecedented initiative among international financial institutions to clearly define the standards for the environmentally acceptable conduct of the private sector receiving funding. These standards were selected from other international environmental treaties and initiatives and mostly reflect those from the UN and OECD, such as prevention, environmental integration through the EIA and EMS, sustainable use of natural resources, public consultations and disclosure of environmental information.[92]

The development of binding norms for environmental protection that cover the activities of multinationals also brings together not only complex issues of substantive regulation but also issues of group liability, procedure, and jurisdiction.[93] We can see that multinationals can be a major source of potential and actual environmental harm but that they can also act as leading sources of technology to combat environmental problems.[94]

Notes

1 Smith, Adam (1776) *Wealth of Nations Books I–III*, London: Penguin Classics, 1999, Book II.iii.26: 441.
2 Kiss, A. and D. Shelton (2004) *International Environmental Law*, 3rd edn, Enschede: Nijhof Brill.
3 Ong, D.M. (2001) 'The Impact of Environmental Law on Corporate Governance: International and Comparative Perspectives', 12 *European Journal of International Law* 685.
4 Kiss and Shelton (2004).
5 ICJ, *Gabcikovo-Nagymaros Project* (Hungary–Slovakia). Judgement (25 September 1997), para 53.
6 Kiss and Shelton (2004).
7 Tomuschat, C. (2001) *International Law: Ensuring the Survival of Mankind on the Eve of a New Century*, Boston, MA and London: Martinus Nijhoff Publications.
8 Sauvant, K.P. and V. Aranda (1994) 'The International Legal Framework for Transnational Corporations', in A.A. Fatouros (ed.), *Transnational Corporations: The International Legal Framework*, London: Routledge, pp. 109–110.
9 Chinkin, C. (2003) 'Normative Development in the International Legal System', in D. Shelton (ed.), *Commitment and Compliance: The Role of Non-binding Norms in the International Legal System*, Oxford: Oxford University Press, pp. 21–42.
10 Morgera, E. (2009) *Corporate Accountability in International Environmental Law*, Oxford: Oxford University Press.
11 OECD, 'Overview of the OECD: What Is It? History? Who Does What? Structure of the Organisation?' http://www.oecd.org.
12 Sauvant and Aranda (1994).
13 Karl, K. (1999) 'The OECD Guidelines for Multinational Enterprises', in M.K. Addo (ed.), *Human Rights Standards and the Responsibility of Transnational Corporations*, The Hague: Kluwer Law International, pp. 89–90.
14 OECD Guidelines, ch. II, para. 10, 11; OECD, 'Roundtable on Corporate Responsibility; Encouraging the Positive Contribution of Business to Environment through OECD Guidelines for Multinational Enterprises' (Background Report, June 2004).
15 Morgera (2009), p. 104.
16 Ibid., p. 105.
17 UN Code of Conduct, paras 41–43.
18 Shelton, D. (2003) 'The Utility and Limits of Codes of Conduct for the Protection of the Environment', in A. Kiss, D. Shelton and K. Ishibashi (eds), *Economic Globalization and Compliance with International Environmental Agreements*, The Hague: Kluwer Law International, p. 213.
19 Pearson, C. (1982) 'An Environmental Code of Conduct for Multinational Companies?', in S.J. Rubin and T.A. Graham (eds), *Environment and Trade: The Relation of International Trade and Environmental Policy*, Totowa, NJ: Allanheld Osmun, p. 154.
20 UN Code of Conduct, para 43.
21 Pearson (1982), p. 155.
22 UN Guide to the Global Compact, p. 58. https://www.unglobalcompact.org/library/241.
23 Ibid., Principle 9.

24 Ibid., p. 64.
25 UN Sub-Commission (2001) 'Draft Universal Human Rights Guidelines for Companies', UN Doc E/CN.4/Sub.2/2001/WG.2/WP./Add.1.
26 Section G, para. 14.
27 UN Norms, Section G, Commentary at (a). https://www1.umn.edu/humanrts/links/commentary-Aug2003.html.
28 Morgera (2009), p. 113.
29 Haufler, V. (2001) *A Public Role for the Private Sector*, Washington, DC: Carnegie Endowment for International Peace.
30 Sands, P. (2003) *Principles of International Environmental Law*, Cambridge: Cambridge University Press, pp. 263–264.
31 Ibid.
32 Ong, D. (2001) 'The Impact of Environmental Law on Corporate Governance: International and Comparative Perspectives', vol. 12, no. 4 *European Journal of International Law* pp. 685–726, p. 695.
33 Sands (2003), p. 800.
34 Morgera (2009).
35 Weissbrodt, D. and M. Kruger (2005) 'Human Rights Responsibilities of Business as Non-State Actors', in P. Alston (ed.), *Non-State Actors and Human Rights*, Oxford: Oxford University Press, pp. 315, 343.
36 OECD (2001) Guidelines for Multinational Corporations, Ch. V, para 3. http://www.oecd.org/daf/inv/mne/ResourceDocumentWeb.pdf.
37 CBD Guidelines on Biodiversity and Tourism, Principle 5, Operational Guidelines. https://www.cbd.int/doc/publications/tou-gdl-en.pdf.
38 Morgera (2009), p. 181.
39 Ibid.
40 OECD Guidelines, Commentary, p. 30.
41 OECD (2004) 'Roundtable on Corporate Responsibility: Encouraging the Positive Contribution of Business to Environment through the OECD Guidelines for Multinational Enterprises: Summary of the Roundtable Discussion', p. 4. http://www.oecd.org/corporate/mne/33805553.pdf.
42 United Nations Conference on Trade and Development (UNCTAD) (2001) *Environment*, Geneva: UN, p. 56.
43 Sands (2003), p. 246.
44 Ibid.
45 OECD Guidelines, Ch. V, para. 5.
46 Sands (2003), p. 247.
47 ICJ (1996) *Legality of the Threat or Use of Nuclear Weapons*, Advisory Opinion, Para 29. The opinion in this case reiterated that customary international law on the prohibition on causing trans-boundary environmental harm applied to the whole of the international community.
48 Fitzmaurice, M. (2002) *International Protection of the Environment*, Hague: Recueil, 13 at 260; Rio Declaration, note 5, Principle 15. http://www.gdrc.org/u-gov/precaution-7.html.
49 UNCTAD (2003) *World Investment Report 2003*, New York and Geneva, p. 111.
50 Rio Declaration, Principle 15.
51 Convention for the Protection of the Ozone Layer (Vienna 1985) Arts I and V(3)(a).
52 UN Framework Convention on Climate Change (New York 1992), Art. 3(3).
53 Cartagena Protocol on Biosafety (Montreal 2000), Art. 10(6).
54 Khokhryakova, A. (1998) '*Beanal v Freeport-Mcmoran, Inc.*: Liability of a Private Actor for an International Environmental Tort under the Alien Tort Claims Act' 9 *Colorado Journal of International Environmental Law and Policy* 463.
55 The UN Global Compact, Principle 7. https://www.unglobalcompact.org/.

56 OECD Guidelines for Multinational Enterprises, Ch. V. http://www.oecd.org/corp orate/mne/1922428.pdf.
57 UN Norms, Section G. https://www1.umn.edu/humanrts/links/norms-Aug2003.html.
58 Guide on the UN Global Compact, p. 54. https://www.unglobalcompact.org/libra ry/241.
59 1992 Convention on Climate Change, Article 3 https://unfccc.int/resource/docs/ convkp/conveng.pdf; 1992 Convention on Biological Diversity, Articles 8 & 10. https://www.cbd.int/doc/legal/cbd-en.pdf; 1994 Convention to Combat Desertification, Articles 4 & 5. http://www.unccd.int/Lists/SiteDocumentLibrary/conventionText/ conv-eng.pdf.
60 UNGA Res 47/191 (1992).
61 WCED (1987) *Our Common Future*, Oxford, Oxford University Press, p. 43.
62 UNEP GC decision 15/2 (1989) Annex II.
63 UN (2002) Report of the World Summit on Sustainable Development, UN Doc A/ CONF 199/20, Resolution 1, para 5.
64 Osborn, D. and T. Bigg (1998) *Earth Summit II: Outcomes and Analysis*, London: Earthscan, ch. 2.
65 UNEP (1996) *Final Report of the Expert Group on International Law Aiming at Sustainable Development*, UNEP/IEL/WS/3/2.
66 Birnie, P., A. Boyle and C. Redgwell (2009) *International Law and the Environment*, 3rd edn, Oxford: Oxford University Press, p. 126.
67 *The Social and Economic Rights Action Centre and the Centre for Economic and Social Rights v Nigeria*. ACHPR Communication 155/96 (2002) paras 52–55.
68 Birnie, Boyle and Redgwell (2009), p. 127.
69 ICJ Reports (1997) 7, para 140. http://www.icj-cij.org/docket/files/92/7375.pdf.
70 *Pulp Mills on the River Uruguay*, ICJ Report (2006) paras 68–84. http://www. icj-cij.org/docket/files/135/15877.pdf.
71 Esty, D.C. (1994) *Greening the GATT*, Washington, DC: Institute for International Economics, p. 41.
72 Laferrière, E. (1996) 'Emancipating International Relations Theory: an Ecological Perspective', 25 *Millennium Journal of International Studies* 53, 54–61.
73 Carlie, M. and I. Christie (2000) *Managing Sustainable Development*, 2nd edn, London: Earthscan.
74 Sands (2003), p. 826.
75 UNCTAD (1989) 'Ongoing and Future Research: Transnational Corporations and Issues Relating to the Environment – Report of the Secretary General', UN Doc E/C. 10/1989/12, 12–13.
76 Gleckman, H. (1988) 'Proposed Requirements for Transnational Corporations to Disclose Information on Product and Process Hazards', 6 *Boston University International Law Journal* 89.
77 Ako, R.T. (2005) 'Issues on Environmental Human Rights and Corporate Social Responsibility in the Niger Delta', 15 *Lesotho Law Journal* 1.
78 The International Council on Human Rights Policy (2002) *Beyond Voluntarism: Human Rights and the Developing International Legal Obligations for Companies*, Versoix: International Council on Human Rights Policy, Bhopal case on p. 13 and, ch. 6. http://www.ichrp.org/files/reports/7/107_report_en.pdf.
79 United Nations Centre on Transnational Corporations (UNCTC) (1985) 'Envir-onmental Aspects of the Activities of Transnational Corporations: A Survey'. UN Doc ST/CTC/55, p. 93, ch. 6.
80 UNCTC (1990) 'Proposed Text of the Draft Code of Conduct on Transnational Corporation', UN Doc E/1990/94 para 42.
81 Guide to the UN Global Compact, p. 58. https://www.unglobalcompact.org/libra ry/1151.

82 Commentary to the UN Norms, (b) and (c); and IFC Performance Standard 1. http://www.ifc.org/wps/wcm/connect/3be1a68049a78dc8b7e4f7a8c6a8312a/PS1_English_2012.pdf?MOD=AJPERES.
83 Protocol on Pollutant Release and Transfer Register (2003).
84 PRTR Protocol, Art. 24.
85 Ibid., Art. 1.
86 Ibid., Preamble, p. 15.
87 UN Norms, para G; UN Global Compact, Principle 7.
88 The sea bed 'Area' was established under the United Nations Convention on the Law of the Sea 1982, Part XI, Section I, p. 66. http://www.un.org/depts/los/convention_agreements/texts/unclos/unclos_e.pdf.
89 Issued by the Legal and Technical Commission. 2002 UN Doc ISBA/7/LTC/1/Rev. 1
90 Morgera (2009), p. 192.
91 IFC (2006) 'Performance Standards on Social and Environmental Sustainability'. http://www.ifc.org/wps/wcm/connect/c8f524004a73daeca09afdf998895a12/IFC_Performance_Standards.pdf?MOD=AJPERES.
92 Morgera (2009), p. 269.
93 See Chapter 1.
94 See Chapter 9.

4 Trade and financial issues

Introduction

John Dyer, as long ago as 1757, wrote:

> Industry,
> Which dignifies the artist, lifts the swain,
> And the straw cottage to a palace turns.
>
> > (*The Fleece* (1757) bk. 3, 1. 332)

Trans-border trade is as old as civilisation, and states have constantly fluctuated in their policies between advocating free trade on the one hand and protecting their domestic enterprises on the other.[1] The international law governing trade and the more recent problems concerning the trans-boundary flow of money continue to be made up of a patchwork of bilateral and multilateral arrangements. Such agreements appear to be drafted more in the style of private law rather than public regulation, with trade matters utilising agreements containing negotiated benefits and burdens. Consequently, sanctions for non-compliance through the withdrawal of benefits appear easier than in other fields. For example, if one side breaches an agreement by raising tariffs, the other side may retaliate with tariffs of its own.[2] However, despite the WTO/GATT regime, international trade and finance are not governed by detailed international agreements and therefore non-binding norms often substitute for binding agreements as a precursor to an existing treaty. Trade agreements, therefore, are usually negotiated to increase market access or limit barriers to trade.

International trade and environmental protection

Since the adoption of the General Agreement on Tariffs and Trade (GATT) in 1947,[3] many states have become parties to what is now a complex system of international trade agreements based on the promotion and liberalisation of free trade in goods and services. Since the Marrakesh Agreement of 1994 entered into force, these agreements have been administered by the World

Trade Organization (WTO), and the WTO now provides the principle forum for negotiations on multilateral trading relations among member states, and for the binding settlement of disputes arising under WTO agreements.

A policy of free trade will inevitably create some conflict between international environmental agreements or environmental protection requirements in national law that have an effect of restricting trade in certain goods. However, international policy does not seek to give free trade priority over environmental protection, but neither does it endorse any general exception for environmental purposes. What the preamble to the 1994 Marrakesh Agreement Establishing the World Trade Organization acknowledges is that the expansion of production and trade must allow for:

> the optimal use of the world's resources in accordance with the objective of sustainable development, seeking both to protect and preserve the environment and to enhance the means for doing so in a manner consistent with their respective needs and concerns at different levels of economic development.[4]

It thus seeks a balance between the two objectives.

Principle 12 of the Rio Declaration consecutively called for states to cooperate to promote an 'open international economic system that would lead to growth and sustainable development in all countries'.[5] Further, the Declaration provides that 'Trade policy measures for environmental purposes should not constitute a means of arbitrary or unjustifiable discrimination or a disguised restriction on international trade'.[6]

Since 1994 a number of important decisions of the WTO Appellate Body have helped clarify how this balance between free trade agreements and environmental protection could be achieved. However, the WTO has been less successful in finding ways to integrate these two concerns. With regard to multilateral environmental agreements concluded since 1994 addressing trans-boundary or global environmental problems, these also have tried to accommodate both concerns, often repeating in preambular terms the exhortations to balance trade and environmental issues. This is due to the fact that there is a risk attached to the consideration of the compatibility of trade related environmental mechanisms (TREMS) with WTO rules at the drafting stage of any multilateral environmental agreements (MEAs) since 'the potential for conflict with WTO rules is near deal breaking in new MEA negotiations'.[7]

The multilateral trading system

The WTO oversees the implementation, administration, and operation of the 'Multinational Trade Agreements', which are legally binding upon its members. In addition to the General Agreement on Trade in Goods (GATT), these Agreements include the General Agreement on Trade and Services (GATS), the Agreement on Trade-Related Aspects of Intellectual Property Rights

(TRIPS), the Agreement on Trade-Related Investment Measures (TRIMS), the Agreement on Technical Barriers to Trade (TBT Agreement), the Agreement on the Application of Sanitary and Phytosanitary Measures (SPS Agreement), the Agreement on Agriculture, and the Agreement on Subsidies and Counter-vailing Measures (SCM Agreement). Environmental measures can fall under any one or more of these agreements; in addition, most of them contain spe-cific environmental exceptions, which mostly came within the Uruguay round of negotiations from which the WTO emerged.[8]

At the core of the WTO/GATT system are two non-discrimination principles which are the most favoured nation principle (MFN) and the national treat-ment principle. Both of these principles are essential for the full implementation of the Schedules of Concessions, i.e. lowered tariffs, which are binding obligations under GATT Article II.

The MFN principle under Article I is designed to ensure equality of treatment of 'like products originating or destined for the territories of all other contracting parties'. This means that 'customs charges and duties', 'all rules and formalities connected with importation or exportation', and internal taxes, charges, and domestic regulation of a product's distribution, sale, and use are given equal treatment 'unconditionally'.[9]

The national treatment provision under GATT Article III broadly applies to all 'internal' requirements applied to imported products, including taxes, charges, and all manner of regulations. The equality of treatment between imported and domestic products required by this provision is delicately worded with two standards to be met. One is positive and the other negative, and must be applied to imported products to accord 'treatment no less favourable than that accorded to like products of national origin'.[10] They must not be applied 'to afford protection to domestic production'.[11]

For internal taxes and charges, two negative criteria apply: they must not be 'in excess of those applied, directly or indirectly, to like domestic charges',[12] or 'applied to imported or domestic products so as to afford protection to domestic production'.[13] However, the question is whether the phrase 'laws, regulations, and requirements' in Article III is limited to the conditions of purchase or sale of products in the domestic market.[14]

Environmental exceptions

The 'General Exceptions' provision under GATT, Article XX, constitutes conditional exceptions to the GATT obligations, including those under Articles I, III, and XI. In addition Article XX may be applied to the envir-onment to justify certain environmentally inspired rules that affect free trade, although the word 'environment' is not used. The relevant wording of Article XX is *inter alia*:

> Subject to the requirement that such measures are not applied in a manner which would constitute a means of arbitrary or unjustifiable

discrimination between countries where the same conditions prevail, or a disguised restriction on international trade, nothing in this Agreement shall be construed to prevent the adoption or enforcement by any contracting party of measures:

a   necessary to protect human, animal or plant life or health;
b   [...]
c   relating to the conservation of exhaustible natural resources if such measures are made effective in conjunction with restrictions on domestic production or consumption.

Also the burden of proof is placed upon the party asserting Article XX as a defence.[15] It is very difficult to discharge this burden, largely because of the strictness with which its provisions are interpreted.[16]

At the meeting held to sign the Final Act Embodying the Results of the Uruguay Round of Multilateral Trade Negotiations in Marrakesh in 1994, the GATT contracting parties adopted a ministerial Decision that formally established a new Committee on Trade and Environment (CTE)[17] under the auspices of the World Trade Organization. The CTE was then charged with making appropriate recommendations on 'the need for rules to enhance the positive interaction between trade and environment measures for the promotion of sustainable development'. However, since 1996 the CTE has taken no decisions on how to reconcile trade and environmental concerns, with its annual reports being notable for their brevity.[18]

Nevertheless one of the great strengths of the WTO is the system of compulsory binding dispute settlement as provided by the Understanding on Rules and Procedures Governing the Settlement of Disputes adopted in 1994.[19] This system is administered by the Dispute Settlement Body (DSB).

The system of dispute settlement is neither self contained nor static, and the jurisdiction of the DSB only extends to matters arising under 'covered agreements'.[20] Most importantly, Article 3(2) of the WTO Dispute Settlement Understanding expressly provides that the existing provisions of the 'covered agreements' are to be classified 'in accordance with customary rules of interpretation of public international law'.[21]

The WTO approach to trade and environment is an expansive one that seeks to accommodate the value systems of both free trade and the environment that were initially perceived to be opposing values. It is doing this in a balanced fashion, but it must be appreciated that the sole promotion of the environmental agenda and its wholehearted adoption, without taking into consideration the importance of trade for economic growth, will result in developmental stagnation. This would not only undermine the goals set in the WTO Agreement but also the poverty reduction goal set by the Millennium Development Goals. It is certainly not the case that the trade promoters and the environmentalists are at opposite ends of the spectrum as they were made out to be in earlier cases. It is apparent from the recent decisions emanating from the WTO that there is some degree of convergence between the free trade promoters and the environmentalists. Without doubt, trade – and thus economic growth and human prosperity – remains an important part of the WTO, but they have shown through their decisions that they are willing to balance the trade interests with state measures that are addressed to protect the environment or health.[22]

Multilateral environmental agreements

So far there has been no dispute before the WTO/GATT dispute resolution panel which concerns whether a multilateral environmental agreement conforms to the GATT rules. However, the validity of some MEA trade restrictions is at least doubtful, in particular those involving process and product methods, discrimination between parties and non-parties, and extraterritorial application.

Leading examples of such MEAs include the Montreal Protocol on Substances that Deplete the Ozone Layer,[23] which adopts trade controls that are more restrictive as to non-parties than parties; the Convention on International Trade in Endangered Species of Wild Fauna and Flora (CITES),[24] which regulates imports and exports in certain species of animals and plants and allows punitive trade restrictions to be imposed on non-complying parties; and the Basel Convention on the Control of Transboundary Movements of Hazardous Wastes and their Disposal and Amendments which came into force in 2014,[25] which prohibit exports and imports of hazardous and other wastes by parties to the Convention to and from non-party states.

There are differing opinions as to whether the creation of the WTO in 1994 would trump any inconsistent provisions of an earlier MEA. Different solutions have been suggested according to whether the incompatibility arises between a measure under the 1997 Kyoto Protocol and the GATT 1994, rather than for the 1973 CITES and GATT 1994.[26] Many of the environmental treaties are also flexible by nature, with subsequent amendment and use of additional trade restricting mechanisms rendering a 'one stop shop' approach to treaty interpretation insufficient to address the trade and environmental conflicts which may arise.

International financial standard setting

The International Finance Corporation (IFC) of the World Bank Group is the largest multilateral source of financing for private sector projects in the developing world.[27] Its environmental guidelines and standards clearly identify the responsibility of the private sector on the basis of international environmental standards.[28] The fact that the IFC has selected standards from the range of available multinational environmental agreements and other international documents is particularly evident by identifying the additions and changes between the new 2006 and the previous 1998 standards.

The International Finance Corporation

Although the legal instruments creating international financial institutions do not mention environmental protection, all of such organisations assert to support sustainable development and condition their funding of development projects on the protection of the environment by the creation of specific procedures for selecting projects, and through mechanisms for reviewing the compliance with such procedures.[29] Any failure to comply with international environmental obligations may entail their international responsibility as well as liability for damages.[30] Environmental NGOs in fact monitor and continuously raise concerns about severe negative environmental impacts of projects which are funded by international financial institutions. The environmental policies developed by these institutions specifically address their international responsibility for the protection of the environment.[31]

The International Finance Corporation is a private sector arm of the World Bank family, which provides loans to private companies for projects in developing countries.[32] It was established in 1956 and is the largest multilateral source of loan and equity financing for private sector projects in the developing world. Assisting private companies in the developing world to mobilise financing in international financing markets is also part of its functions. The IFC also provides advice and technical assistance to business and governments.

In the light of the mission of the IFC to promote private sector investment in developing countries which will reduce poverty and improve people's lives, the IFC can be described as 'at the cross roads of the public and private sectors',[33] as it is a public sector institution committed to working with the private sector, sharing private sector risks in making loans and equity investments without government guarantees. Although the IFC coordinates its activities with other institutions in the World Bank Group, it will normally operate independently under its own legal and financial autonomy with its own Article of Agreement, share capital, management, and staff. However, there remain certain links with the World Bank inasmuch as its safeguard policies are deemed to apply by default to IFC funded projects with the private sector when there are gaps in the IFC's own policies and standards even though they were drafted for public sector projects. Also the World Bank and IFC often cooperate when operating in the same country, thus the procedures of both organisations apply to a single project.[34]

The World Bank Operational Standards

The Operational Standards developed by the World Bank appear to be quasi-administrative in nature, for internal use by the organisation to guide its staff in their activities. Nevertheless they are also applied in the framework of financing development projects through loan and credit agreements negotiated between the World Bank and borrowing countries. This results in the Operational Standards gaining an external dimension, which potentially affects the borrower.

The Operational Standards are not typical of international policy and legal instruments as their purpose is to assist individuals working for an international organisation to fulfil their tasks pursuant to the mandate of the organisation. As policy instruments they do not have legal status *per se* in the legal order but they may be regulated by the law of treaties by being incorporated into a loan or credit agreement. The Operational Standards may also play a crucial part in fostering the emergence of new international practices that seek to promote sustainable development and in facilitating respect for international legal instruments negotiated and adopted in other arenas. Finally, they play an important role in assessing the quality of the World Bank's activities.[35]

The World Bank has developed an array of procedures and mechanisms to ensure compliance with the multifaceted and complex Standards during an operational activity. These take into account their policy nature as well as their contractual character when incorporated into a loan or credit agreement. Further, the Standards promote compliance with international conventions and non-legally binding instruments. Finally, by favouring the participation of the non-state actors, the Standards make such actors the 'guardians' of respect for the World Bank's norms and procedures. The establishment of the World Bank Inspection Panel has significantly reinforced this last element.[36]

Operational Standards in the World Bank's activities

The Operational Standards include the operational policies and procedures and consist of numerous instructions from the World Bank management to its staff. They encompass a wide array of topics which are intended to assist the organisation's staff in its work concerning financed activities falling within the mandate of the World Bank. These include specific investment activities or activities aimed at facilitating investments for productive purposes.[37] The operational policies and procedures have been grouped in general themes and are designed to avoid or mitigate detrimental impacts of financial activities on certain groups of people or the environment.

Compliance with Operational Standards was identified as an important tool for achieving quality control and subsequent shifts in the role of the Operational Standards occurred in 1992 when the World Bank's management clarified the extent to which the Operational Standards are binding, and in 1993 when the World Bank Inspection Panel was established. These Operational Standards are now considered to be normative and procedural benchmarks for assessing the organisation's activities. Additionally, the adoption of the World Bank's general disclosure policy concerning its documents strengthened the normative aspect of the Standards.

Binding nature of the Standards

The Board, which is the World Bank's executive body, is composed of representatives of member states and is involved in the elaboration of the

Operational Standards. The Board's Executive Directors discuss and approve operational policies submitted for their consideration. All policies must be consistent with the Bank's Articles of Agreement. These Articles are interpreted by the Board, and the Operational Standards constitute one of the channels by which the mandate of the organisation is translated into practice.

Some of the Operational Standards are mandatory for World Bank staff, and others are merely of advisory or persuasive value. The management of the World Bank issued a decision in 1992 that specified the extent of the binding nature of the Operational Standards, the objective of the decision to ensure greater clarity of, and compliance with, the Operational Standards.

Operational Policies (OPs) and Bank Procedures (BPs) are binding on World Bank staff within the limits of flexibility provided, whilst the Good Practices (GPs) are not binding. However, this is further complicated by the fact that not all Operational Directives (ODs) include procedures and practices that are binding on World Bank staff, as the binding nature of the provisions of ODs depends on the wording of each standard.[38]

Environmental and Social Operational Standards

The operational policies and procedures range from the protection of specific vulnerable groups of people to water resources management issues, with some instruments being for general application whilst others are more specific. However, all contain provisions that are process orientated, requiring respect for certain patterns of behaviour. Not only do these policies and procedures provide guidelines for World Bank staff, but they also indicate what requirements the borrower must fulfil before the World Bank will finance an operation. These policies are collectively known as 'pillar policies',[39] with the Environment Assessment policy issued as an OP in 1999; the Indigenous Peoples policy and the Involuntary Resettlement policy still being in OD format. These pillar policies aim to integrate the social and environmental considerations into the financial activates of the World Bank as well as the policies dealing with the Involvement of Nongovernmental Organisations (NGOs) in World Bank-Supported Activities, and Disclosure of Operational Information.

Additionally, an important role is played by the Policy on Economic Evaluation of Investment Operations, which integrates environmental concerns in the cost benefit analysis conducted for World Bank financed projects. The World Bank analyses every proposed project in order 'to determine whether the project creates more net benefits to the economy than other mutually exclusive options for the use of the resources in question',[40] including the option of not undertaking the project at all. An assessment of a project's sustainability requires that economic, financial, and institutional risks, as well as environmental risks on the territory of the borrower, on neighbouring countries, and on the global environment, must be taken into account. Impacts on the global environment are considered when (a) payments related to a project are made under an international agreement, or (b) projects or project components are financed by the Global Environment Facility.[41]

The World Bank's Environment Assessment operational policy is the cornerstone for evaluating project activities with potential environmental impacts as it lays down standards and procedures for conducting environmental assessment, and aims at improving decision making by ensuring that the project options are environmentally sound and sustainable. In this regard the Bank screens all projects for classification into one of three categories that determine the appropriate level of environment assessment.[42]

It is the borrower who must conduct the assessment to ensure that development options under consideration are environmentally sound and sustainable, and that possible environmental impacts are recognised early in the project cycle and mitigation is taken into account during the project design. All projects must be consistent with domestic law, and international treaties to which the borrowing country is a party.

The World Bank Inspection Panel

The World Bank Inspection Panel was created in 1993 in order to improve the quality control in its operations during project preparation and implementation. The existence of the Panel was also expected to increase the accountability of the World Bank's management and staff in regard to the Bank's Board and to ensure transparency in its operations. The Panel was therefore established as an independent and permanent organ within the World Bank's organisational structure. The Panel was granted the competence to receive and, subject to the approval of the Board, investigate complaints from groups of individuals whose rights or interests had been or are likely to be directly and adversely affected by the World Bank's failure to comply with operational policies and procedures. The mandate of the Inspection Panel also covers projects financed by the International Bank for Reconstruction and Development (IBRD) and the International Development Association (IDA).[43]

The Resolution also provides in a non-restrictive manner that the 'Panel shall receive requests for inspection presented to it by an affected party in the territory of the borrower which is not a single individual i.e. a community of persons such as an organisation, association, society or other grouping of individuals'.[44] The Clarifications endorsed by the Executive Directors on 17 October 1996 specify that a group of individuals alleging to be affected should be understood as meaning 'any two or more individuals with common interests or concerns'.[45]

Compliance concerns are therefore institutionalised by the establishment of the Panel to conduct investigations, offering the possibility of remedial action by the World Bank if a violation is found.

Compliance with international law

The World Bank, indeed, does not operate in isolation. Its environmental and social operational policies and procedures reflect concerns related to the promotion of sustainable development as expressed in many other fora. Operational Standards are in fact vehicles for achieving this objective, although they are not necessarily exhaustive in covering all of the issues. The relationship between these policies and international law standards highlights their mutually reinforcing contribution to the promotion of sustainable development and the rule of law. The numerous references in the policies to international law promote respect for best practices. Some policy statements make precise reference to various international treaties but do not exclude the possibility of taking into account treaties which are not specifically mentioned. The Operational Policies and procedures also refer to soft law instruments, and in so doing promote respect for them. Both types of instruments are taken into account because they are intrinsically linked to the World Bank's activities.[46]

Control of investment risks

> In the second decade of the 21st century, the World Bank is no longer as financially influential as it once was. The growth of international private sector finance, and of global public lending institutions in newly industrialised nations [...] mean that the Bank has now become just one financial player amongst others.[47]

Not only do developing countries rely on World Bank funding but host states also rely on the private sector. In this regard some major issues can arise between multinational corporations and the host state, which are primarily regulated by international law, so how can multinationals protect their investment?

Legal conflict in these areas was most pronounced in the 1970s and 1980s, in the wake of major renegotiations and nationalisations of foreign owned natural resource operations, particularly in the oil industry.[48] Such matters centred upon the revision or termination of an international investment contract entered into between the host state and a foreign investor, and the expropriation of assets belonging to the foreign investor. In more recent times the incidence of such events has been rare but that cannot rule out the possibility of conflicts over control and ownership of foreign investments, especially in a period where the sense of dependence on foreign investors may be reduced and nationalistic sentiment heightened.

The experience of these major expropriations prompted the establishment of national investment guarantee schemes and the setting up, in 1985, of the Multilateral Investment Guarantee Agency (MIGA). However, the focus has shifted more recently to forms of indirect taking of foreign owned assets, and to the increased use of general standards of treatment, contained in international investment agreements (IIAs), for the assessment of governmental action that interferes with the operation of an investment. Recent arbitral decisions have highlighted the growing importance of the national treatment and most favoured nation standards of non-discrimination, and the fair and equitable treatment standard, as benchmarks for the review of such action.

Questions that arise concern state responsibility for full protection and security of investments, renegotiation of investment contracts, the taking of foreign owned property, and the operation of national and multilateral investment guarantee schemes.

Any international company under its corporate governance policy should look to protect its investors and control the risks involved which could affect all of its stakeholders. This section will outline some of the elements to control any such risks.

The internationalisation of international investment agreements

The question as to whether international investment agreements should be governed by international law arose during the 1970s and 1980s when there were a number of expropriations in the Middle Eastern oil industry. The most controversial of these was the *Texaco* arbitration,[49] in which the arbitrator held that an oil concession agreement between a US oil company and the Government of Libya was 'internationalised', that is it was assimilated into international law on the principal grounds that, firstly, the reference to principles of international law, and to general principles of law, in the choice of law clause in the concession agreement was held to define the extent to which Libyan law could apply.[50] Therefore, only if Libyan law was in conformity with international law should it be applied. Secondly, the fact that the contract was an economic development agreement emphasised the need for international law to prevail. The magnitude of the investment by the US company, the broad subject matter, and the long duration of the agreement meant that a degree of stability was required by which the investor could be protected against legislative uncertainties and governmental measures that may lead to an abrogation or rescission of the contract. Therefore, stabilisation clauses were inserted which removed all or part of the agreement from the internal law and provided for its correlative submission to *sui generis* rules or to a system which properly was an international law system.[51]

The Texaco case was not followed in subsequent oil arbitrations when a number of arbitrators chose to follow the national laws so long as they were not in conflict with international law. However, the decisive factor appears to be the actual content of the agreement; in particular the terms of any express choice of law clause used by the parties and whether there exists a stabilisation clause restricting the host state's sovereign powers.[52]

Therefore, instead of making a simple choice between national law or international law supported by general principles of law as recognised by civilised nations, the above approach serves to avoid the choice of law problem. This transnational approach may also avoid the stultification of dispute resolution procedures that might otherwise have become enmeshed in futile conflicts over the applicable law, with the host state favouring exclusive use of its own law and the foreign investor insisting on the internationalisation of the dispute. Where both parties are of equal bargaining power the compromise of adopting 'transnational law' may be used.

Following on from the 'internationalisation' doctrine, the classic legal doctrine of 'sanctity of contract' has been invoked as a limitation on the absolute sovereignty of the host state over its relations with foreign investors. Stabilisation clauses in investment contracts can be used to exclude rules of the host nation's law from the regulation of the agreement by making international law or general principles of law the proper law of the agreement. Such clauses may also exclude subsequent amendments of host state law from operating upon the investment contract, thus preserving the original terms of the investment contract from subsequent legal challenge.

Renegotiation of international investment agreements

Despite stabilisation clauses in international investment agreements, there is a trend towards renegotiation of these agreements periodically. In order to avoid the inflexibility of stabilisation clauses, there is a view that investment agreements, as a matter of course, should include a renegotiation clause. This would clearly mark renegotiation as being legally acceptable and avoid any argument should there be a need for renegotiation.

Why renegotiate? It may be at the initiation of the host state as a result of a gradual shift in bargaining power away from the international company towards the host state. Or there may be good reason for the international company to seek renegotiation. Thus renegotiation may be a commercially desirable process for both parties.[53] However, if negotiations lead to unreasonable terms being imposed on the company, this may amount to unacceptable economic coercion by way of a diminution of corporate assets, or a partial sale thereof at undervalue, resulting from pressure in negotiations. This would allow the state to achieve a result that it could not achieve lawfully through nationalisation without compensation. This raises the question as to whether there is a doctrine of unfair coercion in international law that can control such abuses of power on the part of the host state in the renegotiating process.[54]

In the absence of established rules of international law on the matter, the control of unreasonable terms imposed on foreign investors by way of contractual renegotiation may be considered under the general principles of contract law found in most modern legal systems.[55]

The taking of foreign corporate assets

It has been argued that not only express policies of nationalisation or expropriation fall to be considered as a 'taking of property', but also methods that do not involve an overt taking but which effectively neutralise the benefit of the property for the foreign owner. These are referred to as 'constructive taking' or 'creeping expropriation', or even 'regulatory taking'.[56] However, collectively they are referred to as 'indirect takings' as they have the common feature of not being a specific, direct measure that deprives the owner of his/her title to the property.[57]

In relations to indirect or regulatory takings, a distinction needs to be made between a legitimate exercise of the state's 'policing powers' and such a taking. For example, where a deprivation of property or other economic loss arises out of bona fide general taxation, regulation, or forfeiture for crime, then this is not generally compensatable.[58] While an expropriation or taking for environmental reasons may be classified as a taking for a public purpose, and thus legitimate, the fact that the property was taken for this reason does not affect either the nature or the measure of compensation to be paid for the taking.

Investment guarantee schemes

The threat of political risks, such as appropriation, is a factor that will increase the perceived costs of investment in a host state.[59] The governments of capital exporting states have sponsored public sector or mixed public/private insurance schemes. Such schemes have traditionally depended on developing host states and have been administered as part of the home state's foreign aid programme, and as such may be more than merely an insurance scheme but may also be an instrument of the home state's foreign economic and development policy.

Bilateral investment treaties

Consequent upon the nationalisation of BP in Iran, the International Centre for Settlement of Investment Disputes (ICSD) Convention[60] was agreed, and came into force in 1966. This led to a further 390 bilateral investment agreements, some of which are very short but contain ten key provisions. These are based on the 2004 US Model Bilateral Investment Treaty which was updated in 2012 by the US Department of State. The 2012 Model Bilateral Investment Treaty encompasses three main principles:

1   There must be enhanced transparency and public participation. The parties must consult periodically regarding how to improve their transparency practice in the context of developing and implementing laws and other measures affecting investment in the context of investor state dispute.
2   Notice and comment procedures oblige parties to publish proposed regulations, express their purpose and rationale.
3   There must be multilateral appellate procedures, which include provisions for transparency and public participation.

The Energy Charter Treaty

The Energy Charter Treaty is the only multilateral investment treaty devoted to the energy sector. This was originally set up in the European Union as the overall dependence of EU countries on energy imports from third countries made it important for the EU to create formal links with producers and transmitters of energy to contribute to the long term stability that energy supply contracts typically require; especially in the case of supplies of natural gas. This reality encouraged an orientation not only to the Gulf region but also to the East. The EU therefore developed a legal instrument for cooperation between East and West Europe called the Energy Charter Treaty (ECT).[61] This multilateral treaty was signed by some 50 states and the European Communities, and is now open to all countries, with its purpose being: 'to establish a legal framework in order to promote long term co-operation in the energy field, based on complementaries and mutual benefits, in accordance with the objectives and principles of the Charter.'[62]

The ECT creates rights and obligations in international law for all of its contracting parties and is principally concerned with the promotion and protection of investments, trade, and the transit of energy goods. The Treaty distinguishes between the 'pre investment' stage, involving the making of investments and setting of access conditions, and the 'post investment' stage concerning investments already in place. But it is the latter stage that is subject to a legal regime of 'hard law' obligations, similar to those common to bilateral investment treaties and enforceable by international arbitration.

Another major feature of the ECT is that it subjects trade in energy materials and products between contracting parties to the provisions of GATT and its related instruments, even where those contracting parties to the Treaty are not yet parties to GATT. The aim is to promote access to international markets for non-GATT parties on commercial terms. As in the investment provisions there was also a Treaty provision for 'second stage' negotiations on trade matters.[63]

Non-discrimination, fair and equitable treatment, and full protection and security

In recent years, the nature of claims made by investors has changed. Whilst expropriation claims have historically been the most important, a significant measure of success has been through the bringing of claims based on breaches of the national treatment or fair and equitable treatment standard.[64] Additionally, the most favoured nation standard has given rise to claims that stronger standards of protection, found in other international investment agreements entered into by the host country, should apply to the IIA underlying the dispute due to the MFN clause in that agreement. The responsibility of states to ensure the full protection and security of investments has given rise to some disputes; however, the approach to compensation cannot be the same as for expropriation claims, as the nature of the loss is different.

National treatment

The national treatment standard requires that foreign investors should receive treatment no less favourable than that accorded to nationals of the host state engaged in similar business activity.[65] The aim is to ensure equality of competitive conditions between foreign investors and domestic investors in a like situation. Although it represents less than the minimum protection accepted under international law, which demands that the treatment of foreigners is better than that given to nationals where the treatment of nationals falls below international minimum standards, it does represent the maximum protection for economic rights accorded to foreign investors under host state law.[66] The basis of any claim brought under the national treatment standard lies in the allegation that the investor and/or their investment have been treated less favourably than a comparable domestic investor/investment.

National treatment provisions are drafted according to a common basic pattern, but with some significant variations. For example, some agreements do not refer expressly to national treatment in order to avoid extending preferential treatment reserved for national enterprises to their foreign counterparts. This was the policy of China in its early agreements, although in its more recent agreements there is an unreserved national treatment provision.

Most favoured nation treatment

Although the MFN has been widely recognised in treaties where states grant each other reciprocal freedom of commerce, it is not recognised in customary international law.[67] It therefore depends on the treaty in which it is included. If a MFN clause is included in a Bilateral Investment Treaty, or other type of IIA, then it has the effect of extending to the home contracting state the more favourable terms of investment granted to a third state by the host contracting state. This prevents any discriminatory terms of investment operating against investors from the home contracting state. Therefore, the MFN standard ensures equality of competitive conditions in the host country market as between foreign investors of different nationalities. The scope of MFN treatment is unconditional in the absence of express limitation.[68] In other words, it can be specifically excluded in relation to certain third countries. However, the standard only operates in relation to the subject matter of the IIA; it cannot be extended by implication to matters covered by other treaties, such as conventions on the protection of intellectual property.

The MFN standard presents few drafting issues as it is a treaty based standard that may be conditional or unconditional. It will be subject to exceptions in relation to taxation and regional economic integration commitments entered into by the contracting parties under other agreements.

In BITs it is common to combine the MFN standard with the national treatment standard in the same paragraph, which has the effect of ensuring that investors can avail themselves of the more favourable standard. In other treaties the beneficiary country will be given the choice between the MFN and national treatment standards.

Fair and equitable treatment

Unfortunately the fair and equitable treatment standard is somewhat uncertain. The concepts of 'fair' and 'equitable' are mostly interchangeable. In English law equitable principles were developed to ensure that the unjust effects arising out of a literal and inflexible application of the common law to a particular case could be avoided.

The application of equity was based on a willingness to review the specific facts of the case to determine whether, in that context, the application of a principle of law was proper or whether it had to be replaced by a view of what would be right and just on those facts. Therefore, in law, equity introduces a degree of flexibility in the interpretation of the rules arising out of sensitivity to apply rules that are 'fair'. This meaning of equity has been accepted as a principle of international law.

Conclusion

Most BITs and other IIAs contain clauses providing for the compensation of the investor for losses due to armed conflict or internal disorder. However, these do not establish an absolute right to full compensation, but they lay down the principle that the investor shall be treated in accordance with the national treatment and/or MFN standard in the matter of compensation.

Some treaties deal with compensation in a single provision, which also deals with compensation for expropriation, whilst others deal with these two types of compensation in separate provisions. Most BITs guarantee the free transfer of compensation to the investor's home state.

Notes

1 See Shelton, D. (2007) *Commitment and Compliance: The Role of Non-binding Norms in the International Legal System*, New York: Oxford University Press, ch. 6.
2 Ibid., p. 243.
3 See WTO (1999) *The Legal Texts: The Results of the Uruguay Round of Multilateral Trade Negotiations*, Cambridge.
4 https://www.wto.org/english/docs_e/legal_e/04-wto.pdf, p. 9.
5 http://www.unep.org/Documents.Multilingual/Default.asp?documentid=78&articleid=1163.
6 Ibid.
7 Birnie, P., A. Boyle and C. Redgwell (2009) *International Law and the Environment*, Oxford and New York: Oxford University Press, p. 756.
8 Ibid.
9 https://www.wto.org/english/res_e/booksp_e/gatt_ai_e/art1_e.pdf.
10 1994 General Agreement on Tariffs and Trade (GATT) Article III(4). https://www.wto.org/english/res_e/booksp_e/analytic_index_e/gatt1994_e.htm.
11 Ibid., Art. III(1).
12 Ibid., Art. III(2).
13 Ibid., Art. III(1).
14 Birnie, Boyle and Redgwell (2009), p. 758.

15 (1984) *Canada – Administration of the Foreign Investment Review Act*, GATT BISD (30th Supp.) para 5.20.

16 Birnie, Boyle and Redgwell (2009), p. 760.

17 *Trade and Environment*, GATT Ministerial Decision of 14 April 1994, 33 *International Legal Materials* (1994) 1267.

18 Birnie, Boyle and Redgwell (2009), p. 763.

19 1947 GATT, Articles XXII–XXIII and 1994 Agreement Establishing the World Trade Organization, Annex 2, in WTO, *Legal Texts*.

20 DSU, Article 22. https://www.wto.org/english/tratop_e/dispu_e/dsu_e.htm.

21 Codified in Articles 31–3 of the Vienna Convention on the Law of Treaties 1969.

22 Carr, Indira (2015) 'International Trade Rules and Environmental Effects', in S. Alam, J.H. Bhuiyan, T.M.R. Chowdhury and E.J. Techera (eds), *Routledge Handbook of International Environmental Law*, London: Routledge, p. 559.

23 Goyal, A. (2006) *The WTO and International Environmental Law: Towards Conciliation*, New Delhi: Oxford University Press, ch. 5.

24 https://www.cites.org/eng/disc/text.php.

25 Basel Convention on the Control of Transboundary Wastes and their Disposal.

26 Birnie, Boyle and Redgwell (2009), pp. 768–769.

27 IFC, http://www.ifc.org/wps/wcm/connect/corp_ext_content/ifc_external_corpora te_site/home.

28 Warner, M. (2006) 'The New International Benchmark Standards for Environmental and Social Performance of the Private Sector in Developing Countries: Will it Raise or Lower the Bar?' London Overseas Development Institute. http://www.odi.org/sites/ odi.org.uk/files/odi-assets/publications-opinion-files/750.pdf, p. 2.

29 Morgera, E. (2009) *Corporate Accountability in International Environmental Law*, Oxford: Oxford University Press, ch. 7.

30 Sands, P. (2003) *Principles of International Environmental Law*, 2nd edn, Cambridge: Cambridge University Press, p. 153.

31 Suerdo, R.A. (2004) 'The Law Applicable to the Activities of International Development Banks', 308 *Recueil des Cours* 1, 123–127.

32 Kiss, A.D. and D. Shelton (2004) *International Environmental Law*, 3rd edn, Enschede: Nijhof Brill, pp. 157–158.

33 Lee, C.F. (2001) 'International Finance Corporation: Financing Environmentally and Socially Sustainable Private Investment', in S. Schlemmer-Schulte and K. Tung, *Liber Amicorum Ibrahim F.I. Shihata*, The Hague: Kluwer Law International, pp. 469–470.

34 See the Chad/Cameroon Pipeline and the Bujagali Hydropower Project in Uganda.

35 Wirth, D.A. (1997) 'Economic Assistance, The World Bank and Nonbinding Instruments', in E. Broen Weiss (ed.), *International Compliance with Non binding Accords*, Studies in Transnational Legal Policy, No. 29, Washington, DC: American Society of International Law, pp. 219, 227–321.

36 Res. No. IBRD 93–10, Res. No. IDA 93–6, 'The World Bank Inspection Panel' (1995) 34 *International Legal Materials* 503.

37 Art. 1(i) of the Articles of Agreement establishes that the primary purpose of the World Bank is to 'assist in the reconstruction and development of territories of its members by facilitating the investment of capital for productive purposes'. Articles of Agreement, 2 United Nations Treaty Series (UNTS) 134, as amended 606 UNTS, 294.

38 Shihata, I.F.I. (1994) *The World Bank Inspection Panel*, New York: Oxford University Press, p. 45.

39 The operational policies and procedures can be found at http://www.worldbank. org.

40 OP 10.04 on Economic Evaluation of Investment Projects (April 1994).

41 Ibid.

42 OP 4.01 on Environmental Assessment also includes a fourth category, 'Category F1'.

43 Boisson de Chazournes, L. (2007) 'Policy Guidance and Compliance: The World Bank Operational Standards', in D. Shelton (ed.), *Commitment and Compliance*, Oxford: Oxford University Press, pp. 281–303.

44 http://ewebapps.worldbank.org/apps/ip/Pages/Panel-Mandate.aspx.

45 Resolution, http://ewebapps.worldbank.org/apps/ip/Pages/Panel-Mandate.aspx.

46 Boisson de Chazournes (2007), p. 297.

47 Rich, B. (2013) 'Foreclosing the Future: Examining 20 years of the World Bank's Environmental Performance', Bretton Woods Project. http://www.brettonwoodsproject.org/wp-content/uploads/2013/10/At-Issue-Bruce-Rich-FINAL.pdf.

48 Korbin, S.J. (1984) 'Expropriation as an Attempt to Control Foreign Firms in LDCs: Trends from 1960–1979', 28 *International Studies Quarterly* 329.

49 *Texaco Overseas Petroleum Co. v Libya* (1978) 17 *International Legal Materials* 1.

50 By clause 28 of the Deeds of Concession: 'This concession shall be governed by and interpreted in accordance with the principles of the law of Libya in common to the principles of international law and in absence of such common principles then by and in accordance with general principles of law, including such of those principles as may have been applied by international tribunals.'

51 *Texaco Overseas Petroleum Co. v Libya* at para 45.

52 Greenwood, Christopher (1982) 'Book Review of "Human Rights in the Israeli Occupied Territories 1967–1982" by Esther Rosalind Cohen', 53 *British Yearbook of International Law* 27.

53 Kolo, A. and T.W. Walde (2000) 'Renegotiation and Contract Adaptation in International Investment Projects', 1 *Journal of World Investment and Trade* 5, 47.

54 Vagts, D.F. (1978) 'Coercion and Foreign Investment Rearrangements', 72 *American Journal of International Law* 17.

55 Ibid.

56 Muchlinski, Peter (2007) *Multinational Enterprises and the Law*, Oxford: Oxford University Press, p. 587.

57 OECD (2005) *International Investment Law: A Changing Landscape*, Paris.

58 *Saluka Investments B.V. v Czech Republic* UNCITRAL Rules Arbitration, Permanent Court of Arbitration award of 17 March 2006. Paras 253–265.

59 Muchlinski (2007), p. 614.

60 The Washington Convention for the Protection of Foreign Investments, 1965.

61 [1998] OJ L69/1. Final Act of the European Energy Charter Conference 69/5–69/114.

62 Article 2 ECT.

63 Cameron, P.D. (2007) *Competition in Energy Markets*, 2nd edn, Oxford: Oxford University Press.

64 Muchlinski (2007), p. 621.

65 This is especially true of North American Free Trade Agreement (NAFTA) cases, where most claims that have succeeded did so on national treatment grounds rather than those of expropriation. Ibid., p. 621, note 1.

66 For further discussion see UNCTAD (1998) *Bilateral Investment Treaties in the Mid 1990s*, New York and Geneva: United Nations.

67 Snyder, R.C. (1948) *The Most Favoured Nation Clause*, New York: Kings Crown Press, Columbia University.

68 UNCTAD (1999) *Fair and Equitable Treatment*, Series on Issues in International Investment Agreements, New York, pp. 13–27.

5 Intangible assets, intellectual property and technology transfer issues

Introduction

Energy, sustainability and the relevance of intangible assets, intellectual property and technology transfer was succinctly put by Ban Ki-moon when he stated:

> Energy is the golden thread that connects economic growth, increased social equity, and an environment that allows the world to thrive ... We need to raise sustainable energy to the top of the global agenda and focus our attention, ingenuity, resources, and investments to make it a reality.[1]

United Nations Secretary-General Ban Ki-moon

Over the last few years multinational companies have focused on issues related to sustainability. A survey carried out in 2012 by McKinsey found that executives have developed practices to manage the long term development of certain activities.[2] The most cited issues by the executives surveyed were reducing energy use, reducing waste and managing reputation. The focuses of the respective companies addressing sustainability, and the value executives expected, was influenced by the particular industry of the companies. Executives from the extractive and energy industries indicated that reputation was a main driver and the executives from these industries are most likely to believe that sustainability programmes add shareholder value in the short term and the long term. According to the McKinsey survey the most effective companies are more likely to work with external partners (either with customers, suppliers or community stakeholders in the value chain) to increase value and mitigate risk.

One particular high profile sustainability initiative was set up in September 2011 by the UN Secretary-General Ban Ki-moon. The global initiative focuses on three interlinking objectives:

- Energy access: ensuring universal access to modern energy services.
- Energy efficiency: doubling the global rate of improvement in energy efficiency.
- Renewable energy: doubling the share of renewable energy in the global energy mix.

A report by the UN Global Compact and Accenture on *Sustainable Energy for All: Opportunities for the Oil and Gas Industry*[3] identified, for each industry, priority actions which were aligned to the vision and objectives of the *Sustainable Energy for All* initiative. The actions included four modes of engagement, i) operations, ii) products and services, iii) social investment and philanthropy, iv) advocacy, and public policy engagement. These modes of engagement are meant to provide different ways that businesses can create value through revenue growth, cost reduction, brand enhancement and risk management.

How companies implement the objectives of sustainability and a multinational's particular focus will be influenced by a number of factors. Innovation and the mobilisation of science technology resources to address sustainability issues have been highlighted as key factors.[4]

Intellectual property rights, climate change technologies and sustainability

Purpose of intellectual property rights

Intellectual property rights, under a general definition, include patents for inventions, utility models, design rights, trademarks, domain names and copyrights. Closely related are legislation rights for unfair competition, trade secrets, confidential information and know-how.

Intellectual property rights are a deal between the creators of the intangible assets and technology innovations and the governments or societies of the countries within which the creators operate. Countries have constructed different legal intellectual property regimes and these differences can affect the speed of innovation and its utilisation.[5] For example, patent law defines what inventions can be patented, what rights the patent proprietor has and the term of the patent protection. In general, an invention must be new, not obvious, and have some industrial application. There are certain exclusions from patentability, including diagnostic, therapeutic and surgical methods; plants and animals other than micro-organisms, and essentially biological processes for the production of plants or animals other than non-biological and microbiological processes.[6]

In return for the creators sufficiently disclosing their intellectual property they are provided with some form of legal protection. This protection provides a mechanism by which the owner of the intellectual property right may seek to prevent the unauthorised use, or abuse by a third party. This right of the intellectual property owner to prevent unauthorised use is not unlimited, as there are certain legal instruments which may override the proprietor's intellectual property rights, such as compulsory licensing and exhaustion of rights. The requirement for some form of publication means that this published knowledge created in one country is accessible to parties from all countries. It is argued that by having such a means to prevent unauthorised use, there is an incentive to share the information about the innovation and to develop the innovation further. It is also argued that intellectual property rights facilitate the collaboration of two or more parties to jointly innovate. Only by providing clearly defined rights to each party's proprietary intellectual property can each party have the confidence when bringing their technology into a joint development project.

There are differing schools of thought on whether intellectual property rights are a barrier or a facilitator to innovation development and technology transfer.[7] It has been found that intellectual property is potentially both an incentive and an obstacle to the transfer of technology and to innovation development. The provision of a certain amount of protection is necessary to facilitate the investment in innovation, but the use of intellectual property rights could potentially hamper further development and technology transfer. It should be understood that intellectual property rights are only one element which may affect innovation development, and other elements such as financial investment, local infrastructure and expertise have a significant influence on the innovation and technology transfer ecosystem.

The justification of the intellectual property protection system, and in particular the patent system, is an optimal balance between the private interests of the party investing resources in technology development and commercial innovation and the public interest in seeing the technologies and commercial innovations implemented and disseminated.[8]

For patents the balance may be placed into two groups. The first question is known as the 'pre-grant questions'; for example, what types of technology should be patentable and what inventions should be excluded? Many national laws allow the patent offices to exclude technologies that would cause damage to the environment if exploited, or that are contrary to morality and public order. These provide an overlap between patent law and practice and environmental and public policy. The concept of damaging the environment formed part of the debate about the patentability of genetically modified organisms (GMOs). The European Patent Office (EPO) board of appeal defined the concept of '*ordre public*' as covering the protection of public security and the physical integrity of individuals as part of society.[9] The EPO has come to the conclusion that in order for the exclusion to patentability on the grounds of '*ordre public*' and damage to the environment, there had to be more than just a possible risk to the ecosystem. One of the key opponents to the patenting of GMOs is the NGO Greenpeace. The Greenpeace organisation raised the debate on damaging the environment with patented technology. This included the knock-on effect of public security and the detrimental physical integrity of individuals as part of society. This wider view of the possible adverse effects of different types of patented technology has also entered the discussions regarding climate change technologies and it is conceivable that as sustainability issues gain more scrutiny, sustainability technologies may also come into the spotlight.

The second question is the 'post-grant question', which focuses on the issues concerning the patented technology in a broader legal and regulatory arena. After the patent is granted there is a focus on how the patent proprietor utilises the rights provided under the patent laws, in the context of the broader public interest and the relevant commercial environment. There are the issues of potential abuses of the patenting system and what steps should be taken to monitor and regulate the use of the patent rights in the commercial arena and what type of intervention may be appropriate. A patent proprietor cannot use the patent rights to engage in abusive anti-competitive practices. Both developed and developing country patent laws provide a number of restrictions on the patent exclusive rights, which places the public interest above the interests of the patent proprietor. Also under TRIPS Article 30 there are certain restrictions to the rights granted to the proprietor and these have in general been implemented into national patent legislations. One notable exception to infringing a patent is the right for a third party to carry out non-commercial scientific research and experiments. Under this exception, further innovation may be carried out on existing patented technology without the concern of infringing patents, thus providing scientists and researchers the freedom to access and develop improvements or alternative technologies. However, there are significantly differing national perspectives as to what falls within the scope of non-commercial research. There has been an interest in the research exclusion as there is an increase in the number of public–private partnerships (PPPs) for research projects focusing on sustainable technologies. One such initiative is the European Commission's Horizon 2020 PPP, which intends to leverage six billion Euros of investment.

In practice, a new technology or innovation is not commercialised on its own, but it will form part of a family of other related technologies. For larger scale technology innovation there will be a number of different parties involved. The licencing strategy of the patent proprietors and their intellectual property management may come under the scrutiny of the regulators and competition authorities. In order to address global issues using technology innovation, various mechanisms have been proposed to encourage collaboration. Forming patent pools is one such mechanism. Under such a structure all collaborating parties provide access to their intellectual property including the licensing of their relevant patents, normally under a cross-licence agreement. The parties join forces in a common commercial cause to create a technical and commercial solution to their collective benefit. These types of arrangements have been particularly successful in the electronics industry and the telecommunication industry; where complex technologies require technical standards and collaboration to facilitate the introduction of an innovation. While there is a general consensus that for complex technologies pooling intellectual property rights is positive and enhances efficiency,[10] without regulatory oversight there is the possibility of competition and antitrust violations. Historically, patent pools have been formed in the developed countries in Europe and the USA. More recently Asian companies have participated more actively following their increased role in technology innovation.[11]

Patent law and policy in the earlier years was focused on public health and the impact of patenting on access to medicines. This focus led to a revision of the Trade-Related Intellectual Property Rights (TRIPs) agreement to promote access to medicines and follow-on work by the World Health Organization which considered means for aligning research and other measures to promote innovation. A parallel has been made by some policymakers between the public health issues and the climate change issues. Clearly, there is a parallel between the climate change and health issues and the sustainability issues.

The patent system has had the most focus rather than the other forms of intellectual property. However, there are other forms of intellectual property legislation which are relevant, such as legislation covering trade secrets and confidential information; commercial reputation building with the use of certification and collective trademarks, geographical indications and other signs used to identify products and services relevant to sustainable technologies; and the protection of traditional knowledge.

In the computer software industry the intellectual property right of copyright law has been transformed by the open source model. The open source model differs from the more traditional model for intellectual property rights. Instead of one party creating a new software and marketing it to the consumer and providing further update developments or versions, under the open source model the software is made available to any party to develop or improve. This creates a community of developers working in an independent and unstructured manner. In the early days of this model, some of the participants developed the software just for interest or professional recognition, while others wanted to improve the quality of the software.

Open source software systems are normally licensed under 'copyleft' licence, the most famous one being the General Public License (GPL). Under a GPL licence the licensee can use the software and develop it for free, but any development versions of the software must also be licensed under a GPL licence.

One possibility is for climate change technology to create similar open source licences, so that a community of technology developers contribute to the innovation process, without concern of infringing a third party's intellectual property rights. The use of open community developments and open collaborations has been accelerated by the increasing access to the internet. The modern generation are more familiar with the concept of sharing ideas and developments openly. Also, industry has seen the advantages of using open innovation to form collaboration projects with other companies, research institutes, customers, suppliers, or communities of developers. Within the area of open innovation there is a part to be played by social media. In the beginning companies used social media to either promote or market their products. However, social media interaction has developed into a forum for activity involving third parties or communities in the decision making process or development of the products. Companies have to form a clear policy on how to manage the social media relationship, because if mismanaged the adverse reaction from social media can happen very quickly and can have a damaging effect on the reputation of the company. In general the social media community responds best to companies being open and honest with their information.

Intellectual property rights and climate change technologies

There has been much debate on the role of intellectual property rights in the role of mitigating climate change issues. This role has focused on the use of climate change technologies and the access to such technologies, mainly by the emerging economies. The role of technology was recognised in the multilateral instruments on climate change and both UNFCCC (Art. 4.1c)[12] and Kyoto Protocol (Art. 10c) mention the development, application and dissemination of technologies relevant to climate change. The instruments included the know-how, practices and processes. Climate change technologies provide solutions to decrease material inputs, reduce energy consumption and emissions, recover valuable by-products and minimise waste disposal problems.[13] The initial focus was on renewable energy technologies, such as solar, wind, wave, geothermal and biofuels, but the types of technologies have increased to include clean coal, nuclear, carbon capture and storage, cleaner fossil-fuels and energy efficiency technologies including smart grids.

Technology transfer has been a discussion point on the agenda of the UNFCCC, which requires developed countries to promote the transfer of technology to developing countries in order to enable the developing countries to implement the provisions of the Convention (Art. 4.5). The UNFCCC Conferences of the Parties (COP) 7[14] established a framework to enhance the implementation of Art. 4.5 of the Convention. There were five key themes identified: technology needs and needs assessments; technology information; enabling environments; capacity-building; and mechanisms for technology transfer. At the UNFCCC 2007 Bali meeting the attending parties presented different views on the role played by intellectual property in the transfer of technology between countries. Some developing countries considered intellectual property to be a barrier to technology transfer and they proposed a number of changes to the international legislation such as the World Trade Organization Agreement on Trade-Related Aspects of Intellectual Property Rights (TRIPS). The issue of the transfer of climate change mitigation technology was discussed at the Beijing International Conference on Carbon Abatement Technology Transfers in 2008. Countries such as China and India proposed that the TRIPS flexibility for medicines (including compulsory licensing) be extended to cover climate mitigation technologies under the argument that, similar to access to medicines, intellectual property rights would be a barrier to the access of climate mitigation technology. The reasoning provided was that the climate is a public health issue and there should be greater access to the technology used to provide a cleaner, heathier environment for the public. However, many developed countries and NGOs such as the World Intellectual Property Organization (WIPO), Japan and the EU argued that the commercial environment for the climate mitigation technologies is not the same as the commercial environment of the health situation. In the pharmaceutical industry generally one company owns the intellectual property (normally patents) for the key technology. In the climate mitigation industry, the intellectual property ownership of these different technologies is spread across a large number of competing companies. Hence, it was argued that the intellectual property rights are not a barrier to technology transfer, but conversely such rights provide a framework under which the owner of the intellectual property has confidence that their valuable property is well protected and this will facilitate the transfer of technology from the companies within the developed countries to companies within the developing countries.

A study into the patenting activity and licensing activity for climate mitigation technologies was carried out by the United Nations Environment Programme (UNEP), the European Patent Office (EPO) and the International Centre for Trade and Sustainable Development (ICTSD).[15] The study showed that patenting activity for climate mitigating technologies had increased at a rate of 20 per cent per annum from 1997 to 2009 and that for certain technologies patenting was dominated by developed countries. The six leading countries innovating and patenting were Japan, the United States of America, Germany, the Republic of Korea, the United Kingdom and France. Some of the emerging countries were ranked highly with India in the top five for solar technologies and Brazil and Mexico the top two countries for hydro and marine technologies. The conclusion of this report was that the patenting activity indicated that for many of the technology sectors there seemed to be sufficient competition in the marketplace, taking account of the market share of the major players.

The discussion between the developing countries and developed countries is currently ongoing (as at mid-2015). Various countries submitted questions, comments, evidence and reports on the subjects of technology innovation, intellectual property protection and technology dissemination. Within this information it became apparent that intellectual property is only one element in the larger issue of how to achieve a good technology innovation framework. Other issues such as access to financial capital (government public funding, private investment, venture capital), collaboration, and investment in education and expertise, played an important role in providing an environment for successful innovation and adaption. It is generally accepted that intellectual property legislation alone cannot support the innovation framework.

There is a continued discussion regarding access to climate change technologies and in particular licensing of intellectual property and transfer of technologies, especially to developing countries and their suggested need for 'accelerated access to critical mitigation and adaption technologies'.[16] The effect of the intellectual property legislation for either promoting or hindering innovation and adaption of new technologies has been a contentious issue. Some commentators suggest the intellectual property system should be completely abandoned, or at least not be applied to climate change technologies.

Intellectual property rights and sustainability

Notwithstanding the debate between the developing and developed countries on the benefits or otherwise of intellectual property legislation for promoting technologies which will mitigate climate change, many multinational companies have accepted the premise that climate change poses a commercial and social risk and that they in some part have an obligation to address this. The concerns about climate change, health, and food security have focused the debate on the role of and access to new technologies in creating an effective response to such global challenges. In an effort to address these global issues, some multinational companies have placed sustainability as part of their business strategy. In this way the issues of energy efficiency, use of renewable energy, waste reduction, recycling, health, safety, anticorruption and reputational damage have become part of the business strategy agenda.

In order to supply the increasing global demand for energy there is a common understanding that there will need to be a use of a more diverse collection of technologies different from the current established technologies used for accessing conventional oil and gas reserves. The technologies required will include technologies for: unconventional oil and gas reserves such as shale gas and heavy oil; renewable energy sources; and for achieving cleaner coal energy production.[17]

Intellectual property and technology transfer

The World Intellectual Property Organization (WIPO) has worked to form global rules on intellectual property, but without a mechanism for enforcement. However, this issue was addressed when intellectual property was linked to trade under the General Agreement on Tariffs and Trade (GATT). Although initially there were a number of developing countries opposed to this, an agreement was formed where there would be a reduction in agriculture subsidies and tariffs for textiles by the developed countries in return for enforceable global rules on intellectual property. Under the Agreement on Trade-Related Aspects of Intellectual Property Rights the developing countries consider technology transfer as part of the bargain in which they agreed to protect intellectual property. Some commentaries are of the opinion that the TRIPs agreement is unduly biased towards the parties in the developed countries who own the majority of the intellectual property rights.[18] With regard to medicines, developing countries initially had to pay more for medicines, and pharmaceutical companies generally did not invest in the major diseases affecting those countries.

In the context of climate change technologies and sustainability one of the key issues addressed is whether the intellectual property rights, which are created from the technology and commercial innovations, are a benefit or hindrance. From a commercial viewpoint technology development and commercialisation requires investment in intangible assets, and the ability to prevent a competitor using the created intellectual property assets will influence whether the investor is able to risk financial capital. Also, at the commercialisation stage normally there will be some collaboration between multiple parties along the supply chain. Here again the ability for the owners of the respective intellectual property to define and protect their intellectual property will help all parties to the collaboration understand the value of the intellectual property within the collaboration. Innovation in the climate change technology arena can be highly complex[19] and the technology value chains for multinational companies can be across multiple jurisdictions and involve multiple parties. There will be a greater likelihood of success when there is a level playing field for all parties contributing to a collaboration and where the contribution of intellectual property receives an equitable value.

Sustainable development together with the protection and preservation of the environment is in the preamble of the Marrakesh Agreement Establishing the World Trade Organization (WTO) lists as part of the principles and objectives of the world trading system. Also mentioned is that the multilateral trading system should take into account the different levels of development and members' asymmetries. Similarly the preamble to the Agreement on Trade-Related Aspects of Intellectual Property Rights refers to the promotion of technology transfer to developing countries. Technology transfer is facilitated by a well-developed intellectual property system. When considering this issue, a company needs to understand that technology is transferred in a different way than the technology product which embodies the technology. Providing a single technology product to a party is different than enabling that party to reproduce that product. In order for the third party to commercially reproduce a product the technical and business know-how has to be transferred and if required the business structures and organisations used to make sure the product is commercially viable. The transferring of these intangible assets is achieved by using the intellectual property rights.

A report[20] by the International Centre for Trade and Sustainable Development discussed the benefits of creating a Sustainable Energy Trade Agreement (SETA). The report discussed the international diffusion of sustainable energy technologies and how to facilitate such diffusion by analysing several issues such as products, industries and countries, as well as a company's modes of technology transfer in an international environment. The report goes on to address all modes of technology transfer used by companies and how these are affected from a macro and micro perspective. The report focuses on the scaling-up and deployment of renewable or sustainable energy sources. Countries face the challenge of controlling the carbon output while ensuring access to energy security by reducing the reliance on fossil-fuel imports. Also, companies are focusing on renewable energy sources and energy efficiencies as part of their sustainable long-term plans. To encourage the development and use of renewable energy technologies and the take-up of such by companies, there have been various incentives such as feed-in tariffs and tax breaks. Also, focusing on lowering the costs of equipment and services used to produce sustainable energy can be a critical influencing factor to the scaling-up process and commercial adoption, along with addressing barriers to trade in sustainable goods and services. Barriers to trade may include tariffs, conflicting standards, or unequal levels of efforts. Under some sustainability strategies there is a heavy promotion of local manufacture and production of renewable energy equipment and services. One negative result of such a strategy could be policies which allow or promote national protectionism, which in turn could cause disputes between commercial actors or national governments.

The ICTSD's proposal for a SETA sets out to address the issue of barriers to trade. The proposal discusses how sustainable development, energy technology and diffusion and trade are integrated in economic and technological processes and that technology diffusion has a spill over effect within developing countries. The technology development includes tangible assets, such as the equipment and physical products, and the intangible assets, such as the intellectual property and know-how. Technology diffusion refers to not only the process of technology transfer, but also the absorption of the technology into the recipient economy. The diffusion of technology by companies into a particular region or country often takes place in a complex group of transactions involving the transfer of capital, equipment, technology and personnel. Also, the particular supply chain of materials for production and the transportation network and infrastructure have to be taken into account. Technology could be transferred by international technology development joint ventures, or by international licensing of existing technology.

There has been a change in the geographic patterns in the technology economic geography. An indicator of technology development is the global patenting activity. Although the developed countries remain dominant in the filing of patent applications, in some areas of technology there is a significant increase in patenting activity from the developing countries.

Changes to intellectual property to assist climate change technology

In some jurisdictions the patent application process for climate relevant or green technology can be accelerated. The UK Intellectual Property Office (UKIPO) was the first office to introduce a 'Green Channel' accelerated patenting process initiative in 2009. Similar programs have been initiated by intellectual property offices in Korea (KIPO), United States (USPTO), Canada (CIPO), Australia (IP Australia), Japan (JPO), Israel, Brazil (INPI) and China (SIPO). Most of the offices use a broad interpretation of what may constitute green technologies and most merely require the applicant to indicate the ecological benefit of the invention. By providing an accelerated prosecution, the patent applicant may have the security of a granted patent much earlier than normal. This may be beneficial for securing financial support, or deterring competitors from unauthorised use of the patented technology.

There has been a proposal to lower the threshold for patentability in the field of climate change relevant technologies, so that the only test for patentability would be one of novelty and thus remove the requirement that the invention should be not obvious. However, such a proposal would be inconsistent with the fundamental principles of patent law and counterproductive to the efforts of recent years by the various national and international patent offices to improve the quality of the patenting process. Such a modification to the patenting process may also provide patent exclusivity on trivial changes to the established technology, so hampering further developments.

Some developing countries have proposed a supplementary requirement to patentability of being an eco-friendly element, such that polluting inventions would not be patentable. This proposal is not widely supported, particularly by the supporters of the view that strong intellectual property protection is needed to support innovation and technology dissemination. There could also be some significant practical problems defining which technologies should be included. In addition, the various patent office examiners are currently not experts in questions related to the environmental effect of an invention.

There are recognised challenges for sustainable technologies, one of which is a need to encourage investment in innovation and in the diffusion and transfer of the technologies to third parties on a worldwide scale. Some parties have proposed creating special compulsory licences for intellectual property covering climate change technology. In particular patent compulsory licensing has been debated. However, those who do not support this type of legal development point to the fact that for many technologies a patent licence on its own is not sufficient to facilitate technology transfer and adoption. To achieve such an adoption there is normally a need to have associated know-how, expertise and other rights such as copyrights. Compulsory licensing is currently addressed in the Paris Convention, under TRIPS, and under national legislation.

Under the Paris Convention, Article 5.A,[21] there is provision for compulsory licences relating to patents and utility models. Each member state can take legislative measures to provide for the granting of compulsory licences to prevent abuses resulting from exercising the exclusive rights given by a granted patent, such as failure to work the patent. A compulsory licence shall be non-exclusive and shall not be transferable. Under TRIPS Article 31[22] there is a provision to allow a member use of a patent without authorisation of the proprietor. This could cover compulsory licences for third parties and governments. The proposed licensee should have made efforts to obtain authorisation from the proprietor on reasonable commercial terms and conditions. It should also be established that the efforts of the licensee have not been successful within a reasonable period of time. A large number of countries have national legislation that provides similar compulsory licensing under certain conditions. However, in practice it has proven difficult for third parties to obtain such licences.

More focus has been on encouraging voluntary sharing of innovation and facilitating collaboration. The World Intellectual Property Office (WIPO) has formed a programme for promoting package technology licensing agreements for green technologies in order to accelerate their dissemination throughout the world, especially in developing countries. The programme is an online interface of available green technologies. The purpose of this programme is to create a global network of partnerships with companies offering a package of all relevant features of a technology, including intellectual property licence, know-how, processes and training.

In the private arena, two patent pools or patent 'commons' have been set up. The Eco-Patent Commons was launched in 2008 by IBM, Nokia, Pitney Bowes and Sony under the World Business Council for Sustainable Development (WBCSD). Members submit patents that have environmental benefits and third parties may exploit the covered technology for free and without notification. The Commons is not a licence, but rather an agreement not to assert patent infringement as long as the patentee considers that the use benefits the environment. The Green Xchange is another patent pool or patent 'commons' set up by Best Buy and Nike in association with the non-profit organisation Creative Commons. Members make their technologies in three ways: allowing patented technology for use by academic research to promote open collaboration, innovation and inventions; contributing to a registry of knowledge and information; submitting patents to be made available under a standard licence agreement for green technology uses.

Corporate governance and the transfer of technology and know-how

Section IX, Science and Technology, of the 2011 edition of the OECD Guidelines for Multinational Enterprises addresses the issues of innovation, technology transfer and access to knowledge. Under the OECD guidelines, an enterprise should have an understanding of the effects and benefits of developing technology and science within the various countries in which they operate to contribute to the development of local and national innovative capacity. The OECD guidelines focus on five key areas: compatibility of the national science and technology policies and plans and contribution to the national innovative capacity; the transfer and rapid diffusion of technologies and know-how with due regard to intellectual property rights; localised science and technology development work; granting intellectual property licences in a manner that contributes to the long term sustainable development prospects of the host country; developing ties with local universities, public research institutions and cooperative research projects with local industry. The guidelines highlight the fact that in a modern knowledge-based and global economy multinational enterprises may be the main conduit of technology transfer across borders and they can significantly contribute to the innovation capacity of the countries within which they operate. Not only should the multinational company have a strategy and policy for addressing these issues, the company can usefully contribute to the formation by the host country governments of policy frameworks to facilitate innovation development.

Sustainability reporting

Multinational companies are providing information about their sustainability performance by producing annual sustainability reports. Many companies have recognised the commercial opportunity to be gained by actively contributing to the global sustainability agenda. One issue that has been discussed is the form of these reports and the type of information and data they should contain. There are also a number of rating organisations which produce questionnaires and carry out evaluations of performance under different criteria. The ratings allow the respective companies to benchmark themselves against their competitors. One agency focusing on this subject is the Global Initiative for Sustainability Ratings (GISR), launched in 2011. Its stated mission is to build and steward a generally accepted, world-class corporate sustainability ratings, ranking, and index standard and associated accreditation process. GISR is complementary to the disclosure focus of the standards forming groups, the Global Reporting Initiative (GRI), the Sustainability Accounting Standards Board (SASB) and the International Integrated Reporting Council (IIRC).

Many key stakeholders, such as investors, find the sustainability ratings offer a valuable instrument for understanding a company's ability to manage risks that could affect its competitiveness, reputation and licence to operate. The ratings and company sustainability reports provide information about the company's strategy for identifying and creating new markets for goods and services and their capacity to innovate. Companies carrying out GRI reporting increased in 2013 in the USA.[23] Although it is not compulsory in the USA to report on sustainable issues, multinational US companies that operate in other countries are expected to comply with legislation and regulation mandating greater transparency. In 2014 the European Parliament approved the draft text for a new directive that requires companies to disclose information on their policies, and risks and measurable results regarding environment issues, social and employee-related issues, and anti-corruption. The directive advises companies to use the existing frameworks for non-financial reporting including GRI guidelines.[24] The categories of the GRI reports include economic aspects, environmental aspects, and social aspects such as labour practices, human rights, society, and product responsibility.

Following the increase of sustainability reports and their subsequent scrutiny, sustainability issues are becoming increasingly common in the boardroom. An area being discussed is a potential link between sustainability performance and executive compensation.[25] There has been a link between executive compensation and corporate performance in the USA since an increase in the 1970s and 1980s with performance-based bonus plans and stock options. In many companies the ultimate responsibility for sustainability oversight is assigned to the board of directors or a board committee. The *Journal of Management* found, in a 2006 article, that there was an increase in the corporate social performance of companies using a long term focus in CEO pay[26] and a Harvard Business School study indicated that companies that are rated leaders in sustainability are more likely to align executive compensation with non-financial sustainability metrics.[27] The development of sustainability performance compensation requires there to be a set of agreed metrics to the measured and valued. A report[28] by Kruse and Lundbergh indicated that non-financial metrics should be measurable, relevant, comparable, stretching and clearly disclosed. The authors recommend choosing relevant and specific metrics that are core to the business and not too vague. The sustainability performance should be aligned with the corporate strategy so that the performance is seen as important to the whole organisation and its corporate goals. The executive compensation could be for achieving both financial and non-financial metrics.

Conclusion

With the increasing use of GRI information on a company's sustainability performance, the reputation of the company will increasingly be linked to its strategy and policy on sustainability issues. This information will be open to the scrutiny of third parties, including direct stakeholders of the company. The company's reputation and the value of the company brand will be linked to the third parties' assessments of the sustainability reports and the various benchmarking sustainability league tables. With the power of social media and the speed of modern communications, the reaction and analysis of the company's sustainability performance will be transmitted globally.

Notes

1 http://www.un.org/press/en/2014/sgsm15839.doc.htm; http://www.un.org/press/en 2012/ sgsm14242.doc.htm.
2 McKinsey Global Survey results, Capturing Value from Sustainability, 2012. http://www.mckinsey.com/insights/energy_resources_materials/the_business_of_ sustainability_mckinsey_global_survey_results. The online survey was in the field from 17 July to 27 July 2012, and received responses from 4,145 executives representing the full range of regions, industries, company sizes, tenures, and functional specialties.
3 (2012) *Sustainable Energy for All: Opportunities for the Oil and Gas Industry*, UN Global Compact and Accenture. https://www.accenture.com/mx-es/~/media/ Accenture/Conversion-Assets/DotCom/Documents/Local/es-la/PDF2/Accent ure-Sustainable-Energy-All-Opportunities-Oil-Gas-Industry.pdf.
4 Henry, C. and J.E. Stiglitz (2010) 'Intellectual Property, Dissemination of Innovation and Sustainable Development', 1 *Global Policy* 3, 237–251.
5 Ibid.
6 Trade-Related Aspects of Intellectual Property Rights, Section 5, Article 27, 3a) 3b). https://www.wto.org/english/tratop_e/trips_e/art27_3b_e.htm.
7 International Centre for Trade and Sustainable Development (ICTSD) (2008) 'Climate Change, Technology Transfer and Intellectual Property Rights', ICTSD background paper, Trade and Climate Change Seminar, 18–20 June, Copenhagen, Denmark.
8 *Climate Change and the Intellectual Property System: What Challenges, What Options, What Solutions?* World Intellectual Property Organisation (WIPO), DRAFT 5.0 14.XI.08.
9 'Plant Cells Resistant to Glutamine Synthetase Inhibitors, Made by Genetic Engineering'. T 0356/93 (Plant Cells) of 21.2.1995, Decision of Technical Board of EPO, ECLI:EP:BA:1995:T035693.19950221.
10 *Patent Pools and Antitrust – A Comparative Analysis*, World Intellectual Property Organisation (WIPO), March 2014.

11 (2011) *World Intellectual Property Report: The Changing Face of Innovation*, Chapter 3: 'Balancing Collaboration and Competition', p. 121. http://www.wipo.int/econ_stat/en/economics/wipr/wipr_2011.html.

12 https://unfccc.int/files/cooperation_and_support/ldc/application/pdf/article4.pdf.

13 http://www.eea.europa.eu/themes/technology.

14 http://unfccc.int/meetings/marrakech_oct_2001/session/6273.php.

15 European Patent Office (2010) 'Patents and Clean Energy: Bridging the Gap between Evidence and Policy', Brussels.

16 Agenda for COP-17 (2011) Durban, South Africa.

17 Park, Patricia (2013) *International Law for Energy and the Environment*, 2nd edn, CRC Press.

18 Henry and Stiglitz (2010).

19 *World Intellectual Property Report* (2011) Bloomberg BNA, p. 29.

20 Brewer, Thomas L. (2012) *International Technology Diffusion in a Sustainable Energy Trade Agreement (SETA): Issues and Options for Institutional Architectures*, Geneva: ICTSD.

21 http://www.wipo.int/treaties/en/text.jsp?file_id=288514.

22 https://www.wto.org/english/docs_e/legal_e/27-trips_04c_e.htm.

23 The Conference Board (2015) *Sustainability Practices 2015; Key Findings* – The Global Awakening Companies Respond to Climate, Corruption and other Risks.

24 Directive 2014/95/EU of the European Parliament and of the Council of 22 October 2014, 'Improving Corporate Governance: Europe's Largest Companies Will Have to Be more Transparent about How they Operate', European Commission, http://europa.eu/rapid/press-release_STATEMENT-14-124_en.htm.

25 Singer, Thomas (2012) 'Linking Executive Compensation to Sustainability Performance', Director Notes, The Conference Board, https://www.conference-board.org/retrievefile.cfm?filename=TCB-DN-V4N11-12.pdf&type=subsite.

26 Deckop, John R., K. Merriman Kimberly and Shruti Gupta (June 2006) 'The Effects of CEO Pay Structure on Corporate Social Performance', 32 *Journal of Management* 3, 329–342.

27 Eccles, Robert G., Ioannis Ioannou, and George Serafeim (2011) *The Impact of a Corporate Culture of Sustainability on Corporate Behavior and Performance*, Harvard Business School.

28 Kruse, Claudia and Stefan Lundbergh (2010) 'The Governance of Corporate Sustainability', 3 *Rotman International Journal of Pension Management* 2.

6 Corporate governance

Introduction

In his book, *Firm Commitment,* Colin Mayer states: 'Your reputation is what determines your success, cramps your style, or opens unlimited opportunities to you. It takes years to establish and minutes to lose.'[1]

This statement encapsulates the theme which came uppermost throughout the interviews carried out over the last two years. Corporate governance has possibly become the most commonly used phrase in the international business vocabulary since the global financial crisis and credit crunch engulfed financial markets and most economies around the world. Increasingly, weaknesses in corporate governance are being put forward as reasons for, and causes of, the economic crisis. The blame is focused on excessive executive remuneration, failures in risk management and internal control systems, including weak monitoring, and lack of independence in the boardroom. The lack of boardroom ethics is also being blamed for the liquidity crisis and its repercussions.[2]

The collapse of Enron in 2001 focused international attention on company failures, in particular in the USA and the UK. The USA responded by passing the Sarbanes–Oxley Act 2002, whilst the UK commissioned the Higgs and the Smith Reports in 2003. However, the effectiveness of the legislation and codes of corporate governance and best practice may be called into question in the light of the 'banking crisis'. Although both the USA and the UK responded swiftly to the Enron failure by strengthening the internal systems of control through internal audit, audit committees and the role of non-executive directors, the 2008 crisis appears to have been based on poor risk management, inadequate internal controls and weak monitoring boards. So what has gone wrong?

Nations around the world have provided far reaching programmes for corporate governance reform, with corporate governance increasingly including stakeholder concerns. In policy terms, society wants corporations to behave in a way consistent with the public good. In economic terms, society does not want corporations to externalise their costs onto the community. How does society make that happen? By looking to accountability.

Defining corporate governance

Corporate governance can mean different things depending on the country or jurisdiction. A relatively early definition of corporate governance sought to establish a broader remit than that enshrined in agency theory, which stated that the governance role is not concerned with the running of the business of the company *per se*, but with giving overall direction to the enterprise, with overseeing and controlling the executive actions of management and with satisfying legitimate expectations of accountability and regulation by interests beyond the corporate boundaries.[3]

But the Walker Review in 2009 defined corporate governance in a much more restrictive way: 'the role of corporate governance is to protect and advance the interests of shareholders through setting the strategic direction of a company and appointing and monitoring capable management to achieve this'.[4] Despite the general acceptance that corporate governance should have a more wide-ranging stakeholder inclusive definition, the Walker Review reverts to the restrictive shareholder centric approach to corporate governance.

The broadest definitions of corporate governance consider that companies should be accountable, not only to the whole of society, but also to future generations and the natural world. Solomon defines corporate governance as the system of checks and balances, both internal and external to companies, which ensure that companies discharge their accountability to all their stakeholders and act in a socially responsible way in all areas of their business activity.[5]

This definition is based upon the perception that companies can maximise their value creation over the long term, by discharging their accountability to all their stakeholders and by optimising their system of corporate governance. The Higgs Report also emphasised a strong link between good corporate governance, accountability and value creation thus: 'the UK framework of corporate governance…can clearly be improved…progressive strengthening of the existing architecture is strongly desirable, both to increase corporate accountability and to maximise sustainable wealth creation'.[6]

It was the introduction of limited liability and the opening up of corporate ownership to the general public through share ownership which had a dramatic impact on the way in which companies were controlled. The market system as exercised in the UK and the USA is organised, *inter alia,* in such a way that the owners, who are the shareholders of a listed company, delegate the running of the company to the company management. In other words, there is a separation between ownership and control. One problem that arises as a result of this system of corporate ownership is that the management do not necessarily make decisions in the best interests of the owners. In finance theory, there is a basis assumption that the primary objective for companies is shareholder wealth maximisation. In practice this is not necessarily the case. It is very likely that company managers prefer to pursue their own personal objectives, such as aiming to gain the highest bonus possible in a display of egoism. This in turn can result in a tendency to focus on project and company investments that provide short run profits, when managers' remuneration is related to this variable, rather than the maximisation of long-term shareholder wealth through investment in projects that are long term in nature.

This short termism is considered to characterise countries that are classified generally as 'outsider dominated'.[7] This means that the economy is not only dominated by large firms controlled directly by their managers but also indirectly through the actions of outsiders, such as institutional investors.[8] In this environment, managers are tempted to supplement their salaries with prerequisites leading to a reduction in shareholder value. It follows from this divergence in objectives that shareholders have a need to control the company management.

This raises the question as to how can shareholders exercise control over company management? One way is by monitoring by the shareholder, but this is expensive and involves shareholder engagement which institutional investors do not necessarily consider to be desirable. One pension fund director interviewed by Solomon commented that there is a weakness in the present system of corporate governance in that responsibility for ownership rests with people who do not want it and are not seeking it. Institutional investors are investing in shares because they give a good return and it is coincidental really that they bring with them this responsibility.[9]

Reflecting this view the Hampel Report[10] suggested that institutional investors do not want to be involved in companies' meetings and business decisions. There are also important legal issues involved in the content and results of these meetings and decisions, such as 'insider dealing'.

Therefore, if the market mechanisms and shareholders' ability to express themselves are not enough to monitor and control managerial behaviour, then regulation or formal guidance is needed. In fact, if markets were perfectly efficient and companies could compete in an efficient market for funds, then artificial initiatives aimed at reforming corporate governance would not be needed.

However, markets are not perfectly competitive and therefore intervention is necessary in order to improve corporate governance, help companies to raise finance and make companies more accountable to all stakeholders.

Corporate governance failure

Severe corporate governance problems emerged from the Enron case which involved unfettered power in the hands of the chief executive. It was not usual in the USA for the chairman and the chief executive to be separate positions at that time, although this has changed somewhat since Enron. There were also numerous examples of unethical activity within the Enron organisation that continued to come to light long after its demise. There have been many books published aiming to explain why events transpired as they did, and as stated, the USA and the UK responded swiftly to the Enron collapse. Corporate governance has been highlighted as a major factor in the Enron collapse as a result of the weaknesses in the Enron corporate governance system.

The European Union also had its scandals with regard to corporate governance in the shape of Parmalat, an Italian company which specialised in long life milk. The company grew exponentially accompanied by rising debts, which led to the founding family selling 49 per cent of its control over the company in 1990. The company continued to expand which led to further debts. These debts were covered by a 3.9 billion Euro bank account in the Cayman Islands, which turned out to be based on forged letters from the bank. The company then admitted £10 billion worth of debt and went into administration. However, Parmalat survived and is now in profit. Further, Parmalat filed a lawsuit against the auditors in order to recover funds as the auditors failed to identify the fraud and it was claimed must therefore have been 'active conspirators' with the company's former management.

However, the case was dismissed in 2009, on the grounds of the *pari delicto* doctrine, which means that no one can sue to recover damages from a fraud in which it was a willing participant.

Corporate governance failure and the collapse of the world's banking sector

In 2007 there was a growing realisation that banks had been lending excessively in the subprime market, which means that borrowers were not in a financial position to repay mortgages and loans. The mortgagees were defaulting and the banks were facing a major liquidity crisis.

The Turner Review[11] was published in March 2009 and described the events which led up to the complete loss of confidence in the banking sector. It has become increasingly obvious that decision making by banks on interest rates offered, loans and mortgages granted, and terms agreed with borrowers had thrown caution to the wind, and despite the huge salaries attracted by executives in the world's leading banks, their performance in terms of risk management, ethical behaviour and judgement was flawed.[12] Although both the US and UK governments put together financial bailout packages for the banks to try to put the economies back on track, the corporate governance failure of the banking sector has led to a world recession with a slowdown in business activity with consequential job losses.

The Turner Review of the banking crisis identified that many of the problems encountered pre-Enron were the causal factors in the banking crisis, identifying negative human characteristics and the failure to raise serious questions as to why the financial and corporate sectors had not learned from previous mistakes. More care should have been taken in developing a robust risk management system and acquiring a more detailed understanding of the business of their own organisation.

However, the corporate governance checks and balances can only detect, not cure, unethical practices with the intangible issues of fraud and ethical breakdown.

The role of boards in corporate governance

The tradition of 'the board' began with the earliest form of corporate organisation, the joint stock companies. The group of people who oversaw the company would meet regularly, but in those days furniture was expensive and very few had large tables around which to accommodate the group. So the men sat on stools, around a long board placed across two sawhorses from which the name 'the board' was taken. The leader of the group, to denote his importance, sat upon a chair, rather than a stool, and so he was named 'the chair man'.[13]

The responsibility of today's boards of directors has not changed over many years with most jurisdictions identifying two main duties, being the 'duty of care' and the 'duty of loyalty'.

The 'duty of care' means that a director must exercise due diligence in making decisions. They must discover as much information as possible on the question at issue and be able to show that, in reaching a decision, they have considered all reasonable alternatives.

The 'duty of loyalty' means that a director must demonstrate unyielding and undivided loyalty to the company's shareholders. If the director were to hold such a position in two like companies which could be in competition, then the director must resign from one board because they could not demonstrate loyalty to the shareholders of both companies at the same time.[14]

Thus directors' conduct will be judged by the 'business judgement rule'. In other words, when directors can demonstrate that they have acted with all due loyalty and exercised all possible care, the courts will not second guess their decision, but defer to their business judgement. That is unless a decision is made by the directors or managers which is clearly self dealing or negligent. So as long as a director can show care and loyalty the decision will not be challenged by the court.

As noted in the *Disney* decision: 'Fiduciaries who act faithfully and honestly on behalf of those whose interests they represent are indeed granted wide latitude in their efforts to maximise shareholders' investments.'[15] Times may change but fiduciary duties do not.

The litigation was about the decision to pay Michael Ovitz US $140 million compensation for his short and stormy 14 month tenure as Disney's President. However, what is important about the decision is that it signalled that the protection it granted to the Disney Board would not be available for future directors. The judge indicated that the 'business judgement rule', and what had been permitted under the pre-Sarbanes–Oxley Act, would not be permitted again.

The role of non-executive directors in corporate governance

The collapse of Enron during 2001 focused attention on the effectiveness of the non-executive director function. The Higgs Report and the related Tyson Report in the UK clearly responded to the considerable impact of ineffective non-executive directors. The Reports identified the function of the non-executive director as having an essential role to play in achieving the appropriate balance between outside and inside directors on boards, stating that this is an essential ingredient for an effective board.

The Tyson Report[16] specified that the role of a non-executive director was to:

1 Provide advice and direction to a company's management in the development and evaluation of a strategy;
2 Monitor the company's management in strategy implementation and performance;
3 Monitor the company's legal and ethical performance;
4 Monitor the veracity and adequacy of the financial and other company information provided to investors and other stakeholders;
5 Assume responsibility for appointing, evaluating and, where necessary, removing senior management; and
6 Plan succession for top management positions.

It was the Higgs Report which emphasised that the non-executive directors needed to have more than simply the experience and ability to perform these functions and stipulated that they also needed to have integrity and high ethical standards, sound judgement, the ability and willingness to challenge and probe on issues, as well as strong interpersonal skills. In fact the Tyson Report went further and suggested that an ideal non-executive director should include '*no crooks, no cronies, no cowards*'.[17]

Non-executive directors have not escaped criticism in the current financial crisis as some have been blamed for ineffective monitoring contributing to the global financial meltdown.[18]

One suggestion following on from the Higgs Report is the extent to which the non-executive director's monitoring role can be made more effective through the introduction of 'gatekeeper liability' in which the non-executive director could be made personally liable for the misdeeds of executive directors. A further suggestion from the Higgs Report was that corporate secretaries should play a leading role in corporate governance affairs, stating that they should provide a source of corporate governance information and should support the effective performance of non-executive directors.

Following the global financial crisis the Walker Review[19] in 2009 emphasised the need for non-executive directors in the banking sector to devote materially more time to their duties. The Review highlighted the need for executives to be challenged more substantially before strategic decisions are made. In the banking sector, executives need to be challenged more robustly by non-executive directors on issues such as risk, risk management and related strategy. This was woefully missing from the banks' boards of directors in the period leading up to the crisis.

The recent financial trauma around the world has emphasised the delicate nature of corporate governance and the need for greater accountability and ethics in all types of organisations. The main issues seem to revolve around an urgent need to nurture a more responsible corporate environment and improve the effectiveness of the non-executive director function in monitoring company management.

Management performance

Unquestionably the biggest challenge a company faces is not failure, but success. When a company is failing, it will try almost anything. On the other hand, a company that is successful generally does not know where the roots of that success lie. There is consequently a tendency to fall into a pattern of not changing anything.

It took the abuses of the takeover era to wake up the institutional investors, and almost before they got started, the takeover era had ended. But by that time, there was a new issue to provoke outrage: excessive CEO compensation. In some ways, this was an ideal corporate governance issue for the new activists. It was the first corporate governance issue to go from the financial pages to the front pages to the editorial pages to the comic pages.

However, no one complained about the money Bill Gates made at Microsoft; but when pay was not related to performance, the business press was just as outraged as the shareholders. Even *Forbes*'s cover story on executive pay bore a banner headline: 'It doesn't make sense'.[20] It was also a perfect issue to be addressed by shareholders. Compensation for performance could have no more direct connection to shareholder value. However, if compensation is unrelated to performance all the shareholder resolutions in the world cannot make a difference. Some people dismiss the issue of executive compensation as immaterial because the amounts involved are a tiny fraction of the company's market capitalisation, even its annual budget. But every dollar/pound of executive compensation, like every other asset allocated by the company, must meet the same rigorous standards for return on investment. However, the record of American and UK corporations in providing a competitive rate of return on the money spent on CEO compensation is very poor. As a CEO shelf life shrinks, new candidates insist on even more downside protection in their contracts, ensuring that the contracts will have even more tenuous ties between pay and performance.

The role of the shareholder with regard to compensation starts with one simple point: compensation presents an investment opportunity. The CEO's compensation plan is a clear indication of the company's value as an investment. Therefore, a shareholder should want to invest in a CEO whose compensation depends on the money the shareholder will receive. Compensation plans also reveal what the company's goals are and how confident the CEO and board are of the company's future.

CEOs are paid a lot for one reason, and that is because they take risks. Their compensation should provide the appropriate incentives for those risks and to the extent that the shareholder can better align these incentives, is an investment with substantial returns. The question then is not whether there will be increased activism by shareholders on the subject of compensation but what form will that activism take. With few exceptions, shareholders have not objected to CEOs earning a lot of money, as long as they created a lot of value for shareholders first. What shareholders have objected to is CEOs being paid a lot of money without earning it. Their focus has been on strengthening the link between pay and performance.

The issue is not only matching compensation to performance as there is almost always some standard that can be used to support a bonus, and compensation consultants are good at providing a mix of 'performance plans' that ensure that at least one of them will pay off. The real issue that shareholders should focus on is not just tying compensation to performance, but really improving performance. All the incentives in the world cannot work if there are other impediments to getting the job done with some incentive plans being manipulated.

The question then is 'Who is in the best position to make a given decision about the direction of a corporation, and does that person or group have the necessary authority?'[21] The person or group in the best position to make any decision about the corporation's direction is determined by two factors: conflicts of interest and information. Decisions should be made by those with the fewest conflicts and the most information.

The corporate structure has been so robust that it has outgrown most of the structures, including the political structures, designed to control it. Accountability must come from within; and that requires an effective governance system that itself is accountable. The ultimate aim of a corporate governance structure must be that it is continually re-evaluated so that the governance structure itself can adapt to changing times and needs.

The role of institutional investors in corporate governance

The ownership structure of corporations has in recent times become more concentrated. In fact the growing concentration of shareholding by a relatively small number of institutional investors is resulting in the evolution of a capitalist system in the USA and the UK that bears little resemblance to the fragmented and dispersed stock market of yesteryear. Mainly, this is a result of the gradual transference of ownership from individuals to investment institutions with millions of pounds invested in the shares of listed UK and foreign companies, as well as in other forms of financial asset. These include pension funds, life insurance companies, unit trusts and investment trusts, and now represent the dominant shareholder class.[22]

However, it is not only the growth of institutional ownership that has transformed the ownership structure but also the increase in ownership concentration, which in turn affects corporate governance. Increasingly, listed companies are owned by a small number of large institutions and in the UK the pension fund sector now represents the most significant group of institutional investors in the country. This increase in ownership concentration and the transferral of ownership from individuals to institutions has important repercussions for corporate governance in the USA and the UK.

One problem with institutional investors as monitors of company management is that they are not actually the shareholders. Their relationship with companies and with the true shareholders involves a complicated web of ownership and accountability. The real shareholders are the clients of the institutional investment organisations. In other words, most company employees are members of an occupational pension scheme; the pension scheme is run by a fund manager; the pension fund manager selects companies for the portfolio and purchases the shares, using pooled funds entrusted to him/her by all the employees in the company. Therefore, the employee is the ultimate 'owner' of the companies in which the pension fund manager invests. It is the employee who is the ultimate beneficiary of the investment through his/her pension payouts. A further layer in the complexity of ownership and accountability is the existence of the trustee under pension fund law. The trustee is entrusted with ultimate responsibility over the pension fund assets and it is the pension fund trustee who has a fiduciary responsibility to ensure that the eventual pension is maximised and that the funds of pension fund members are invested to the greatest effect.[23]

So we can now see that the existence of these intermediaries, such as trustees in institutional investment, can obscure the corporate governance monitoring function. A major problem arising from this complex ownership structure is that of 'short termism' in investment. This happens when the institutional investors wish to maximise their short-term profits in order to make their investment returns look as healthy as possible in the short run. They then pressure companies to focus on short-term profits rather than long-term profits. This is detrimental to long-term company survival and sustainability as companies need to invest in long-term projects in order to ensure that they grow and prosper in the long run.

As long ago as the 1930s John Maynard Keynes recognised that the professional investor is largely concerned, not with making superior long-term forecasts of the probable yield of an investment over its whole life, but with foreseeing changes a short time ahead of the general public.[24]

According to Melvin,[25] this complicated ownership structure has contributed to a complete breakdown in trust between companies and their shareholders. It is, therefore, these institutional shareholders who need to examine their own governance structures in order to actively rebuild trust among their beneficiaries.

Trustees are therefore in an influential position in their pension funds. They have a fiduciary duty to maximise the investment returns for the members of the pension fund. They are responsible for the asset allocation decision and for the pension fund's investment policy. However, they are traditionally undertrained and unprepared for such major responsibilities. In fact in his research Myners[26] found that:

1 62 per cent of trustees had no professional qualifications in finance or investment;

2 77 per cent of trustees had no in-house investment professionals to assist them;

3 Over half the population of trustees had received less than three days training when they assumed their responsibilities;

4 44 per cent of trustees had not attended any course since their initial 12 months of trusteeship;

5 49 per cent of trustees spent three hours or less preparing for pension investment matters. (This implies that given four meetings *per annum*, trustees spent less than 12 hours a year on investment matters.)

Myners commented that the lack of investment understanding among trustees in general was a serious problem.[27]

The recent financial crisis has revealed a lack of effective engagement between banks and their core institutional investors, which has contributed to the collapse of the global banking sector. Therefore the remit of the institutional investor is broadening, such that the areas of corporate management and business strategy affected by active institutional shareholders are constantly expanding. Risks, especially reputational risk, are driving institutional investor dialogue with investee companies which should have a positive effect on corporate governance and company value.

Transparency, internal control and risk management

Transparency is an essential element of a well functioning system of corporate governance, as is risk management, and an effective system of internal control. Corporate disclosure to all stakeholders is the principle way in which companies can become transparent.

The term disclosure encompasses many different forms of information produced by companies, including the annual report which includes the director's statement, the Operating and Financial Review (OFR) in the UK, and the Management Discussion and Analysis (MDA) section of the annual report in the USA; profit and loss account, balance sheet, cash flow statement and other mandatory items. It also includes all forms of voluntary corporate communications, which will be discussed in more detail in the next chapter.

Academic research has shown that investors perceive a value to corporate disclosure and Brennan and Solomon stressed that mechanisms of transparency, in the form of accounting, financial reporting and voluntary disclosures, represent an important element in corporate governance.[28]

In respect of the use of accounting information to control management it is through their remuneration, because there is a direct link between company performance and managerial remuneration. According to Healy and Palepu,[29] the contract should require management to disclose relevant information that enables shareholders to monitor their compliance with the contractual agreements, and so evaluate the extent to which management has utilised the company's resources in the interests of the shareholders.

The role of internal control, internal audit, external audit and audit committees in effective corporate governance

Recent events in the international banking sector have focused attention on companies' systems of internal control and risk management. Previous corporate governance agendas for reform had marginalised risk and risk management by focusing on the board composition and remuneration issues; however, the current financial crisis has pushed risk to the forefront of corporate governance concerns. It is essential, therefore, for good corporate governance that the audit committee, the internal audit function and the external audit are effective in themselves, and also that they are linked effectively. Merely operating effectively in isolation is in itself inadequate.[30] Information flows between these elements of corporate governance are essential for effective corporate governance. Likewise, the linkages and disclosures to the board of directors are crucial for effective corporate governance. It is clear from the recent banking crisis that these linkages and disclosures have not been operating adequately.[31]

Risk disclosure and corporate governance

Corporate risk disclosure represents an important, specific category of corporate disclosure. As Moxey and Berendt[32] highlighted in their report in 2008, risk reporting is an area where banks and other organisations have been remiss. This was also highlighted by the Turnbull Report,[33] which focused attention on this aspect in the Turnbull framework for internal control. Emphasis on the reporting stage of the internal control system is essential, both for corporate accountability and for the future success of the business. Both the USA and Canada had in fact recognised the need to improve corporate risk disclosure before the publication of the UK Turnbull Report, and this need was also acknowledged a little later by interested parties in the UK. The Cadbury Report in 1992 had highlighted the relevance of risk disclosure to the corporate governance agenda by suggesting that validating the company as a going concern and improving the disclosure of internal control should lead to improvements in the communications between investors and their investee companies. In fact, if the aim of company management is to reduce the cost of capital by raising confidence in the market, then the communication of risk management policies must be a significant factor.[34]

Corporate disclosure, and particularly financial accounting information, plays an essential role in corporate governance. The importance of improving risk disclosure and the essential role of the audit function all need to be considered in the context of corporate governance.

International corporate governance

In the early days of the twenty-first century it seemed that all clashes between cultures, political systems, and religions had been overshadowed by the triumph of one overarching belief system; that of the belief in capitalism. The cold war was not won by any particular creed but free enterprise and corporations can go where diplomats cannot.[35] However, the twenty-first-century edition of the global corporation varies substantially from its predecessors. As an example, take ExxonMobil, which is the largest earning corporation in the history of commerce. Its headquarters are in Dallas, Texas, but its legal domicile is New Jersey. Its stock trades on the New York Stock Exchange. It has principle operations in virtually every industrialised country in the world, and less than one third of its earnings are derived from operations within the USA. The sense that corporations have nationality, and therefore some sort of accountability to the law and customs of a host nation, is at best a convenient fiction. Corporate governance is, therefore, demonstrably of greatest importance in those countries having a need to attract capital.

The most important fact to keep in mind in examining global corporate governance is that it is changing very rapidly. Every country from the most established economy to the emerging economies is undergoing extensive examination of every aspect of its governance codes and practices as a matter of risk management and competitiveness. However, just as companies exist in a variety of forms throughout the world, so the same word may mean something different in each country. For example, accounting firms have operations in dozens of countries and prepare audited financial reports with the same letter heads and logos, but the outputs differ because accounting standards differ. Another term, 'executive compensation', may be called 'remuneration' in some countries and is almost impossible to compare across boundaries, not because cultures and amounts differ, but because disclosure rules differ so enormously.

Just as there is a distinction between rules based and principle based accounting, there is a distinction between governance codes that are mandatory and those that are 'comply or explain'. This gives companies the opportunity to adapt provisions to their circumstances and encourages innovation.

Most countries have one board of directors, but some have dual boards. For example, in Germany the two tier board structure dates back to the 1870s when public companies had to have a management (insider) board and a supervisory (outsider) board. In Israel, almost all public companies are still controlled by the first or second generation of the founding families. In Japan, under the well-established system of *keiretsu*, interlocking business holdings and share ownership are centred around a bank.

In the UK, government retains more oversight over private power than in many of the other established economies. It was as recent as the 1980s that the principle British institutions providing infrastructure services such as transportation, mail, phone, coal, steel and energy were in fact owned by the government, and this pattern of private accountability to a public authority remains meaningful in the twenty-first century. Likewise in many other industrialised countries corporations continue to be instruments of national policy to a greater or lesser extent. It is important to keep in mind the extent to which chartering countries are prepared to empower private individuals to create sources of wealth, and therefore, legitimate power that is independent of the political authority.

At one end of the spectrum is the USA where there is almost no tradition of government ownership of commercial enterprises. This may well account for the success of the private sector and its capacity for wealth creation, but the risk is that there will occasionally be circumstances when corporate power may acquire an inappropriately large influence. At the other end of the spectrum are countries that maintain extensive government control, even of 'public companies' open for investment. For example, the Chinese government has the controlling shareholding in PetroChina, although Warren Buffett, the legendary investor, holds 1.3 per cent through his company Berkshire Hathaway.

On a global scale, there is a fundamental asymmetry of state control of corporate governance laws in the USA. A country's capacity to control conduct stops at its borders and yet the preponderance of corporate activity takes place across the globe. The traditional notion that corporate conduct can be controlled by the country of its domicile is obsolete. At the risk of discouraging further investment from abroad, countries plainly have the power to control activities within their borders.

The institutional investor as proxy for the public interest

The only actor having the same motivation, scope, and power as management is the previously discussed institutional owners, who are trustees for a significant part of the population, especially the pension fund. By definition, they are looking for sustainable growth from companies that provide useful goods and services and good jobs at good wages. Pension funds and the corporation have the same scope and ultimate objectives, thus optimising the long-term value. These vehicles of pooled savings for retirement in the USA, UK, Canada, Australia, Scandinavia, and the Netherlands are not only important, but are increasingly the controlling owners of publically traded enterprises throughout the world. Like the companies in which they invest, these ownership groups can transcend national boundaries and therefore regulations.

As identified earlier, majority stock ownership is managed by fiduciaries and the exercise of ownership rights can be compromised by conflicts of interest and the collective choice problem. Both public and private entities have failed to enforce the legal obligations of the trustees to act as owners of portfolio companies 'for the exclusive benefit' of plan participants; the effect has been to disenfranchise a substantial portion of the ownership group. This dysfunction of the fiduciary duty in the mercantile context tends to mislead.

The Norwegian Government Pension Fund has many of the characteristics necessary for the ideal corporate owner. Notwithstanding its name, it is not a pension fund with liabilities to present and future retirees, but is a fund for the benefit of the Norwegian people into perpetuity. The Norwegian government determined that the wealth extracted in the form of oil from within its jurisdiction should be used to purchase ownership of publically traded corporations on behalf of the entire population of Norway. It was formerly known as the Petroleum Fund of Norway but its name was changed in 2006. The government, the Norges Bank, and a skilled cadre of managers carry out the difficult task of trying to combine wealth maximisation with sensitivity to the ethical consequences of certain investments and has established an Advisory Council on Ethics to make recommendations about companies whose activities 'constitute an unacceptable risk of the Fund'. These companies include a number of armament producers, certain technology companies and those involved in the nuclear industries. In 2006 the Advisory Council also suggested that the Fund divest itself of more than US $400 million holdings in Walmart in protest over policies of employment and compliance with the law. The Fund attempted to contact Walmart to initiate discussions on the issues but Walmart did not respond and so it was determined that divestment was appropriate.[36]

Governance of the Norwegian Government Pension Fund involves a balance between the government, which makes decisions to disinvest from particular sectors and companies, and Norges Bank, which is committed to an activist programme of global corporate governance in order to assure the continuing integrity of the equity sector of publically traded companies.

It is well known that the Minister of Finance, who is the 'owner' of the Pension Fund, requires the Pension Fund to be highly diversified in compliance with prudent investment principles. Accordingly, the manager of the Fund, Norges Bank, has invested 60 per cent of the Fund in bonds and 40 per cent in more than 3,000 publically traded companies in over 30 countries. To protect the interests of the Fund the Norges Bank also engages in active long-term corporate governance initiatives and has established a corporate governance group whose primary objective is to assist Norges Bank in its efforts to maximise the Fund's long-term financial returns.

This active corporate governance implies that an owner uses their ownership stake to push for changes in the company. Active corporate governance is important because costly conflicts of interest may arise in some of the underlying portfolio companies of the Pension Fund wherever the Fund's ownership is in the form of stocks or bonds. However, by cooperating with other large pension funds, and by maintaining the reputation for integrity, the Pension Fund enjoys an unprecedented opportunity for helping promote improved corporate governance practices around the world. In turn, the Pension Fund helps to safeguard its own financial return in the long run.

Throughout the world, nuances of governance orthodoxy may differ but concern is universally the failures of ownership to protect the rights of the minority, which is usually the public shareholder. In addition the language of accountability differs from that in the English speaking world, which has traditions of trusteeship and the language of fiduciaries, whereas the rest of the world relies on its civil law history.

For example, in the USA and the UK, corporate governance addresses in large part the problems caused by an absence of effective ownership, whilst in the rest of the world, the problem is the existence of a controlling owner, whether it is family, another corporation, or the government.

International harmonisation of corporate governance

International harmonisation is now common in most areas of business, in particular in accounting and financial reporting, with the International Accounting Standards Board driving towards a comprehensive set of internationally acceptable standards for accounting. This has resulted in the rise of international trade and transnational business links with the development of internationally comparable business practices and standards becoming increasingly necessary. Thus the need for a global convergence in corporate governance derives from the existence of forces leading to international harmonisation in financial markets, with increasing international investment, foreign subsidiaries and integration of international capital markets. Companies are no longer relying on domestic sources of finance but are attempting to persuade foreign investors to lend capital. The standardisation of corporate governance is one way of building confidence in a country's financial markets and of enticing investors to risk funds. Consequently there are several initiatives aimed at standardising corporate governance at the global level.

One of the most significant influences at the global level has been the introduction of the OECD Principles in 1999. However, one of the problems with the OECD Principles and code of practice is their impotence, as they have no legislative power. Nevertheless, their impact has been substantial by countries using them as a reference point for self assessment and for developing their own codes of practice in corporate governance. The World Bank has researched many countries around the world to assess the extent to which they have complied with the OECD Principles, and all are available on the internet.

In 2004 the OECD revised the Principles on Corporate Governance with the preamble that: 'if countries are to reap the full benefits of the global capital market, and if they are to attract long term "patent" capital, corporate governance arrangements must be credible, well understood across borders and adhere to internationally accepted principles'.[37]

The International Corporate Governance Network (ICGN) was established in 1975 and now includes membership overseeing more than US $10 trillion in assets with its four primary purposes being:

1   To provide an investor led network for the exchange of views and information about corporate governance issues internationally;
2   To examine corporate governance principles and practices;

3   To develop and encourage adherence to corporate governance standards and guidelines; and
4   To generally promote good corporate governance.

It sets forth what owners expect of companies, but it also focuses on the obligations and conflicts of its own members and other institutional investors. The ICGN has been instrumental in promoting the OECD Principles and produced a statement to this effect in 1999 confirming that the OECD Principles were the foundation stone of good corporate governance, in addition to providing guidance on how companies should put the Principles into practice.

Conclusion

On a global scale, conflicts occur as corporate interests and political interests try to control one another. Corporations rely on sovereign countries for permission to operate and for protection from liability and competition. Political regimes rely on corporations for money, job creation, and the contributions they make to a stable economy and community.

In the twenty-first century most of the public policy focus and energy, especially in the emerging economies, is on the 'supply side' of corporate governance. In other words, what managers and directors must do. But it is just as important to make sure that the 'demand side' is set up with the authority, ability, and incentives aligned to enable effective oversight and market response. In addition, particular attention should be given to financial accounting standards and open disclosure in respect of climate change.

Notes

1   Mayer, Colin (2015) *Firm Commitment: Why the Corporation is Failing us and How to Restore Trust in it*, Oxford: Oxford University Press, ch. 3, p. 44.
2   Solomon, Jill (2012) *Corporate Governance and Accountability*, 3rd edn, Chichester, UK: Wiley, p. 3.
3   Tricker, Robert Ian (1984) *Corporate Governance: Practices, Procedures and Powers in British Companies and Their Board of Directors*, Aldershot: Gower Press.
4   Walker, David (2009) *A Review of Corporate Governance in UK Banks and other Financial Industry Entities*, London: Walker Review Secretariat, 16 July, p. 19.
5   Solomon (2012), p. 6.
6   Higgs Report (2003) *Review of the Role and Effectiveness of Non-Executive Directors*, London: Department of Trade and Industry, January, p. 12, para. 1.13. http://www.ecgi.org/codes/documents/higgsreport.pdf.
7   Mayer (2013), p. 219.
8   Solomon (2012), p. 9.
9   Ibid., p. 11.
10 Hampel Report (1998) http://www.ecgi.org/codes/documents/hampel_index.htm.
11 http://www.fsa.gov.uk/pubs/other/turner_review.pdf.
12 Solomon (2012), p. 41.
13 Ibid., p. 226.
14 Monks, Robert A.G. and Nell Minow (2008) *Corporate Governance*, 4th edn, Chichester: Wiley, p. 231.

15 *The Walt Disney Co. Derivative Litigation.* http://courts.delaware.gov/opinions/download.aspx?ID=7740.
16 Tyson Report (2003) *The Tyson Report on the Recruitment and Development of Non-Executive Directors*, report commissioned by the Department of Trade and Industry following the publication of the Higgs Review.
17 Ibid., p. 5.
18 Laura F. Spira and Ruth Bender (2004) 'Compare and Contrast: Perspectives on Board Committees', 12 *Corporate Governance: An International Review* 4, 489–499.
19 Walker Review (2009) *A Review of Corporate Governance in UK Banks and other Financial Industry Entities*, London: Walker Review Secretariat, 16 July.
20 *Forbes*, 27 May 1991.
21 Monks and Minow (2008), p. 346.
22 Dobson, Gavin R. (1994) *The Global Investor*, Cambridge: Probus Europe; Solomon (2012), p. 117.
23 Ibid., p. 118.
24 Keynes, John Maynard (1936) *The General Theory of Employment, Interest and Money*, Basingstoke: Macmillan, pp. 154–155.
25 Melvin, C. (2006) 'Ownership, Conflict and the Universal Investor', Presentation at the Symposium on Shareholder and Stakeholder Relations, London: Association of Chartered Certified Accountants (ACCA), 9 February.
26 Myners, Paul (2001) *Institutional Investment in the United Kingdom: A Review*, London, Report to HM Treasury.
27 Ibid., p. 43.
28 Brennan, Niamh M. and Jill Solomon (2008) 'Corporate Governance, Accountability and Mechanisms of Accountability: An Overview', 21 *Accounting, Auditing and Accountability Journal*, guest editorial, 1, 885–906.
29 Healy, Paul M. and Krishna G. Palepu (2001) 'Information Asymmetry, Corporate Disclosure, and the Capital Markets: A Review of the Empirical Disclosure Literature', 31 *Journal of Accounting and Economics*, 405–440.
30 Solomon (2012), p. 160.
31 Ibid.
32 Moxey, Paul and Adrian Berendt (2008) 'Corporate Governance and the Credit Crunch', ACCA Discussion Paper, London, November.
33 https://www.governance.co.uk/resources/item/259-the-turnbull-report.
34 Solomon (2012), p. 172.
35 Monks and Minow (2008), p. 352.
36 Ibid., p. 366.
37 OECD (2004) *Principles of Corporate Governance*, Paris: OECD, p. 13.

7 Sustainability through social responsibility

Introduction

In his inaugural address as Chairman of Solomon Brothers in 1991, Warren Buffett said: 'Lose money for the firm, I will be very understanding; lose a shred of reputation for the firm, I will be ruthless.'[1] Again the issue of reputation was raised which is now inextricably associated with sustainability and corporate social responsibility.

Sustainable development as an overarching societal goal, integrating the objectives of environmental protection, social justice, and economic protection, has been increasingly acknowledged as an important principle of international law. While the world population is growing at an accelerated pace, the threat of climate change, loss of biodiversity, exhaustion of natural resources, and social inequality are becoming an unavoidable reality. A paradigm shift towards more sustainable economic and business models is, therefore, urgently required.

Although sustainable development has been a high priority in international politics, any practical application is still far from clear. This is particularly reflected in the regulation of multinational companies, which are the basic economic entities, without which no progress can be made towards sustainable development. The recent financial crisis and subsequent downturn in the global economy shows that in order to obtain a competitive advantage in the long term, business should move from the old, shareholder value model towards the rebalancing of purely achieving profit and contributing to social development and environmental protection. Sustainable companies recognise the potential to contribute independently, creatively, and actively towards sustainable development and thus focus on the decision making process to consider barriers for the necessary changes and propose solutions to overcome these barriers and contribute to preserving the sustainability of the company for the future.

The orthodox conception of corporate social responsibility (CSR) assumes that the company is composed of different constituencies, including shareholders, employees, consumers, creditors, and local communities. However, because non-shareholder interests often conflict with shareholders' interests, in respect of profit maximisation, efforts to promote the interests of the wider stakeholders are inconsistent with the view, referred to as 'shareholder primacy', that profit maximisation is the primary purpose of the company. This creates problems for CSR policies. However, Professor Millon proposes a different way of thinking about CSR that focuses on the long term sustainability of the company.[2] Because this focuses on the well-being of the various stakeholders on whom the future of the company depends, then a long term approach to management can achieve significant CSR results in ways that are consistent with shareholders' economic interests. Thus, the managerial vision may become less myopic once it acknowledges the interrelationship between multiple constituent interests, the context in which the company operates. Furthermore, the consequences of its operations in various contexts can be better cultivated from the vantage point of the longer term perspective that a sustainability approach to CSR would require. Although the sustainability approach to CSR's emphasis on long term economic interest may not require industry to be as proactive as a CSR approach rooted in ethical considerations would, it nevertheless may provide a promising start for creating new possibilities and informing practical reforms.

The dramatic growth of the market for social responsibility investment (SRI) in the past decade, accompanied by some regulatory measures, has for some raised hopes that environmental law may have gained an invaluable new means of influence. However, the SRI remains rather limited and we come back to the principle that investors should be held legally accountable for social and environmental problems that they have helped to fund; in particular the institutional investors under their fiduciary duties. Given that institutional investor ownership dominates shareholding in the developed countries, this reflects an important shift over that recent decade.

Information brought forward in the form of mandatory disclosures of social and environmental risks plays a significant role in the future development, whereby the role of voluntary reporting like that required by the Global Reporting Initiative should not be neglected.

Shareholder primacy and CSR

The shareholder primacy concept and profit maximisation, as practiced in the US corporate system, is not a legal requirement but rather a social norm firmly entrenched in American business. However, the shareholder primacy concept is now being gradually replaced by the more enlightened stakeholder norm which is essential to facilitate intergenerational environmental justice and sustainability, by ensuring that future generations have the opportunity to benefit from, and to enjoy, the natural environment as the current generation have.

There is a great unexplored potential within current state company law to move away from the path of 'business as usual' onto a path towards sustainability. It is accepted that business has to contribute to the mitigation of climate change, the protection of biodiversity and to ensure that future generations are able to meet their needs. Profit for shareholders is but one function of companies, and even if where, exceptionally, company law turns this function into the primary goal by requiring directors to prioritise the shareholder interest, it is still understood that this is a means to increase the welfare of society.

Shareholders themselves could use their power and influence to demand a shift away from 'business as usual' as many jurisdictions give broad powers to the general meeting which would allow them to alter the business of the company from unsustainable to sustainable; however, research has shown that socially responsible investment is but a small part of the financial economy.

Alternatively company law in many jurisdictions gives the board of directors surprisingly broad powers to steer the company towards greater sustainability. In some jurisdictions, environmental sustainability has become part of the duties of the board, and all jurisdictions expect boards to ensure their companies comply with environmental law. Some boards go beyond the requirements of environmental law and internalise the externalities, so long as they can make out a good business case to do so. In fact the business judgement rule now adopted in most jurisdictions broadens this discretion to a considerable degree.

A European perspective

The European Commission previously defined corporate social responsibility as 'a concept whereby companies integrate social and environmental concerns in their business operations and in their interaction with their stakeholders on a voluntary basis'.[3]

In order to update the European perspective on CSR the Commission released a Communication in October 2011 outlining its new strategy for 2011–14 for corporate social responsibility. This document emphasises the multidisciplinary nature of CSR and gives a new updated definition as 'the responsibility of enterprises for their impacts on society'. This is expanded at length but does identify a number of principles which are internationally recognised. The Communication[4] states that:

> For companies seeking a formal approach to CSR, especially large companies, authoritative guidance is provided by internationally recognised principles and guidelines, in particular the recently updated OECD Guidelines for Multinational Enterprises, the ten principles of the United Nations Global Compact, the ISO 26000 Guidance Standard on Social Responsibility, the ILO Tri-partite Declaration of Principles Concerning Multinational Enterprises and Social Policy, and the United Nations Guiding Principles on Business and Human Rights.[5]

Under these principles and guidelines, CSR at least covers human rights, labour and employment practices, environmental issues, and combating bribery and corruption. Therefore, community involvement and development, the integration of disabled persons, and consumer interests, including privacy, are all part of CSR under the EU agenda. The promotion of social and environmental responsibility through the supply chain, and the disclosure of non-financial information are also recognised as important cross cutting issues. The Commission has also adopted a 'Communication on EU Policies and Volunteering' in which it is acknowledged that employee volunteering is an expression of CSR.[6]

The Commission also promotes the three principles of good tax governance[7] in relations between states. In addition, enterprises are encouraged, where appropriate, to work towards the implementation of these principles.

The Commission expresses that CSR should be led by corporations themselves and that public authorities should only play a supporting role through a mix of voluntary measures and, where necessary, complementary regulation. Public authorities should make policies which create market incentives for responsible business conduct, and ensure corporate accountability. The Commission also requires businesses to work together with trade unions and civil society organisations to identify problems and bring pressure for improvement to work constructively. Not only that, but businesses are required to work together with trade unions to put consumers and investors in a position to enhance market reward for socially responsible companies through consumption and investment decisions.

The Commission also recognises the influence of the media to raise awareness of both positive and negative impacts of enterprises. We will look at the influence of social media in the next chapter.

In 2013 the Commission released draft guidance for the oil and gas sector on respecting human rights. This is based on the UN Guiding Principles and is specifically to advise the oil and gas sector about how they can observe and implement the UN Guiding Principle on Business and Human Rights.[8]

Although neither the EC Draft Guidance nor the UN Guiding Principles are legally binding on oil and gas companies, they provide a useful framework for addressing the human rights impacts of their business. In a political, economic and regulatory environment which is increasingly expecting oil and gas companies to take active steps to respect human rights, the EC Draft Guidance provides a sensible platform to engage with such issues.

The Guidance focuses on the rights and perspectives of potentially affected stakeholders. It accepts the internationally recognised human rights as the standard for assessment through meaningful consultation, relationship building, and prioritisation according to severity of impact in the assessment process and in consequent action. It extends to the business relationship (based on linkage not leverage), including legacy issues and contextual factors not under the company's legal control.[9]

Corporate social responsibility and the oil and gas sector

The Deepwater Horizon oil spill in the Gulf of Mexico has highlighted once more the magnitude of the risks assumed by those engaged in oil and gas development. Oil and gas companies face environmental, health and safety, liability, and ultimately reputational risks, the management of which is central to the company's long term success. As in the Deepwater Horizon example, the exploration and production of oil and gas is often technically challenging. Oil and gas producers tap into unseen, pressurised underground petroleum resources and try to extract those resources safely from the ground. Once extracted, the product is often transported long distances in pressurised pipelines or oceangoing tankers. It may be refined or transformed using any of a variety of complicated chemical processes at high temperatures and pressures. Each of these stages of the production process is managed by people and subject to human error. At the same time, despite these risks, oil and gas production can be an extremely lucrative business for those who are good at it.

However, the general public is very ambivalent towards the oil and gas sector. On the one hand, the availability of fossil fuels has driven economic growth for more than a century, enabling people to achieve higher standards of living, and feeding the public coffers of oil rich nations. On the other hand, oil and gas production imposes significant costs on society including air pollution, oil spills, injuries, and deaths. It is also sometimes associated with second order costs, including social dislocation and conflict. Indeed, these phenomena are sufficiently common that some scholars refer to 'the oil curse'.[10] This is the idea that the presence of oil wealth in a nation can do more harm than good.

This ambivalence means that governments, NGOs, and civil society will constantly seek means to control oil and gas development in order to minimise the risk of harm and provide redress in the event of harm being done. As we have seen in the OECD countries this is typically accomplished through laws and regulations. However, it is also accepted that in such a technically challenging industry accidents do happen. Therefore, societies look to the oil companies to self regulate, and do more to guard against risks to society than merely comply with the law. The outcome is that, perhaps more than in any other industrial sector, people demand CSR from oil and gas companies.

Modern CSR programmes reflect the recognition that business, including the energy sector, does not happen in a social vacuum. Today's oil and gas companies work within an ever broader and more complex set of social institutions with norms and expectations that coexist with market forces. As we have seen these can take different forms of regulation; however, some reflect ethical norms which are every bit as important to companies in respect of sustainability as laws and regulations. Many of these expectations come from society, governments, NGOs, and the community at large, whilst others may arise from business leaders themselves who wish to 'do the right thing'. In an age of instantaneous communication and lowered regulatory and trade barriers, more and more business is transparent, when customers, suppliers, investors, employees, neighbours, governments, and NGOs can see what is happening almost immediately. If an energy company employs child labour in Indonesia or dumps toxins into an African river, activists, investors, and customers in Europe and North America will learn about it not long afterwards. Transparency and globalisation have strengthened the ability of external stakeholders to detect and publicise wrongdoing, and to press their concerns on business people. When almost everyone has a smart telephone, there is an increasing probability that business wrongdoing will not only be reported by media outlets, but will be posted for all to see on YouTube or some other website.

Defining corporate social responsibility

There are many definitions of CSR but essentially it refers to the kind of things that companies do in their efforts to navigate the ever changing expectations of governments and civil society. It would be difficult to find a Fortune 500 company that does not publish some form of annual CSR or Sustainability Report outlining its investments in environmental sustainability, social progress etc.[11] Most of this is taking credit for the company's pursuit of its self interest which provides social benefits, so demonstrating Adam Smith's concept of the 'invisible hand'.[12] However, CSR implies more than the operation of the invisible hand and is linked to the idea that companies owe *duties* to their external stakeholders beyond those enshrined in law. The word 'responsibility' implies a duty to someone or something; whereas the word 'social' implies that companies owe duties to society at large.[13] Managers and employees are the people who give the company life and make the decisions that we attribute to the company. In fact, in practice, firms balance duties owed to a variety of stakeholders, including, but not limited to, their owners.[14]

CSR is not new. For decades companies have given money to charitable organisations. Heavily regulated companies have explored ways in which they could move beyond compliance, particularly with respect to the environmental impacts of their actions.[15] Much of the initial action was on environmental issues under the banner of 'sustainability'. This is a term which has taken on many meanings in the CSR discourse with the economist's idea of 'sustainable development', or 'sustainability', growing out of the tragedy of the commons[16] and focusing on long term production of a natural resource. Industry has faced myriad environmental concerns for decades. And different industries have responded in different ways. For example, in the 1980s the Chemical Manufacturers Association established their 'Responsible Care' programme, which is a system of voluntary rules and regulations for their members, governing the handling and disposal of chemicals and chemical wastes.[17] Companies who join the European Union's 'Eco-Management and Auditing Scheme' (EMAS) agree to continuously improve their environmental performance over time, beyond anything which is required of them by law.[18] These programmes achieved high levels of voluntary participation by member companies, and environmental management consulting is now a mature sector which goes far beyond helping companies comply with environmental rules. The rise in recent years of climate change as a major environmental issue has stimulated various efforts by companies to reduce their 'carbon footprint'.

CSR can be divided into three general categories.[19] The first and oldest is corporate philanthropy, that is, giving money to worthy causes. The second is the 'CSR as risk management' or investment in reducing legal and reputational risk,[20] which means that because stakeholders can help or hinder a company, their opinions and expectations matter. The third form of CSR includes the kinds of actions companies take that provide a social benefit and save money, such as being more energy efficient, reducing the use of toxic chemicals as manufacturing inputs etc. The *Economist* survey called these 'win-win' CSR and claimed that companies should have been doing these things anyway, irrespective of social concerns or outside pressures.[21]

However, as both a normative and a strategic question are these the sort of things that companies should be doing? Adam Smith's description of the 'invisible hand' includes the line 'I have never known much good can be done by those who affect to trade for the public good'.[22] Disagreement over whether CSR is the right thing to do can also be traced to different views of the relationship between business and society. In many of the continental European nations, the law requires that external stakeholders are represented on company boards of directors, reflecting an expectation that companies will play a role in addressing the needs of those external stakeholders. Sometimes this role is enshrined in law, sometimes not, but European companies are embracing environmental sustainability more widely and eagerly than their American counterparts.[23]

There is no doubt that many CSR activities are motivated by self interest with self regulation as practised by the Chemical Manufacturers Association being a strategically sound response to pressure for government regulation of the industry. By self regulation, it relieves the pressure, and industry can have more say in the design and implementation of the regulatory regime. Some CSR activities are designed to enhance the reputation of the company, which may then attract new and socially aware customers and investors. Customers will be willing to pay a premium for 'green' electricity or oil that comes from a relatively green oil company, and, similarly, employees like to work for a socially conscious company, which may lead to improvements in employee productivity and better retention of good employees. It is not difficult to see how the second and third CSR categories of risk management and 'win–win' situations may advance shareholder interests in the long run and the short run. They save money now while helping society; and investments which address broader stakeholder concerns can pay off in today's transparent, interconnected world.

However, for modern oil and gas companies, the task of behaving responsibly is complicated by the multiplicity of environments within which they operate. Much of their work takes place in places where laws can be few, governments are relatively corrupt or inefficient, and violent conflict is endemic.[24] In these difficult environments, the modern oil company which is concerned about protecting its reputation must find out just what governments, international NGOs, and local neighbours expect of the company, and just how many of those expectations it can fulfil.

CSR in the absence of law

In industrialised democracies, it is expected that law will structure the relationships between international oil companies and their external stakeholders, and that any conflict with stakeholders will be managed in part by governmental institutions. A good example is that the harm caused by the Deepwater Horizon disaster will be redressed by a well developed legal and governmental system. The USA has legal rules for apportioning liability for the environmental and other harm caused by the explosion and subsequent oil spill, in addition to a relatively efficient court system to see that the rules are applied. A contributing factor to the accident was the failure of the Minerals Management Service to be sufficiently vigilant in its application of the law and regulations which were designed to mitigate any environmental or safety risks.[25]

By contrast, in developing countries' environments, legal standards may be weak or non-existent, and governments may be corrupt, inefficient, or both. In fact, governments may lack legitimacy in the eyes of their people, and social conflict must be resolved not through politics but in other ways. This poses a dilemma for oil companies, which they have come to understand, sometimes through a painful learning process. To give an example: Royal Dutch Shell began exploring for oil in Nigeria in the 1950s, with its early production predating Nigerian independence, but coinciding with the first years of Nigeria as an independent country. Blessed with very large reserves of oil, particularly in the Niger Delta, those blessings never reached the people and Nigeria became known for the concept of 'the oil curse'.[26] Shell paid royalties to the Nigerian state, but much of that money found its way into the pockets of corrupt governmental officials.[27] Although the Nigerian government owned 51% of the shares in Shell Nigeria, environmental, health and safety regulations were weak or poorly enforced, and oil production in the Niger Delta became associated with extensive environmental contamination. Due to the fact that the Nigerian government owned 51% of all oil companies operating there many Nigerians associated large oil companies with the government, and with plunder and exploitation.[28] Shell eventually began to recognise and address its reputational problems by undertaking social investment and making concerted efforts to cultivate positive relationships with all of its important stakeholders in Nigeria. However, by that time most of the reputational damage had been done; and so, in spite of pouring resources into social projects and stakeholder relations in Nigeria in the late 1990s and 2000s, protest against Shell became stronger and more organised. The Movement for the Survival of the Ogoni People (MOSOP) challenged Shell's right to operate within Nigeria, sometimes in extralegal or violent ways.[29] Ken Saro-Wiwa, an author and journalist, was the founder of MOSOP, and in 1994 the Nigerian government arrested him and other Ogoni defendants on the charge of incitement to murder. The government convened a special tribunal, which convicted all the defendants, and sentenced them to death. This sentence was carried out in 1995. Both the trial and sentence were widely criticised by environmental and human rights organisations, some of which charged Shell with aiding and abetting the prosecution of the defendants. After Saro-Wiwa's execution a number of human rights organisations supported litigation by the families of the victims against Shell in American courts under the Alien Tort Claims Act (ATCA), seeking to hold the company liable for the persecution of Saro-Wiwa and others.[30] It was claimed that Shell supplied weapons to Nigerian security forces, and participated in security operations that included the shooting of Ogani people.[31] Shell denied these allegations. However, before the trial Shell settled with the families of the defendants for US $15.5 million, denying liability, but claiming that the settlement was 'a "humanitarian gesture" meant to compensate the plaintiffs, including Mr Saro-Wiwa's family, for their loss and to cover a portion of their legal fees and costs'.[32]

However, Shell was not the only international oil company caught up in host state affairs. ExxonMobil found itself in the middle of armed conflict in Indonesia. Mobil Oil began operating the Arun gas field in the Indonesian territory of Aceh, Sumatra, in the 1960s. Throughout the 1990s the region was subject to considerable unrest by, and violence associated with, separatist movements. In 2001, 11 villagers brought an action against ExxonMobil (the successor company) in an American court under the ATCA, claiming that the company had aided and abetted human rights abuses by hiring members of the Indonesian military as company security, who had subsequently committed human rights abuses. The NGO International Labour Rights Fund (ILRF) supported the action by providing legal representation.[33] After many hours of procedural disputes, the federal judge dismissed the action on grounds of lack of standing by the plaintiffs.[34] In each case the company found that its reputation had been damaged by its association with a repressive government.

Many other cases have been documented[35] all of which damaged the reputations of the international oil companies involved. Because the licence to operate comes from governments, and oil and gas are found where they are created by nature, they can be in places with unresolved social conflict. International oil companies can find themselves caught up in that conflict which illustrates the complexity of the stakeholder environment.[36] In each of the documented cases, the national government lacked the capacity to resolve contentious issues and enforce regulatory standards. The governments and the international oil companies were perceived by disaffected groups and NGOs as partners and therefore as opponents of local interests.[37]

CSR and reputational risk

NGOs consider that CSR within the oil and gas sector is merely window dressing.[38] They consider that international oil companies, as rational maximisers of shareholder returns, will take advantage of absent or inadequate laws and regulatory standards, and will pollute and exploit local populations as long as they can avoid liability. However, this is a very one-sided view and does not take account of the forces that have put CSR at the centre of business decision making over the last 20 years. International oil companies have been in the vanguard of embracing CSR because they believe that it is wrong to leave a legacy of toxic contamination, poverty and social dislocation.[39,40]

However, during interviews with oil company executives, it was the recognition that reputational harm can be equally as damaging to the bottom line as legal liability that supported the decision for investments in socially responsible behaviour and would earn positive returns for the sustainability of the company.[41]

All the oil companies, of course, must prioritise shareholder interests and basic management goals associated with profitability and market share. Despite the prominence of CSR discourse of 'win–win' scenarios and the business case for CSR, there are numerous tensions between these traditional objectives and CSR. Skilful company leadership is crucial for managing these tensions. Indeed, the McKinsey Global Survey of Business Executives believes overwhelmingly that the key responsibility for promoting CSR within corporate structures rests with Chief Executive Officers or Chairs.[42] However, even the most senior executives are highly constrained in what they can do, and their tenure can prove fragile if traditional shareholder interests are not protected.

The uneven trajectory of CSR, both within and between companies, is explained partly by its opportunistic and strategic value which varies by company. This is apparent not only in terms of its usefulness for risk and reputation management, but also in relation to competitive and political advantage.[43] The ongoing tightening and improvement of CSR policies and performance in proactive companies can be explained by the need for such companies to ensure that they gain an advantage by cultivating stronger relations with civil society organisations 'to distinguish themselves from other companies, turning their ethical advantage into competitive advantage', as well as greater political influence.[44]

Variations also arise from differences in the way that CSR is internalised within corporate structures. It may be championed by specific individuals or public or corporate affairs departments, but in the case of CEOs or chairpersons, such individuals may carry considerable weight. However, the company may be located in remote locations where the institutional environment and corporate culture is hostile to CSR.

Varieties of capitalism contrast the legalistic tradition and culture of the USA, and the political strategising of UK companies not simply to resist regulation, but also to gain legitimacy and appease government and society.[45] This is contrasted with the Nordic model characterised by consensus building and a relatively strong corporatist pact between state, capital and labour,[46] and helps to explain why Statoil was in the vanguard of implementing CSR.

The case of France is unique inasmuch as it could have been expected that French companies take a lead role given their association with the stakeholder model of capitalism; however, the CSR of French oil companies in Africa and Burma has been extremely negative. This is partly due to the fact that transnational activists tend to target 'Anglophone' companies and have largely ignored French companies.[47] However, it is also explained by the history of the French oil industry and its close relations with the state, which had a fundamental policy priority of securing independent energy sources and so turned a 'blind eye' to malpractice of French oil companies in developing countries.[48]

Variations in the institutional contexts and policy regimes of host countries also need to be taken into account, notably those related to regulatory frameworks and capacities, and in particular, government structures.[49]

Oil companies and corporate social responsibility in Nigeria

The Nigerian economy is heavily reliant on the oil sector. The International Monetary Fund (IMF) estimates that the oil and gas sector in Nigeria accounts for over 95 per cent of the foreign export earnings and about 65 per cent of the Nigerian government revenue.[50] The *Oil and Gas Journal* posits that Nigeria had an estimated 37.2 billion barrels of proven oil reserves in January 2011.

The Niger Delta is where international oil companies maintain a significant presence but it has become a theatre of violent conflict. The Federal Government has joint venture agreements with the oil companies operating in the sector and owns and controls the land including its natural resources in the subsoil. Under the Land Use Act 1978 the government can acquire any land for 'over-riding public purposes'.

The negative impacts of the activities of the oil companies in Nigeria include gas flaring, oil spills, environmental pollution, negative social impacts, conflict and violence amongst others. However, under CSR many international companies are seen as sources of solutions to some of the pressing problems facing the peoples in developing countries.

International oil companies are involved in many CSR activities in the Niger Delta which include *inter alia* the building of hospitals, schools, markets and provision of pipe borne water. In fact it is becoming increasingly apparent to oil companies that pollution prevention pays while pollution does not; therefore, under pressure from stakeholder groups, oil companies now routinely incorporate environmental impact assessments into their corporate strategy. CSR in Nigeria is culture specific and is the product of historical and cultural influences, and as such philanthropy in the guise of CSR is seen to be a way of addressing the economic and development issues in Nigeria.

Nigeria is a signatory to some international agreements, including the Extractive Industries Transparency Initiative (EITI), which carries out regular audits of the extractive sector in Nigeria. This is in order to reconcile the amounts the companies pay to the federal government and the amount the government states it gets from the companies. It could be argued that publication of the reports of these audits promotes accountability and fairness; however, this is not the case. Corruption in the oil and gas industry and lack of political will on the part of the government to implement the EITI, amongst other inherent difficulties, have accentuated the problem. Furthermore, the Nigerian government promotes CSR impliedly through the National Economic Empowerment and Development Strategy (NEEDS). The private sector is expected to play a major role in updating the strategy, in addition to providing jobs, enhancing productivity, quality of life and being more socially responsible with regards to the activities in Nigeria. Thus, international oil companies are expected to contribute their own quota to the corporate, economic and social development of Nigeria. Furthermore, Nigeria is part of the International Standards Organisation National Committee on Social Responsibility ISO 26000.

However, the Nigerian government has been blamed for a parlous regulatory framework in respect of international companies, with structural and systemic deficiencies inherent in CSR practices, which limits the effectiveness of CSR as a vehicle for conflict prevention and reduction in the Niger Delta.

Chinese oil multinationals' corporate social responsibility in Nigeria

Although Western international oil companies operate in Nigeria, a number of Chinese companies are also investing in the oil and gas sector in Nigeria.

China is now a major investor in the Nigerian economy; for example, in the area of international trade, from about US $2 billion in 2000, trade between China and Nigeria rose to about $18 billion in 2010, and between 2003 and 2009 Nigeria was the second largest recipient in Africa of foreign direct investment from China.[51] The CSR practices espoused by Chinese companies in Africa are, inevitably, accentuated by China's cultural and regulatory background, thus, Chinese companies promote CSR with Chinese characteristics[52] in Africa. For example, non-interference and philanthropy are the cornerstones of the Chinese foray into Africa, but human rights appear to be missing from their codes of practice.[53] One explanation is that the companies are following the values and culture of their home state where Chinese companies are not normally subject to the degree of criticism encountered in the West. Whereas the Western companies are constrained by a plethora of actions such as the activities of NGOs, judicial activism, public perception/consumer power and government regulation, this is not the case in China. It has been argued that many of the state owned or controlled multinational companies in China do not have a tradition of transparency in their business operations. Chinese multinationals owe their duty of transparency to their home government and not to the shareholders or other stakeholders of the company. Thus, it is contended that Chinese multinationals have triggered a race to the bottom by African states.[54]

Beyond corporate social responsibility

After brand threatening publicity in the 1980s and 1990s, the international oil companies needed to devise a new and higher standard, so with increasing challenges from Asian national companies for contracts, the international oil companies reached for CSR to deliver sustainability. The difficulty for these multinationals is that, having accepted more responsibility, they are expected to do even more, maybe even more than business priorities can justify. International oil companies have been required to take on increasing responsibilities in oil producing countries where the often dysfunctional local governments have been unable to fulfil them.[55]

Environmental CSR is the big success story, and although many problems remain, the major international oil companies have made great progress in reducing spills, cutting flaring, and reporting on impacts. The companies have been proactive both because environmental harm creates publicity and because the business case for cleaning up has added up. Environmental reforms have been win–win; selling gas instead of flaring it can be profitable; installing slower rusting pipelines can reduce costs. Moreover, environmental reforms are kinds of challenges which are embraced by the managers and engineers who dominate the industry: these are discrete, technical initiatives with clearly quantifiable outcomes.

The multinationals have not tried to address the more unwieldy social tasks, such as poverty reduction in oil producing countries. Poverty reduction, as development professionals know, is hard. Success usually requires dedicated staff with excellent local knowledge and human skills crafting long term projects that are 'owned' by the beneficiaries. The oil companies have instead tended towards short term spending heedless to the needs of the poorest. Even when a company builds a town hall or a hospital, closer inspection reveals a rather shallow business motive: funding high profile projects that keep local leaders, investors or employees happy. But real poverty reduction very rarely flows from such projects.[56]

Lessons learned: CSR and reputational risk

Some NGOs and other observers contend that the oil and gas industry merely uses CSR as window dressing or 'green wash'. This is consistent with the view that multinational oil companies, as rational maximisers of shareholder returns, will take advantage of absent or inadequate laws and regulatory standards, and will pollute and exploit local populations as long as they can avoid liability in the process. However, this view does not take account of the fact that CSR has been close to the centre of business decision making during the last two decades. Some international oil companies may be embracing CSR because they believe that it is wrong to leave a legacy of toxic contamination, poverty and social dislocation.[57] More likely, they may recognise that reputational harm can be just as damaging to the bottom line as legal liability, and that investments in socially responsible behaviour may earn positive returns.[58]

In order to protect the company's reputation effectively, international oil companies must understand the perceptions and forces that determine that reputation. Therefore, developing more productive working relationships with external stakeholders, including governments, is now the *sine qua non* of company CSR programmes.[59] All of the oil majors now devote significant time and energy to stakeholder engagement as a key component of risk management. All of the companies within the energy sector interviewed by the authors highlighted reputational risk management as a major influence on their sustainability strategy.

Extra-legal standards

In the absence of effective or sufficient governmental regulatory standards, international companies have turned to soft law guidelines and global minimum environmental standards, such as the ISO 14000 environmental management system, or to particular environmental goals, such as the maximisation or elimination of flaring of natural gas.

With respect to social issues such as safety and human rights within the workplace, most oil companies adhere to the International Labour Organization (ILO) standards. Although the ILO started as an NGO, it came under the auspices of the UN after the Second World War, and exists to promote the rights and interests of workers. In addition to the ILO standards, the UN provides guidance for companies on questions relating to human rights. The UN Special Representative, Professor John Ruggie, issues regular reports addressing the challenges businesses face in this field. Ruggie charges governments with the responsibility to protect human rights, and companies with the responsibility to respect those rights.[60]

However, sometimes governments fail to perform their duties to protect human rights, and may even violate those rights themselves, leaving the local population feeling powerless and exploited. Therefore, it becomes more important for the international oil company to develop good relations with stakeholders and make good any promises made to adhere to existing international standards, particularly in the absence of effective local government regulation.

Partnership agreements

A further approach to CSR and sustainability and managing reputational risks is for international oil companies to partner with their stakeholders, including governments, to develop new standards for addressing social and environmental issues in the absence of legal standards. In fact, large mining companies have participated in several collaborative attempts to address problems associated with governmental capacity, transparency and accountability. For example, the World Bank developed an initiative that involved money, which was devoted to social programmes and community investment, actually being spent on the intended recipients instead of into the pockets of corrupt officials. This initiative was then taken up by the Extractive Industries Transparency Initiative.[61]

Conclusion

In the oil and gas sector, CSR and sustainability activities represent an attempt to fill the legal regulatory void. It is no secret that many oil rich nations have been poorly governed, and that international oil companies have extracted valuable resources from such countries in the past, while paying inadequate attention to the attendant environmental and social costs. It is also true that these companies have paid reputational costs for that lack of attention. However, it appears that most investor owned oil and gas companies have reached the conclusion that their long term best interests will be served by paying greater attention to the needs and wants of external stakeholders, and to environmental and social legacy in those places they do business.[62]

Notes

1 http://blogs.wsj.com/marketbeat/2010/05/01/buffetts-1991-salomon-testimony/.
2 Millon, D. (2010) 'Enlightened Shareholder Value, Social Responsibility, and the Redefinition of Corporate Purpose without Law', Working Paper, Washington & Lee Public Legal Research Paper Series.
3 'Green Paper Promoting a European Framework for Corporate Social Responsibility'. COM(2001)366.
4 'Communication from the Commission to the European Parliament, the Council, the European Economic and Social Committee and the Committee of the Regions'. COM(2011) 681 final.
5 Ibid., para 3.2.
6 'Communication on EU Policies and Volunteering: Recognising and Promoting Crossborder Voluntary Activities in the EU'. COM(2011)568.
7 Namely transparency, exchange of information and fair tax competition.
8 www.ohchr.org/Documents/Publications/GuidingPrinciplesBusinessHR_EN.pdf.
9 EC Draft Guidelines, p. 12. http://ec.europa.eu/growth/industry/corporate-social-responsibility/.
10 Pipes, Daniel (1982) 'The Curse of Oil Wealth', *The Atlantic*, July, pp. 19–25.
11 See CSRwire, The Corporate Social Responsibility Newswire, 2010, http://www.csrwire.com.
12 Smith, Adam (1776) *The Wealth of Nations, Books I–III*, London: Penguin Classics, 1999, Book 2, ch. 2 p. 1. 'He intends his own gain, and he is in this, as in many other cases, led by an invisible hand to promote an end which was no part of his intention.'
13 Spence, David B. (2010) 'Corporate Social Responsibility in the Oil and Gas Industry: The Importance of Reputational Risk', 86 *Chicago-Kent Law Review* 59, 59–85, at 62.
14 Freeman, R. Edward (1984) *Strategic Management: A Stakeholder Approach*, Cambridge: Cambridge University Press.
15 Spence, David B. (2001) 'The Shadow of Rational Polluter: Rethinking the Role of Rational Actor Models in Environmental Law', 89 *California Law Review* 917, 951–965.
16 Hardin, Garrett (1968) 'The Tragedy of the Commons', *Science*, vol. 162, issue 3859, pp. 1243–1248.
17 http://www.icca.org/en/Home/Responsible-care/.
18 http://www.ec.europa/eu/environment/emas/index-en.htm.
19 *A Survey of Corporate Social Responsibility: Just Good Business, Economist*, 17 January 2008.
20 Ibid.
21 Ibid.
22 Smith (1776), supra note xxii at p. 181.
23 Spence (2010), p. 67.
24 Ibid., p. 70.

25 Ibid., p. 70. Spence states that the MMS was particularly lax in its implementation of the National Environmental Policy Act (NEPA), where the statute requires preparation of an environmental impact statement before approving any project that may significantly affect the quality of the human environment. NEPA 1969 §4332 (2006). NEPA 1969§4332 http://www.fws.gov/r9esnepa/RelatedLegislativeAu thorities/nepa1969.PDF.
26 Usoroh, Ini (2011) PhD thesis. 'Corporate Social Responsibility in Nigeria: A Study of the Energy Sector', Southampton Solent University, validated by Nottingham Trent University.
27 Ibid.
28 Ibid.
29 Eaton, Joshua P. (1997) 'The Nigerian Tragedy, Environmental Regulation of Transnational Corporations, and the Human Right to a Healthy Environment', 15 *Boston University International Law Journal* 261, 270.
30 *Wiwa v Royal Dutch Petroleum Co.*, 626 F. Supp.2d 377 (S.D.N.Y. 1996).
31 Greenpeace Press release (1995) 'Ken Saro-Wiwa and Eight Ogani People Executed: Blood on Shell's Hands', 10 November.
32 Mouawad, Jad (2009) 'Shell to Pay $15.5 Million to Settle Nigerian Case', *New York Times*, 8 June, p. B1.
33 *John Doe v ExxonMobil Corp.*, 2006 U.S. Dist. LEXIS25860 (D.C. Cir.2006). John Baxter of the ILRF listed as counsel for the Aceh plaintiffs.
34 Kendall, 30 September 2009. *Update: Judge Dismisses Indonesian Suit against Exxon,*http://www.nasdaq.com/aspx/stock-market-news-story.aspx?storyid=20090930 1400dowjonesdjonline00633&title=update-judge-dismisses-indonesians-lawsuit-aga inst-exxon.
35 Spence (2010), pp. 73–75.
36 Frynas, Jedrzej George (2009) *Beyond Corporate Social Responsibility: Oil Multinationals and Social Change*, Cambridge: Cambridge University Press, pp. 49–63.
37 Spence (2010), p. 75.
38 Karliner, Joshua (1997) *The Corporate Planet: Ecology and Politics in the Age of Globalization*, Berkeley: University of California Press, pp. 170–175.
39 Spence (2010), p. 62, n.6.
40 Watts, Michael J. (2005) 'Righteous Oil? Human Rights, the Oil Complex, and Corporate Social Responsibility', 30 *Annual Review Environmental Resources* 373, 393–398.
41 Interviews carried out by the authors during 2014/15 with high level decision makers in a number of major oil companies.
42 McKinsey & Co. (2006) 'The McKinsey Global Survey of Business Executives: Business and Society', *McKinsey Quarterly*, January.
43 Utting, Peter and Kate Ives (2006) 'The Politics of Corporate Social Responsibility and the Oil Industry', 2 *STAIR* 1, 11–34.
44 Ibid., p. 25.
45 Van de Hove, Sybille, Marc le Menestrel and Henri-Claude de Bettignies (2002) 'The Oil Industry and Climate Change: Strategies and Ethical Dilemmas', 2 *Climate Policy* 1, 4–5.
46 See Chapter 8.
47 Utting and Ives (2006), p. 26.
48 Assemblée Nationale de France (1998) *Rapport d'information no 1859 sur le rôle des compagnies pétrolières dans la politique internationale et son impact social et environnemental* : http://www.assemblee-nationale.fr/rap-info/i1859-02.asp.
49 *UN Special Representative of the Secretary-General for Business and Government, Interim Report on the Issues of Human Rights and Transnational Corporations and other Business Enterprises.* https://www1.umn.edu/humanrts/business/RuggieRep ort2006.html.

50 IMF (2013) *Nigeria: 2012 Article IV Consultation.* IMF Country Report No. 13/
116. Available at http://www.imf.org/external/pubs/ft/scr/2013/cr13116.pdf.
51 Egbula, Margaret and Qi Zheng (2011) 'China and Nigeria: A Powerful South-South
Alliance', *West African Challenges*, 5. http://www.oecd.org/china/49814032.pdf.
52 See Chapter 8.
53 Ekhator, Eghosa (2014) 'Corporate Social Responsibility and Chinese Multinationals in the Oil and Gas Industry of Nigeria: An Appraisal', 28 *Cadernos de
Estudos Africanos*, 119–140; Tallio, Virginie (2014) 'Multinational Enterprises in
Africa: Corporate Governance, Social Responsibility and Risk Management', 28
Cadernos de Estudos Africanos, 133.
54 Bosshard, Peter (2007) 'China's Role in Financing African Infrastructure', *International Rivers Network*. Available at: http://www.iese.ac.mz/lib/saber/fd_384.pdf.
55 Frynas (2009), p. 36.
56 Ibid.
57 Spence (2001), pp. 951–965.
58 Watts (2005), pp. 393–398.
59 Laplante, Lisa J. and Suzanne A. Spears (2005) 'Out of the Conflict Zone: The
Case for Community Consent Processes in the Extractive Sector', 11 *Yale Human
Rights and Development Law Journal* 69, 71, 116.
60 Ruggie, John. UN Special Representative of the Secretary-General (2007) 'Business
and Human Rights: Mapping International Standards of Responsibility and
Accountability for Corporate Acts', ¶ 6, UN DOC. A/HRC/4/035.
61 Duruigbo, Emeka (2005) 'The World Bank, Multinational Oil Corporations, and the
Resource Curse in Africa', 26 *University of Pennsylvania Journal of International
Economic Law*, 40–46.
62 Spence (2001), p. 84.

8   Law as a communal resource

Introduction

This chapter builds an analytical framework for investigating the role of legal systems in foreign investor/government/civil society relations. In Chapter 6 we considered how investors, and in particular institutional investors, could influence management through investor control and in Chapter 7 we considered the principle of corporate social responsibility and sustainability. Here we will build on these issues by considering the societal interaction between global business and local law.

Foreign direct investments create and alter relations between many types of human actors; buyers and sellers, employers and employees, suppliers and retailers, consumers and producers, shareholders and company officials, regulators and the regulated. These may be located in the home states from which investments originate, the host states in which investments are made and beyond. Here we will consider the triumvirate of the foreign investor, host state legal system and civil stakeholders.

Social action

Roger Cotterrell suggests that 'the sense of community is not limited to or "imprisoned within" distinct social groups'; instead he 'refers to the degree of development of certain aspects of social relationship',[1] that is, stable interactions and a sense of belonging. He suggests that the full range of stable and sustained interactions can be captured in four ideal types, based on Max Weber's types of social action.[2]

Weber identified four forms of social action.

1   Rational action: individuals have expectations about the behaviour of others and act to take account of these expectations in order to attain their own rationally chosen outcomes.
2   Evaluative action: individuals take account of absolute values (beliefs, ethics, aesthetic or other form of behaviour) entirely for their own sake and independently of any prospects of external benefit or success.

3   Emotional actions: action based on feelings and emotions of the individual
    and other actors.
4   Traditional actions: actions that are based on long established and habitually
    practised traditional expectations.

Cotterrell suggests that those who have a convergence of interest, such as
business associations, are linked in 'instrumental' relations which may cross
into several of Weber's ideal types.[3] For example, civil society actors may be
engaged in primarily instrumental relations with each other, with foreign
investors and with government actors; but they often seek to represent the
interests of those who are engaged in relations of other kinds, such as those
based in tradition or belief.

Cotterrell proposes that what allows relations of community to exist and
flourish is mutual interpersonal trust, which with the relations of community,
form a virtuous circle. He claims that trust is the cause and the effect of the
interactions and sense of belonging that characterise relations of community.
Conversely where trust does not exist, there will be none of the stable, sustained,
productive social interactions that characterise community.

Indeed, Tapscott and Ticoll argue in *The Naked Corporation* that businesses
depend on 'sustained, trusting relationships' with five categories of stakeholder:
employees, partners, customers, shareholders and communities.[4] They propose
that in the context of these relationships trust is the expectation that others
will be honest, accountable, considerate and open. They present a detailed model
of the relationship between 'values' and 'value', and suggest that when businesses
have integrity, then their stakeholders will trust them, which in turn strengthens
relationships between business and stakeholders, which will then produce value.

Francis Fukuyama[5] takes a broader view noting that social capital, the habits
of reciprocity, moral obligation, duty towards community, and trust, are inherent
in all societies, to a greater or lesser degree. He claims that in successful
economies, such social capital 'leavens' the economic building blocks of law,
contracts and rationality.[6]

International organisations have been influenced by this literature, with the
Seventh Global Forum on Reinventing Government focusing on the topic of
'Building Trust in Government', and arguing that when trust in government is
compromised, then the general public interest is undermined.[7] The World
Bank's World Development Report in 2005 notes that high levels of 'trust
between market participants' help to keep transaction costs low; and the level
of trust that citizens have in firms and markets determines the extent to which
a liberal market economy will prove successful. 'Governments influence, and
are influenced by, both forms of trust.'[8]

Colin Mayer continues this theme of trust[9] when he discusses the potential
for directors to abuse their fiduciary responsibilities with directors' and
shareholders' interests increasingly being viewed as being 'at odds'. This
damaging cycle of shareholder mistrust prompts greater shareholder activism,
which in turn prompts a more self-interested response on the part of directors.

Mayer considers that there needs to be found a resolution to both the excessive mistrust and interference by investors, with directors needing to be able to balance the interests of owners and other parties.

Cotterrell's work on trust is influential inasmuch as it firstly draws attention to the fundamentally interpersonal, social nature of trusting relationships. For example, he observes that interpersonal systems of confidence, including systems of governance, are often indirectly underpinned by an idealised relation of mutual interpersonal trust.[10] Secondly, he emphasises that trust is vital to all types of stable, productive social interactions. In other words trust can serve as a reference point for a systematic and integrated analysis of relations within and between multiple networks of community; for example, those between foreign investors, civil society and government. Thirdly, Cotterrell identifies and elaborates on the role of law in nurturing trust and, thereby, relations of community.

Legal mechanisms

Econocentric approaches to law such as investment climate discourse tend to treat law as a resource for facilitating private transactions between individuals. Although these are real and legitimate roles for law, Cotterrell argues that the function of law cannot be limited to the 'facilitation and regulation' of interactions between individual citizens. Its 'aspiration is towards...something more than the society of morally unconnected, rights possessing individuals'.[11] Later he urges us to 'keep a firm attachment to the idea of law as a communal resource'.[12]

According to Cotterrell, law functions as a communal resource by approving and protecting the empirical conditions that facilitate mutual interpersonal trust. He identifies three specific mechanisms through which a legal system can and should function as a communal resource.[13] Firstly that legal systems *express* what already holds the participants together; secondly that legal systems draw those participants in further by ensuring their actual *participation* in social life; thirdly that legal systems *coordinate* the differences that hold the participants apart.

Expression

The first communal function of state law is to express the trusting relations which characterise the various networks of community. These networks are founded in traditional relations which, in the economic field, will require that individuals have interpersonal trust in each other's 'honesty, fair dealing and good faith'.[14] Law supports the existence of such trust by stabilising the basic components of commercial interaction, such as organisations and their transactions. This idea was first put forward by Macneil who has observed that contracts are instruments of social cooperation. The role of the state is to provide legislation to offer general stability as a background to such social relations and to facilitate them by supporting cooperation and the continuation of interdependence between the parties.[15]

Participation

The second communal role for the legal system is to ensure participation in social life. In other words, each individual must be given sufficient material and cultural resources as well as the opportunity and freedom to be involved fully and actively in determining the nature and projects of those networks of relations of community. Legal systems facilitate participation in two ways. First, they cultivate and protect the general security and autonomy of individual actors so that they may participate effectively in shaping the conditions of collective life.[16] Second, legal systems (in particular, bureaucracies and judiciaries) can facilitate specific instances of participation by creating and maintaining gateways through which it can occur.

The benefits of widespread participation in one aspect of social life, namely governance, are widely recognised. The active participation of the governed in their own government, even their resistance, is at the centre of liberal thought and political practice. The benefits of participation, and in particular of tripartite participation by civil society, private sector and state actors, have accordingly been noted at the international level with increasing frequency as we have seen in the environmental field; rights of public participation, access to information and access to justice were declared in Principle 10 of the 1992 Rio Declaration. That aspiration found concrete expression in the Aarhus Convention on Access to Information, Public Participation in Decision-making and Access to Justice in Environmental Matters, signed in 1998 under the auspices of the United Nations Economic Commission for Europe.[17]

The call for participation was widened in 1999 when Kofi Annan, the then Secretary-General of the United Nations, called upon business leaders to join UN agencies and civil society actors in a Global Compact to support progress in relation to social and environmental issues. By 2007, the Global Forum for Reinventing Government defined governance itself as 'the process of interaction between three sets of actors – the State, civil society, and the private sector – in making political, administrative, economic, and social decisions that affect citizens'. The Forum went on to observe that trust in government is enhanced by participation of the private sector in the form of public–private partnerships, and civil society through 'effective society engagement'.[18]

The Fourth Global Forum on Reinventing Government, organised by the UN in Marrakech in 2002, had the theme of 'Citizens, Businesses, and Governments: Partnerships for Development and Democracy'. The tripartite theme was also emphasised in the Sixth Global Forum on Reinventing Government, when addressing the title 'Towards Participatory and Transparent Governance'. The outcome of this Forum was the Seoul Declaration which stated that 'by encouraging networking to create mutually reinforcing relationships and broad based collaboration among all actors in society' governments can improve governance.[19]

Indeed, the importance of tripartite participation is now widely accepted by each category of actor. In the joint statement responding to the UN

Millennium Development Goals, the International Chamber of Commerce (ICC) and the International Organisation of Employers (IOE) have suggested that although governments hold the main responsibility for poverty eradication 'addressing these challenges will require concerted effort and partnership by all actors...at the local and international levels',[20] which emphasises the need for corporate social responsibility. Even those civil society actors who are expressly anti-globalisation often accept that they must work with the private sector and governments to make the system of globalisation more equitable.

Coordination

A state legal system must be able to coordinate, integrate, and respect the experiences of social existence characteristics of different relations of community.[21] Coordination is the most sophisticated of the three communal legal mechanisms as it marks and consolidates multiple existing networks of community by balancing their values and interests.

In a community approach to law, the individual's responsibility is to maintain mutual interpersonal trust in the form necessary to the form of communal relations in which they are involved, and when there is a betrayal of trust this gives rise to liability. However, because individuals may be members of several communities, and because communities and their needs may be barbarous as judged by the standards of other networks, individuals may find that they simultaneously breach and fulfil obligations across networks of community.[22] Cotterrell states that in cases of inter-network conflict 'where no other means of reconciliation are possible, the most powerful regulation...puts an end to disagreement about where responsibility lies and what it entails'.[23] In other words, the law adjudicates between the claims of different communities, and purports to rule conclusively about liability.

Influence of third parties

Influence of the World Bank

The World Bank has argued that host state legal systems must be efficient and predictable, and that these qualities are best achieved in the context of stable, accessible and clear legislation; limited bureaucratic discretion; low corruption; and the separation of executive, judicial and legislative powers.

Although the World Bank, historically, has tended to take a fundamentally economic approach to the matter of poverty reduction, and to the role of law in poverty reduction, the organisation's large number of staff come from 160 different countries and represent a diverse range of ages, functions and perspectives. It employs specialists in a wide variety of disciplines, including political scientists, lawyers, sociologists, anthropologists, environmentalists, financial analysts, and engineers. Within this diverse range of disciplines the most influential is that of the economists. For example, while World Bank lawyers would regard the honouring of human rights as an independently legitimate normative goal, World Bank economists tend to require that the 'value added' by human rights to a project be demonstrated in economic terms.[24]

However, recently non-economic values and interests such as equity have gradually found their way into World Bank policies and projects. Although during the 1970s the then President of the Bank, Robert McNamara, was generally regarded as having introduced a heightened sense of moral urgency by insisting that more attention should be paid to understanding the causes and effects of unequal income distribution, and the responsibility of governments to meet the 'basic needs' of their populations, it was not until 1984 that a more social component was introduced into the project appraisal process. It was not until the 1990s that a proactive commitment to enhance the social impact of its projects was made.[25]

Responding to criticisms that the neo-liberal emphasis of the preceding years had been remarkably narrow, the then President of the World Bank, James D. Wolfensohn, drafted a Comprehensive Development Framework presenting freedom from poverty as the new target, and economic and social development as part of an 'interdependent whole'.[26] This Framework was largely based on the work of Amartya Sen.[27] Development was now understood to encompass more than economic growth, but something more equitable and sustainable. Law was no longer restricted to facilitating and encouraging economic growth, but also directly charged with promoting social development. This theme was elaborated at length in the 2006 World Development Report *Equity and Development*, which emphasises repeatedly that equity and efficiency are often mutually reinforcing objectives.[28]

The World Bank's environmental strategy refers to its objectives of promoting participatory and community driven development approaches, and private sector participation to improve the design of laws and institutions, securing certainty and saving costs in the long term. However, the central question for those in the World Bank who are concerned with participation and civil engagement is whether public institutions can simultaneously improve their accountability, by increasing civil participation, and their decisiveness, thereby meeting public expectations for improvements in operational efficiency, whilst simultaneously increasing civic participation.[29]

Influence of foreign investors

Investment climate discourse pays special attention to participation by foreign investors in the creation and implementation of law, which encourages the sense that businesses are the 'partners', rather than the 'victims' or 'adversaries', of government.[30] In fact, since their first appearance in the mid 1990s, World Bank surveys of investors, such as the Enterprise Surveys produced by the Rapid Response Unit, have benchmarked the extent to which investors are notified and consulted when their host states undertake legal reform. Such opportunities were welcomed as a way of ensuring the 'credibility' of the investment climate.[31]

Research has shown that uneven access to participation among investors leads to 'state capture', in which 'firms that are part of the favoured circle tend to face a more attractive policy environment than other firms'.[32] This is anti-competitive, therefore inefficient and undesirable. Left unchecked it can lead to cronyism, corruption and inter-ethnic strife.[33] However, the legal system can mitigate the negative effects of such bonding capital, and maximise the benefits of relatively inclusive bridging capital, by ensuring that participation by foreign investors is broad.

As we have seen, in recent years the World Bank has begun to emphasise the importance of participation by civil society actors in governance. The World Development Report 2005 notes that the 'broad public trust' plays a part in nurturing the investment climate and that 'open and participatory policymaking and efforts to ensure that the benefits of a better investment climate extend widely in society can help to build that support'.[34]

The 2005 Report showcases the investment climate approach, indicating a growing acceptance that it is reasonable to expect variation in legal perceptions and expectations at least amongst foreign investors. However, the Report emphasises that 'there is no single vision of an ideal investment climate', with references to empirical proof and Geert Hofstede's work on variations in attitudes across cultures, of which more later.

Nevertheless, the Report also adopts a very narrow interpretation of what perceptions and expectations such varied actors might have of the legal system, because investment research mainly considers what it sees as the perennial inefficiency of the public sector, and so recommends regulatory formalism and limited bureaucratic discretion in the hope that this will improve efficiency. This emphasis on formalism can be problematic, inasmuch as such a rigid style of regulation can lead to creative compliance.[35] Not only that, but bureaucrats in different jurisdictions have different interpretations of their role. For example, in the USA bureaucrats are relatively formalistic and rule bound in their approach, whereas their counterparts in Japan and East Asia prefer an emphasis on cooperation and flexibility.[36] This is understandable when considering that law is an aspect of the social culture, and that the daily tasks of the administrators are guided by a combination of formal rules and social norms.[37] Most importantly, from a law and community perspective, bureaucratic discretion offers potential spaces for coordination and thus the ability of the legal system to act as a communal resource.[38]

Just as social life takes diverse forms, so does law. It reminds us that all actors, investors, government and civil society, share the need for trust. This may be fulfilled in different ways with the community approach striking a delicate but essential balance between 'seeking similarity' and 'appreciating difference'.[39]

Cultural differences to regulation

When multinationals consider investing in a host country with which they are unfamiliar they will assess any risks including uncertain responses from consumers and competitors which remain a commercial consideration. However, host governments have an important role in helping companies cope with risks associated with the security of their property rights. The 2005 World Development Report identifies 'policy uncertainty...and unpredictability in the interpretation of regulations' as major concerns of multinationals considering investing. 'Almost 95 percent of firms report a gap between formal policies and their implementation.'[40] The evidence produced by the Report shows that there are large variations in investment climate conditions not only between countries, but also within them. For example, in China there are major differences between the cities of Beijing, Chengdu, Guangzhou, Shanghai, and Tianjin in respect of the numbers of days it takes to obtain a mainline telephone connection, to clear customs for imports, and the number of production days lost because of power outages.[41]

Cultural norms play a large part in the mechanics and interpersonal relationships of multinational corporations from one 'home' state operating in another 'host' state. When individuals as well as companies 'grow up' in a particular culture, the cultural norms of behaviour are taken for granted. Little thought has to be given to reactions to a particular issue, preferences, and feelings. However, when transferring to another country with a foreign culture, situations can be confusing. Not only dealing with the regulatory culture but with customers, employees and civic society.

Even the work of senior managers is constrained by its cultural context. Peter Drucker once stated that what mangers do is the same the world over, how they do it is determined by culture and tradition.[42] It is, therefore, impossible to understand the actions of people without an understanding of their values, beliefs and expressions. Different cultures define desirable expertise and competences differently. For example, a desirable trait in a senior manager working for an American company, such as straight talking, would not work in their Japanese subsidiary where the preference for indirect communication is preferred.

Some consequences of culture

When considering the influences of cultural differences, one of the most fundamental elements to take into account is the difference in thinking patterns and reasoning between cultures that score either high or low on the Uncertainty Avoidance dimension. Most Anglo-Saxon countries have a low Uncertainty Avoidance score as their approach to thinking is pragmatic. The American philosopher John Dewey defined truth in the following way: 'truth is truth when it works'. Some of the main attributes of this way of thinking include; a greater focus on practice as opposed to theories or philosophies and high esteem for practitioners rather than experts. There is a focus on empiricism and a preference for action rather than reflection, and a tendency to value being 'persuasive' in communication.[43]

On the other hand people in countries that have a low score on Uncertainty Avoidance, like France, consider Dewey's definition of truth as superficial and prefer a deductive way of thinking after the French philosopher Descartes who wrote 'I think therefore I am'. This way of thinking emphasises defining principles for behaviour or developing a philosophy before action. Experts are given the highest esteem as they create the framework for understanding, and the focus in communication is on challenging and/or validating expertise.

As identified by the 2005 World Development Report, no society is homogenous and there are deviations from the norms found. Happily, extensive research has been carried out by Geert Hofstede[44] and others comparing cultures. In his research he found five fundamental value dimensions that are used in order to explain the cultural diversity in the world. This model is the most validated by research and perhaps the only model based on rigorous culture research. A sixth dimension was added later.

Hofstede's cultural dimensions[45]

Based on cultural statistics of many countries, Hofstede analysed the results and found clear patterns of similarity and difference which were stratified into five dimensions. In order to eliminate any differences in company culture the research was carried out amongst IBM employees only. The sixth dimension was added later. The six dimensions are identified as:

1 Power/Distance (PD)
This refers to the degree to which people accept and expect that power is distributed unevenly within a group or society.

2 Individualism (IDV)
This refers to the degree to which taking responsibility for yourself is more valued than belonging to a group, who will look after their people in exchange for loyalty.

3 Masculinity (MAS)
This refers to the degree to which people value performance and status deriving from it, rather than quality of life and caring for others.

4 Uncertainty/Avoidance Index (UAI)
This refers to the degree to which people develop mechanisms to avoid uncertainty.

5 Long Term Orientation (LTO)
This refers to the degree to which people value long term goals and have a pragmatic approach, rather than being normative and short term orientated.

Added later

6 Indulgence (I)
This refers to the extent to which people try to control their desires and impulses. A relatively weak control is called indulgence and strong control

is called restraint. Cultures are, therefore, described as indulgent or restrained.

Cultural implications in ten major energy producing countries

These will be: Argentina, China, Nigeria, Norway, Russia, Saudi Arabia, United Kingdom, United Arab Emirates, USA, Venezuela.

Here we will analyse the impact of cultural differences in the way people think in these energy producing countries through the prism of six competences which senior managers/CEOs should possess.

- Sound judgement implies that the CEO analyses issues and problems thoroughly, systematically, and from multiple perspectives; makes timely, well-reasoned decisions; makes effective decisions in face of uncertainty.

None of the key words above relating to sound judgement are culturally neutral, but the underlying dimension creating most of the bias is Uncertainty/Avoidance. In those countries with a weak UAI such as the USA, UK, and China, a thorough and systematical analysis should always be done with effectiveness and time constraints in mind. This means that in comparison to cultures with a strong UAI attitude thorough analysis takes more time. For weak UAI countries the thinking process goes from the specifics or practice to a conclusion or to a general theory which is inductive.

In countries with a high UAI score such as Argentina, the UAE, Russia, Saudi Arabia, and Venezuela, a thorough and systematical analysis means a deductive approach. There is a need to first understand the principles, philosophy or context of a certain proposal, then develop a theory, and as a last step take meaningful actions.

Also the Long Term Orientation affects sound judgement as a competence. The majority of our countries had a low LTO including Nigeria, Norway, Argentina, Saudi Arabia, Venezuela, UK, and the USA; with only China and Russia having a high LTO. These countries with a low score are characterised by the assumption that there is one, undividable truth. However, in the long term orientated countries such as China and Russia multiple truths may coexist. This means that the thorough and systematic analysis sought in the Western world will take the shape of synthetic abilities in China and Russia. What is true or who is right is less important than what works. How the efforts of individuals with different thinking patterns can be coordinated towards a common goal is a part of sound judgement in cultures with Long Term Orientation focus.

- Strategic vision is used to initiate programmes of research and work that are consistent with the company mission and broader departmental strategies; ensures that work in the short term is aligned with the longer term objectives of the organisation.

In long term oriented cultures (China and Russia), long term thinking takes the shape of the next 10 or 20 years. In short term orientated countries (Argentina, UK, USA, Nigeria, Norway, Saudi Arabia, Venezuela), long term thinking is confined to the next six months or year. How will the CEO/senior manager decide on what behaviour is needed to align with the longer term objectives of the organisation? Should the focus lie on cost cutting, or investing in the future to make all stakeholders feel secure in return for loyalty in difficult times?

In strong UAI cultures, consistency over time is appreciated in addition to very detailed planning procedures and systems. When a strategic vision is introduced, it is presented in detail. In weak UAI cultures, the tendency is to be flexible. Pinpointing desired results is good, but descriptions on how to get there will not be too rigid.

• Planning and organising skills include prioritising, and effective management.

Planning is different in its emphasis across cultures. In strong UAI cultures it takes the most dominant form with agreed planning systems being sacred. In weak UAI cultures planning takes the form of a broad framework of negotiated objectives. How to achieve those objectives is not sacrosanct. The higher the score for UAI the higher the tendency to avoid risks, and the more there is a tendency to prepare contingency plans; the lower the score for UAI, the more the tendency to cope with problems as they arise. However, what is considered effective planning in one culture may be perceived as time consuming, too detailed and unfocused in another.

• Drive for closure and results; persists when faced with challenges.

In cultures with a high score on Masculinity (UK, China, USA, Nigeria, Saudi Arabia, Venezuela) is found a strong appreciation for words like challenges, success and persistence. In Feminine cultures (Norway, Russia) the emphasis is on cooperation and relationships. In these cultures, results are not necessarily considered in terms of best, the highest or the most. Evaluation of results is also done in a different way. In a Masculine, low Power Distance country like the USA it is done through formalised assessment instruments, which check if fixed targets are met. In the Feminine Scandinavian countries there is a tendency for constant scans to see how actions are working out in practice, and the targets are renegotiable.

• Adaptability demonstrates openness and flexibility when faced with change; copes effectively with pressure and adversity.

The appreciation of openness and flexibility depends on a strong or weak UAI. Pragmatism is seen as sloppy, unpredictable behaviour in strong UAI cultures (Argentina, UAE, Saudi Arabia, Russia, Venezuela). In these countries the need for control is high and too many changes create demotivation. On the other hand, the weaker the UAI (USA, UK, China), the quicker people will be willing to react. The way people cope with pressure and adversity is also dependent on the scores on Masculinity and Individualism. For example, in Masculine countries (USA, UK, China, Argentina, Nigeria, Saudi Arabia, Venezuela,) the tendency is to think in terms of winning and losing. Admitting failure in practice is difficult. Whereas in collectivist cultures (UAE), losing face is the biggest punishment people can have.

• Delegating effectively matches people with tasks; adjusts directions.

The concept of delegation is different in different cultures. In low Power Distance countries (USA, UK, Norway) the subordinates are supposed to work in an autonomous way. They are expected to take responsibility for their content areas and need to react to a changing environment. On the other hand, in high Power Distance countries (China, Russia, UAE, Nigeria, Saudi Arabia, Venezuela), subordinates expect strict instructions about what to do and how to do it. If unforeseen things happen, the subordinate first needs to go back to their direct boss to ask for instructions before they can act.

Rewarding the CEO from a cultural perspective

By recognising how the different skills needed for a good CEO/senior manager, and how s/he may use them, can be influenced by the culture of a country, we turn to the cultural differences in respect of rewarding them for their performance.

Rewarding is about providing consequences, good or bad, to reinforce desired behaviour.[46] It can be done in financial terms such as bonuses, profit sharing, and incentive schemes; but it should also involve negative consequences to avoid repetition of undesired behaviour. The important thing, which is so often overlooked, is that people will do what they are rewarded for, and not necessarily what they are asked to do. It is interesting how often that CEOs/senior managers are asked to do one thing and yet are rewarded for something different. This can lead inexorably to the failure of the organisation.

Reward is the component that can often ruin everything else. The cash-oriented approach of individual performance related bonuses is considered in the USA and the UK to be the only way to incentivise people and is promoted globally by Masculine cultures. However, when it reaches countries with a more Feminine culture, in which greater responsibility, and a larger span of control are perceived to be more relevant, then cash rewards are considered to be 'petty', 'mercantilist', 'reductionist', and 'narrow minded'. If bonus plans are to work in other cultures, they need to be tied to other criteria. In some cultures, team incentives, or allegiance/reputation of the company will work much better than individual rewards.

Conclusion

A global solution?

Unfortunately, according to the research by Geert Hofstede there is no such thing as a global solution. However, there are many different solutions for different cultures. Huib Wursten describes a true success story.[47] Wursten's story describes a manager who took time to read about the different cultures in the various parts of the world where his company operated. This resulted in his knowledge influencing the decisions he made when he was sent to 'turn around' a failing company in Eastern Europe. He was then sent to Mexico to 'turn around' another failing company. In both companies, his predecessors had been good managers, but were applying their own cultural norms within a different cultural environment. Eventually the outcome for all stakeholders was a win–win situation.

Notes

1 Quoted in Perry-Kessaris, Amanda (2008) *Global Business, Local Law*, Aldershot, UK: Ashgate, p. 9.
2 Weber, M. (1922) *Economy and Society*, ed. Guenther Ross, vol. 1, Berkeley: University of California Press, 2013, p. 9: the 'acting individual attaches a subjective meaning to his behaviour – be it overt or covert, omission or acquiescence. Action is "social" insofar as its subjective meaning takes account of the behaviour of others and is thereby oriented in its course.'
3 Cotterrell, Roger (1997) 'A Legal Concept of Community', 12 *Canadian Journal of Law and Society* 2, 75–91, pp. 80–82.
4 Tapscott, Don and David Ticoll (2003) *The Naked Corporation*, Toronto, Canada: Penguin Group, p. 77.
5 Fukuyama, Francis (1996) *Trust: The Social Virtues and the Creation of Prosperity*, New York: Free Press Paperbacks.
6 Ibid., pp. 7 and 11.
7 Global Forum on Reinventing Government (2007) Preamble. Vienna Declaration on Building Trust in Government. Vienna, 26–29 June 2007.
8 World Bank (2005) *World Development Report*, pp. 50–51. http://web.worldbank.org/WBSITE/EXTERNAL/EXTDEC/EXTRESEARCH/EXTWDRS/0,,content MDK:23062314~pagePK:478093~piPK:477627~theSitePK:477624,00.html.
9 Mayer, Colin (2013) *Firm Commitment*, Oxford: Oxford University Press, pp. 200–201.
10 Cotterrell (1997), p. 87.
11 Cotterrell, Roger (1996) *Law's Community: Legal Theory in Sociological Perspective*, Oxford: Clarendon, pp. 18 and 334.
12 Cotterrell, Roger (2002) 'Subverting Orthodoxy, Making Law Central: A View of Socio-legal Studies', 29 *Journal of Law and Society* 4, 643.
13 Ibid.
14 Cotterrell, Roger (2006) *Law, Culture and Society: Legal Ideas in the Mirror of Social Theory*, Aldershot: Ashgate, p. 164.
15 Macneil, Ian R. (1980) *The New Social Contract*, New Haven, CT: Yale University Press.
16 Cotterrell (1996), pp. 299–301.
17 http://www.unece.org/fileadmin/DAM/env/pp/documents/cep43e.pdf.

18 Global Forum on Reinventing Government (2007) paras 5 and 8 and Aide Memoire. https://publicadministration.un.org/en/globalforum.

19 Global Forum on Reinventing Government (2006) para. 8. http://www.i-p-o.org/GF6-Seoul_Declaration-27May05.htm.

20 ICC/IOE (2005) 'Joint Views of ICC and IOE: The Millennium Development Process and Business', Paris and Geneva, p. 2

21 Cotterrell (1996), p. 334.

22 Perry-Kessaris (2008), p. 17.

23 Cotterrell (2006), pp. 163–165.

24 Sarfaty, Galit A. (2007) 'Doing Good Business or Just Doing Good: Competing Human Rights Frameworks at the World Bank', in B. Morgan (ed.), *The Intersection of Rights and Regulation: New Directions in Sociolegal Scholarship*, Aldershot: Ashgate.

25 World Bank, *Social Analysis Source Book: Incorporating Social Dimensions into Bank Supplied Projects*, social analysis policy team, Washington, DC: World Bank. http://go.worldbank.org/RVPWNZ7H80.

26 Wolfensohn, J.D. (1999) 'A Proposal for a Comprehensive Development Framework', made to the Board, Management, and staff of the World Bank Group, 21 January. http://go.worldbank.org/QMTT620DQ0.

27 Sen, A. (1999) *Development of Freedom*, New York: Knopf.

28 World Bank (2006) *Equity and Development*. http://www-wds.worldbank.org/servlet/WDSContentServer/WDSP/IB/2005/09/20/000112742_20050920110826/Rendered/PDF/322040World0Development0Report02006.pdf.

29 Reuben, W. (2003) 'The Role of Civil Engagement and Social Accountability in the Governance Equation', 75 *Social Development Notes*, Environmentally and Socially Sustainable Development Network, Washington, DC: World Bank, p. 3.

30 Bakan, Joel (2004) *The Corporation: The Pathological Pursuit of Profit and Power*, London: Constable, p. 107.

31 Perry-Kessaris (2008), p. 25.

32 Helman, J.S., G. Jones and D. Kaufmann (2000) 'Seize the State, Seize the Day: State Capture, Corruption and Influence in Transition', Working Paper No. 2444, Washington, DC: World Bank.

33 Chua, Amy (2002) *World on Fire: How Exporting Free Market Democracy Breeds Ethnic Hatred and Global Instability*, Toronto: Doubleday.

34 World Bank, http://siteresources.worldbank.org/INTWDR2005/Resources/FNL_WDR_SA_Overview6.pdf.

35 McBarnet, Doreen and Christopher Whelan (1991) 'The Elusive Spirit of Law: Formalism and the Struggle for Legal Control', 54 *Modern Law Review* 6, 848–850.

36 Kagan, Robert A. and Lee Axelrad (eds) (2000) *Regulatory Encounters: Multinational Corporations and American Adversarial Legalism*, London: University of California Press, chs 2 & 3.

37 Haines, Fiona (2005) *Globalisation and Regulatory Character: Regulatory Reform after the Kader Toy Factory Fire*, Aldershot: Ashgate.

38 Perry-Kessaris (2008), p. 28.

39 Ibid., p. 31.

40 World Development Report (2005) *A Better Investment Climate for Everyone*, p. 23. http://siteresources.worldbank.org/INTWDR2005/Resources/complete_report.pdf.

41 Ibid., p. 24.

42 Drucker, Peter F. (2003) *The Essential Drucker*, New York: Harper Business.

43 Wursten, Huib 'Intercultural Issues in Recruitment', *itim Intercultural Management*, p. 5. http://itim.org/en/consultants/huib-wurster (accessed January 2015).

44 Hofstede, Geert (2003) *Culture's Consequences: Comparing Values, Behaviors, Institutions and Organizations Across Cultures*, Thousand Oaks, CA: Sage.

45 Hofstede, Geert (1984) *Culture's Consequences: International Differences in Work-Related Values* (2nd ed), Beverly Hills, CA: Sage Publications.
46 Wursten, Huib, Fernando Lanzer and Tom Fadrhonc, *Improve Efficiency in your HR Capital: Managing People across Cultures is now more Urgent than ever*, p. 3. http://geert-hofstede.com/tl_files/managing%20people%20across%20cultures.pdf (accessed January 2015).
47 Wursten, p. 5.

9 Sustainable development and decision making in large multinational corporations

Introduction

The number of corporate scandals that have occurred over the past years have exposed flaws in the decision making process of large public companies. Many of these failures have caused constituencies outside the corporation to suffer the consequences of strategic choices that did not take into consideration the broad range of stakeholders, including employees, creditors, local communities and the environment.

The recent global financial crisis[1] has caused a depression that increased unemployment in most Western economies,[2] in addition to social unrest and suffering. The various bank bailouts that were funded with taxpayers' money have reduced the public resources available, *inter alia* for education and healthcare. Beyond the financial crisis, the BP oil spill in 2010 reawakened concerns about the environmental dimensions of corporate failures. In addition to the unquantifiable ecological damage, the oil spill has compromised the economic life of the local fishing and tourism industries along the coastal areas hit by the spill, leaving a legacy of social problems among the local communities.[3]

It is arguable that these financial and environmental disasters were characterised, *inter alia*, by the wrong decisions being made at the wrong time. One notable reason for this is that risk management and control functions were not properly factored in to the companies' strategies[4] as such activities are not conducive to profit making. Decisions were myopically geared towards the maximum of shareholders wealth, which entailed pursuing increases in the value of stock on the part of management, to the detriment of long term objectives.[5] This resulted in the failure to take account of different social interests.

The decision making process in multinational corporations needs re-calibrating to align it with more socially inclusive and sustainable goals.

Challenges

In recent decades, cognitive psychologists and behavioural economists have been incorporating empirical findings about human behaviour into economic models. Those findings have transformed understanding of regulation and its likely consequences. They are also providing instructive lessons about the appropriate design of 'nudges', that is, low cost, choice preserving, behaviourally informed approaches to regulatory problems, including disclosure requirements, default rules, and simplification.

The most general lesson is that choice architecture, understood as the background against which decisions are made, has major consequences for both decisions and outcomes. Small, inexpensive policy initiatives, making modest design changes, can have large and highly beneficial effects.

In the USA, regulatory efforts have been directly informed by behavioural findings, and behavioural economics has played an unmistakable role in numerous domains.[6] As a result, behavioural findings have become an important reference point for regulatory and other policy making in the USA. Also, in the UK, Prime Minister David Cameron has created a Behavioural Insights Team with the specific goal of incorporating an understanding of human behaviour into policy initiatives.

Behavioural economics has drawn attention in Europe more broadly. The Organisation for Economic Co-operation and Development (OECD) has published a *Consumer Policy Toolkit* that recommends a number of initiatives rooted in behavioural findings.[7] In the European Union, the Directorate General for Health and Consumers has also shown the influence of behavioural economics.[8] A report from the European Commission, called *Green Behaviour*,[9] enlists behavioural economics to outline policy initiatives to protect the environment. Private organisations are making creative use of behavioural insights to promote a variety of environmental, health related, and other goals.

It is clear, therefore, that behavioural findings are having a large impact on regulation, law, and public policy all over the world and with increasing global interest in low cost regulatory tools, that impact will inevitably grow over the next decades.[10] In these circumstances, it is particularly important to review what we know and what we do not know in order to consider the use of behavioural science nudge theory to encourage senior corporate decision makers to make the right decisions.

What do we know?[11]

1 Based on Sunstein's findings we know that both private and public institutions often establish 'default rules' that determine the result if people make no affirmative choice.
2 That 'procrastination can have significant adverse effects'. People will take account of uncertainties when considering the long term, i.e. the future may be unpredictable, and significant changes may occur over time. 'It may be better to have money now rather than a decade from now. In practice, however, some people procrastinate or neglect to take steps that impose small short term costs but would produce large long term gains.'

3 When people are informed of the benefits or risks of engaging in certain actions, they are far more likely to act in accordance with that information if they are simultaneously provided with clear, explicit information about how to do so.

4 'People are influenced by how information is presented or "framed".'[12] For example, if people are informed that they will *gain* a certain amount of money by using a certain product, 'they may be less likely to change their behaviour than if they were told they would *lose* the same amount of money by not using a particular product'.

5 'Information that is vivid and salient usually has a larger impact on behaviour than information that is statistical and abstract. ...Attention is a scarce resource, and vivid salient, and novel presentations may trigger attention in ways that abstract or familiar ones cannot.'

6 'People display loss aversion; they may well dislike losses more than they like corresponding gains.'

7 'In multiple domains, individual behaviour is greatly influenced by the perceived behaviour of other people.'[13]

8 'In many domains, people show unrealistic optimism and believe that they are less likely than others to suffer from various misfortunes.'[14]

9 People often use heuristics, or mental shortcuts, when assessing risks.[15]

10 People sometimes do not make judgements on the basis of expected value, and may neglect or disregard the issue of probability, especially when strong emotions are triggered.[16]

Incentives and choice architecture

The experiments described by Sunstein, and his conclusions, demonstrate that the strong effects of context go beyond what is reasonable, beneficial, or adaptive, and that individuals often have little awareness of these effects. Sunstein also suggests that policymakers should design policies that improve people's well-being through gentle nudges rather than through coercive measures. In other words, choices can be presented in a manner that will help individuals act in their own interest without restricting their choices. Indeed, in respect to the method of setting defaults, Thaler and Sunstein note that most people end up staying with the preset default option in situations such as savings decisions, organ donations, and privacy choices.[17] In many of these situations, law inevitably must provide a default. In fact one of the primary roles of the central planner is to supply defaults and as such policymakers should consider which default will be the most sensible.

Social norms and nudges

'Social scientists have emphasised the importance of social practices and norms, which have a significant influence on individual decisions. If people learn that they are using more energy than similarly situated others, their energy use may decline, thus saving money whilst also reducing pollution.'[18] It is the behaviour of others in a similar situation which can influence an individual into making decisions. In fact, research demonstrates that decision makers will look to either their predecessors or others in similar situations as informal guides to any particular course of action. In illustrating the possible methods of choice architecture, including smart defaults and feedback systems, the nudge theory develops a vision of how policymakers can steer people towards better decisions without imposing views from above. In other words, policymakers can serve as the architects of choices, supporting, but not mandating, those choices that are wealth-minimising.

Nudges in themselves cannot be expected to produce results, as a sole strategy of intervention, where the causes of the identified problem go beyond individual choice. When the problem relates to matters involving the economic and cultural environment a given nudge is liable to be affected by the particular conditions and modes of implementation. Even though neoclassical economists are generally averse to regulation, they do allow that under certain conditions of imperfect information, regulation may be an appropriate response to a problem.[19] Once that one accepts that many of our decisions are based on imperfect, and sometimes biased, and inaccurate calculations of expected benefits and costs, then it becomes clear that market failure is pervasive. The question is whether policy can and should strive to correct for imperfect decisions. Observing the many deviations from rational behaviour we argue that appropriate corrective measures must consider that the various biases have unique origins and must therefore be counteracted in different ways.

Behavioural research has shown that people are far more likely to respond when certain facts, risks, or possibilities are salient, and we use this to put forward some suggestions in the next chapter.

Nudge theory

'Nudge' theory was proposed originally in US 'behavioural economics', but it can be adopted and applied much more widely for enabling and encouraging change in people, and in particular high level decision makers in companies.

It can be used to explore, understand, and explain existing influences on how people behave, especially influences that are unhelpful, with a view to removing or altering them. There are lots of these unhelpful 'nudges' everywhere, for example in advertising and government; some are accidental, but many are very deliberate.

Nudge theory is credited mainly to American academics Richard H. Thaler and Cass R. Sunstein, who built much of their theory on the 'heuristics' work of psychologists Daniel Kahneman and Amos Tversky, which first emerged in the 1970s in psychological journals. The name and concept of 'nudge theory' was popularised in the book *Nudge: Improving Decisions about Health, Wealth, and Happiness* in 2008.[20] Kahneman's book *Thinking, Fast and Slow* from 2012[21] contains much of the theory which underpins the Thaler–Sunstein 'Nudge' concept.

Nudge theory, in essence, is mainly concerned with the design of choices, which influences the decision maker. It proposes that the designing of choices should be based on how people actually think and decide, which can be instinctively and rather irrationally, rather than how leaders and authorities traditionally, and typically incorrectly, believe people think and decide, that is logically and rationally.

In this respect, *inter alia,* nudge theory is a radically different and more sophisticated approach to achieving change in people than traditional methods of direct instruction, enforcement and punishment by law. This use of nudge theory is based on indirect encouragement and enablement. It avoids direct instruction or enforcement.

The theory accepts that people have certain attitudes, knowledge, capabilities, etc., as outlined above, and allows for these factors; whereas autocratic methods, such as 'command and control', ignore them. The theory is based on understanding and allowing for the reality of situations and human tendencies, unlike traditional forcible instruction, which often ignores or discounts the reality of both situations and people.

Fundamentally nudge theory operates by designing choices for people which encourage positive helpful decisions, for the people choosing, and ideally for the wider interests of society and the environment. It is very relevant to leadership, motivation and management and seeks to minimise resistance and confrontation, which commonly arise from more forceful 'directing' and autocratic methods of 'changing' behaviour.

For example, the command and control methods are confrontational and are liable not only to provoke resistance but also senior decision makers will either create a minimal compliance culture or find ways around the directive; whereas nudge methods are indirect, tactical, and less confrontational. Nudge methods aim to be cooperative and pleasurable; significantly, and easily overlooked, the theory can also be used to identify, explain, and modify existing heuristic effects on people and society groupings, especially where these effects are unhelpful or damaging to society or the environment. Finally the theory was initially developed as an ethical concept for the improvement of society, not as a mechanism for commercial exploitation, or government manipulation.

From this basic theory the concept now offers a vast array of implications and applications. Here we aim to use it as a tool for organisational leadership in business to influence and improve decision making in the interests of a sustainable business.

How behavioural economics informs law and policy

To stumble is human. With every choice we make, individual motivation interacts with emotions, cognition, and social norms. Our decision making stumbles are often the result of the ways in which information is presented and choices are constructed before us. Finding patterns of how we stumble and designing systems that can prevent common behavioural failures is the subject of the new field of behavioural economics which attempts to incorporate the vast knowledge accumulated by cognitive and social scientists into predictive models. The legal community in recent years has focused on creating policies that take into account the limits of human rationality. To do so, law has turned to developments in social science research because, as Richard Epstein recently wrote:

> There is little doubt that the major new theoretical approach to law and economics in the past two decades does not come from either of these two fields. Instead it comes from the adjacent discipline of cognitive psychology, which has now morphed into behavioural economics.[22]

By understanding the ways in which individuals are susceptible to biases and flawed decision making, law and policy can help improve individual and group behaviour.

Humans stumble frequently because we are rather bad at predicting what will make us happy.[23] Moreover, principled ideas about our desires and preferences are often at odds with our immediate choices. *Predictably Irrational*,[24] by Professor Dan Ariely of MIT's Sloan School of Management, is a tour de force analysis of the field of judgement and decision making.

Neoclassical economics, while generally averse to regulation, allows that under certain conditions of imperfect information, regulation may be an appropriate response.[25] The behavioural insights enormously expand the world of imperfect information. Once one accepts that many of our decisions are based on imperfect, biased, and inaccurate calculations of expected benefits and costs, then it becomes clear that market failure is pervasive. The question of whether policy can and should strive to correct for imperfect decisions, however, depends on the prior question of whether and how behavioural biases can be subject to corrective measures. Observing the many deviations from rational behaviour, often referred to as biased behaviour, it is argued that appropriate corrective measures must consider that the various biases have unique origins and thus must be counteracted in different ways.

A vast body of research in psychology, neuroscience, and decision making focused on determining the types of mechanisms that may generate biases, points to two types of biases: those that stem from reflexive or intuitive processes governing behaviour unchecked (Type 1 biases derived from System 1 processes), and those that arise precisely because of processes that are meant to control, monitor, and override the intuitive responses (Type 2 biases derived from System 2 processes).[26] In lay terms, one may think about this as a distinction between biases that are caused by people not thinking carefully and those that are caused by people thinking, or indeed thinking too much. Nudge theory[27] describes System 1 induced biases as cases in which our 'automatic system' induces us to continue making the wrong choices even after we cognitively know about the bias. According to Thaler and Sunstein, de-biasing can occur in such cases when our 'reflective system' disciplines the automatic system.[28] The distinction between System 1 and System 2 failures traces a plethora of dual-processes cognitive models, such as automatic–controlled, emotional–cognitive, reflexive–reflective, and many others; but the logic that manifests in all of them with respect to overcoming biases is almost the same.

Rational choice theory

Although there are multiple interpretations of rational choice theory (RCT)[29] a common assumption is that individuals are rational actors whose decisions are driven by the desire to maximise utility given resource constraints.[30] RCT, at its core, assumes that individuals hold stable preferences and seek out the necessary information regarding their set of options prior to making a decision. Ultimately, decisions are made on the basis of a deliberate analysis of the expected payoffs of a set of options, considering both their desirability and their probability of occurring. A choice is considered rational if there is no alternative that provides a more optimal outcome to the individual.[31] This approach remains prominent within law and economics, at least implicitly, as seen in the types of policy mechanisms that are often advocated.[32]

In the broadest application of RCT, individuals are conceived of as rational in the sense that they act deliberately to maximise their own interests; yet the individual's interests are subjectively defined. Thus, an individual could act to maximise objectively defined monetary outcomes or subjectively defined social outcomes. However, in both cases it should be expected that the individual will act in a manner that is consistent with his/her own goals. It is this version of RCT that has been most often applied by psychologists and those in the social sciences, as well as a growing number of economists, because it accommodates both monetary and social drivers of behaviour such as group membership and social norms.[33] The emphasis on subjective, rather than objective, well-being is largely due to a growing field of research that has revealed a host of non-monetary motivations that influence decision making, sometimes to the point of overwhelming the role of financial self interest.

In addition to questions about the definition of self interest, additional work within the behavioural sciences has questioned whether it can be assumed that individuals actually make calculated considerations of costs and benefits, even when self interest is expanded to include non-economic drivers of behaviour. For example, empirical studies have challenged the view that individuals truly hold a set of stable preferences, as is presumed by RCT. Psychologists and behavioural economists have found that preferences are highly contingent on factors such as how choices are framed and the temporal distance between costs and benefits.[34] However, despite its shortcomings, RCT continues to be a dominant model in legal policy frameworks.[35] Nevertheless it is nudge theory which is used, with some reference to RCT, in our suggestions in the next chapter.

New governance as third way ordering

Thaler and Sunstein suggest that lessons from experimental psychology and economics can revolutionise the field of law and policy, informing a new species of regulation, which they identify as 'libertarian paternalism'.[36] This concept refers to the idea that law can be formulated as default rules which use behavioural insights to help individuals reach their preferred choices, whilst allowing them to maintain the freedom to make their own choices, including mistakes, by an opt out.

Nudge defines 'libertarian paternalism' as including 'actions, rules and other nudges that can be easily avoided by opting out'.[37] However, the lessons of behavioural economics suggest that people tend to remain with the default presented to them.[38] Therefore preferences are endogenously shaped by the framing and setting of defaults. Preferences are adaptive and can change within the same individual over time as expectations and desires continue to be heavily influenced and shaped by social situations. In other words, defaults themselves are norm generating. This points to the inevitability of a normative stance in any legal order. Nevertheless, while human preferences can be a moving target, one feature of individual preferences is well established in the behavioural literature; that is that individuals value the ability to control their lives, paths and choices. Just as voluntariness, agency and choice are matters of degree, there are no bright lines between coercive intervention and mere 'soft' guidance. There are, however, real and important differences among education, manipulation, and coercion.

However, an alternative school of thought, termed 'new governance', of influencing senior managers' decision making is put forward. New governance offers a comprehensive vision for policy reform, one that integrates design with incentives, collaboration with control, process with monitoring and enforcement.[39] These 'new governance' approaches aim to bring together insights from interdisciplinary research on regulation and the changing demands of a new global economy. New governance scholars have a different starting point from that of behavioural law and economic scholars. Whilst the latter begin with the limits of the individual choice, new governance scholars begin with the limits of traditional regulation. Ultimately, however, the two circles of scholarship find themselves in similar territories: much like individual decision making, law is a problem solving venture.[40] Improved decision making becomes both a goal for regulation and a challenge for regulators, who are themselves decision makers with human fallibility.

Looking at business regulation around the world, Braithwaite and Drahos have described the 'rise of a new regulatory state, where states do not so much run things as regulate them or monitor self regulation'.[41] In other words, the focus is on providing 'nudges' in the form of carrots, information, design, and processes, rather than rigid commands and sticks.

New governance theory views adversarial commands as potentially counterproductive. Behavioural insights about social norms and motivation indicate that adversarialism reduces the willingness of companies and individuals to share information and to engage in mutually beneficial problem solving. Lobel[42] states that the exclusive focus on enforcement impedes the ability of industry to consult with regulators as expert authorities. Firms are more reluctant to share information on cost reduction and innovative techniques. They are also reluctant to freely deliberate with the agency in order to find mutually beneficial solutions. In order to allow for such continuous improvement through the self monitoring of corporations, government regulations can be phased in as standards and norms rather than rigid rules and commands. In fact, regulations are often deliberately ambiguous and open to multiple interpretations. Instead of regulating the details of behaviour, agencies increasingly use broad policy goals such as 'risk management' and allow the regulated industries to implement and interpret these mandates.[43] These initiatives also build on the insight that law has a norm generating value in addition to its direct control over individuals and corporations. The law offers principled reasons and justifications for action beyond its direct tangible prohibitions and results,[44] such that as matters of external normative judgement, laws are judged according to their effects rather than any articulated rationales. Sunstein states that many people support law because of the statements made by law, and disagreements about law are frequently debates over the expressive content of the law.[45] In other words, the regulatory regime creates a relational contract between government and industry that in turn supports the generation of private norms.[46] In fact, ends and means of our actions and choices are inextricably linked; not simply preferences, but also principles and values are contingent on our environments and experiences.[47]

Together with behavioural economics, which studies individual behaviour, judgement, and decision making, the fields of organisational behaviour and the sociology of institutions provide lessons for regulators about the impact of internal processes on compliance. Empirical evidence indicates that institutional culture and design have a significant impact on the likelihood that individuals will engage in unlawful behaviour.[48] For example, in the discrimination context, policymakers increasingly recognise that employers' organisational choices can both facilitate and constrain the development of discriminatory work cultures.

After Enron and other more recent corporate scandals, Securities and Exchange Commission Chairman in the USA, William Donaldson, declared that 'the most important thing that a Board of Directors should do is determine the elements that must be embedded in the company's DNA'. He continued by explaining: 'In humans, DNA encompasses the very building blocks of life and determines or influences almost every aspect of our physical development. So too should the moral DNA of a company.'[49] This idea of corporate DNA finds much support in recent behavioural economics and social psychology literature.[50]

CEOs as decision makers

Having considered the contribution of the social sciences to how people make decisions we consider the Chief Executive Officer's dominance or centrality, which describes the power of the CEO within corporate ranks and his/her influence over the board of directors.[51] CEO dominance occurs when the board permits the CEO to exert too much power and influence over corporate decision making and abdicates the board's responsibility to rein in CEOs who engage in behaviour contrary to the best interests of the corporation and its shareholders. CEO dominance can be a problematic corporate governance issue because by the time the problem manifests, it is often after the fraud, illegal activity, or mismanagement has caused harm to the corporation and its reputation.

Recent corporate scandals have revealed that, in some instances, strong willed CEOs manipulated the governance process.[52] Although boards corrupted by influence of a dominant CEO may engage in dubious decision making, social science researchers conclude that charismatic leaders, like individuals typically leading public companies, run corporate affairs by sheer force of personality.[53] The leadership qualities of the CEO combined with the group thinking of the directors coalesce to form a corporate governance environment in which few individuals are willing to disagree with or speak honestly to the CEO.[54]

Corporate scandals continue to generate debate over solutions, yet a long history of social science research suggests that dominant leaders can readily corrupt the group. In cohesive groups such as boards, certain psychological behaviour of the group and its leader is predictable.[55] Notwithstanding the research on dominant individuals and group behaviour, state corporate law does not directly address the organisational structure in which CEOs corrupt the corporate governance process. And yet it is quite normal for active CEOs to sit on boards of other companies.

However, literature posits that some CEOs who are overconfident may benefit the company by forcing through certain policies. Whilst CEO over-confidence is associated with innovation,[56] it is also associated with over investment and risk taking,[57] potentially leading to increased CEO turnover.[58] However, improving internal governance and disclosure can help restrain overconfident CEOs. Therefore, appropriate changes to governance and advisory structures could help capitalise on the optimism of overconfident CEOs to create stakeholder value. In the USA the Sarbanes–Oxley Act has increased oversight and exposure to diverse view points from majority independent boards which improves decision making by overconfident CEOs.[59]

Can boards control the CEO?

Over 70 per cent of outside directors rely exclusively on executive management for information.[60] Fewer than half of CEOs believe their board of directors understands the strategic factors that determine their corporate success,[61] in fact, some long term directors 'confess that they don't really understand how their companies make money'.[62] Yet corporate law expects that boards of directors will stop managers from behaving badly. It assumes that the ultimate governing authority within the corporation rests with their boards, and not with the managers who run them.[63] State company law, judicial decisions and a significant body of legal scholarship are reliant upon the uniquely powerful position that boards control within the corporate hierarchy.

Regulations have been designed to move boards from an 'arms length' monitoring role to a more hands on monitoring role, as the normative propositions that inform them support the idea of more active board involvement. However, for this to be effective board members need more knowledge and familiarity with the corporation on whose boards they sit. Regulations have, nevertheless, done the opposite. Policymakers have ignored the importance of decision making processes and have reduced director knowledge and familiarity through increasing director independence. As a result boards are designed to fail.[64]

In practice, corporate boards of directors do not have the authority granted to them in theory and law. As a normative matter, dominant theories of corporate control and legal reforms meant to improve corporate governance require directors to monitor managers and exercise authority in doing so. Boards of directors cannot exercise the authority granted to them in theory and law unless they have better mechanisms with which to make decisions. By utilising insights into group decision making from organisational behaviour theory they can help to establish the board's decision making authority. In other words, an effective process provides power, and without one, board authority is only a theory and not reality.

CEO remuneration

The corporate governance debate has recently focused on executive compensation. Whilst defenders of the status quo assert that CEO compensation, and corporate governance generally, is efficient, critics contend that the boards have been captured by powerful CEOs who demand excessive remuneration packages unconditional on their performance. Critics argue that the problem lies with the incentives of the board of directors, which has the sole authority to hire the CEO and negotiate his/her compensation. The board owes a fiduciary duty to represent the corporation's interests,[65] but the critics contend that directors' self interest lies with the CEO, not the corporation. Directors realise that the CEO exercises enormous influence over the corporation's nominees to the board, and that the corporation's candidates are almost always elected. Both sides argue that the evidence garnered from CEO compensation justifies their positions on legal reform of corporate governance as a whole. Nevertheless, defenders of the status quo argue that the system works well as it is, pointing to the enormous success of US corporations as evidence. Critics concerned about managerial power propose reforms that will increase the board's responsiveness to shareholders, thus enhancing the board's willingness to act as a check against untrammelled CEO power. Michael Dorff argues that the problem with CEO compensation in public corporations may be caused by the decision making flaws rooted in group dynamics, in particular groupthink and social cascades.[66]

Behavioural economists and social psychologists have for decades studied a set of behavioural phenomena termed as 'groupthink'. This stems from membership of a cohesive group, such as a public corporation board of directors. Irving Janis, who is the leading pioneer in the field, identified seven flaws that often recur in the decision making processes of such groups.[67]

Other group decision making defects stem from social cascades.[68] Social cascades form when individuals in a group possess little knowledge about the subject at hand and therefore rely on others who profess knowledge to make the decisions. This leads to the majority following the early lead of those who profess knowledge which they may not necessarily have.[69] This 'may result in a "cascade" effect, in which large numbers of people repeat the leader's actions.'[70]

These decision making flaws provide an alternative explanation for many of the executive pay structure weaknesses observed by critics. In other words, directors may use inefficient mechanisms to pay senior executives because flaws in their decision making processes interfere with their selection of more efficient compensation devices.

Under group dynamics theory, the role played by CEOs is more ambiguous than under Management Power. Executives may actively manipulate the process in an effort to garner greater compensation, taking advantage of the board's vulnerabilities, playing a role similar to that outlined by managerial power theorists.[71] Most managerial power theorists have cited the *amount* of executive compensation as evidence of a flaw in the compensation setting system.[72]

Recently however, managerial power theorists have taken a great leap forward with the work of Lucian Bebchuk and Jesse Fried, in their groundbreaking book *Pay Without Performance: The Unfulfilled Promise of Executive Compensation,* in which they turn to the structure of executive compensation, rather than the absolute amount, for evidence of managerial power's impact.

Managerial power theory

Managerial power focuses on directors' self interest in explaining the apparent inefficiencies found in many executive compensation packages and the large amount of total executive compensation.[73] The theory argues that directorships are highly desirable, lucrative, and prestigious positions, which individuals are eager to gain and reluctant to give up.[74] It could be argued that directorships' desirability, therefore, would induce board members to pursue shareholders' interests, to secure re-election, but research demonstrates that directors wish to serve management's interests, not shareholders'.[75] Board elections are rarely contested, outside of the hostile takeover context, so the candidates nominated by the corporation nearly always secure election.

Group dynamics theory

Groupthink consists of a set of decision making flaws characteristic of cohesive groups which strive for unanimity.[76] In other words, cohesive groups often forgo the opportunity to consult with experts from outside the group who might provide data or opinions that undermine the favoured option. Even when confronted with contrary data, cohesive groups tend to ignore information that argues against the favoured policy, and to highlight the information that supports that policy. Finally, cohesive groups neglect to form contingency plans to deal with foreseeable obstacles to success.[77] However, some cohesion is useful, but too much cohesion leads to groupthink.

Groupthink seems likely to develop on many corporate boards, as Janis argued that both friendship and prestige tend to promote group cohesiveness.[78] He also argued that a groups' lack of diversity in training and background also contributes to groupthink.[79] Public company boards overwhelmingly consist of white, middle aged men from privileged backgrounds who have spent their careers working for large corporations. Although this homogeneity can contribute to the board's effectiveness by facilitating communication, such lack of diversity also reduces dissent, contributing to groupthink.[80]

Nevertheless, there are limits to the power of groupthink to produce inefficient outcomes. As groupthink depends on the power of consensus, and not self interest, the phenomenon should have more difficulty producing decisions that are obviously wrong.

Social cascades

When people make a decision sequentially, and that decision is public, at some point in the chain individuals may begin to ignore their private information in favour of the crowd's views.[81] This response may be a rational calculation that the crowd has more information than any single individual. Alternatively, it may represent an attempt to preserve reputation, at the expense of making an incorrect decision.[82] Reputation induced cascades in this way share many of the characteristics of groupthink, but cascades caused by lack of private information may respond differently.

The behaviour of individuals involved in social cascades may be rational, particularly when the board member has little other information. Most board members are generally either CEOs of other public companies or company lawyers, investment bankers, or former politicians.[83] Directors therefore, tend to be highly intelligent, educated, sophisticated, and busy. They have little incentive to spend time working through the details of a complex compensation package, much less to consider alternatives to the traditional forms of compensation. They are far more likely to defer to the status quo, assuming that the sophisticated boards that have made this decision before them have acted correctly.

In addition, CEOs functioning as directors of another company can be expected to experience cognitive dissonance in regard to payment structures that they themselves enjoy.[84] Payment types that are inefficient from stakeholders' perspectives, because they fail to motivate the CEO to act on their behalf, are correspondingly advantageous to CEOs, who are thereby left free to pursue their own interests. Admitting to themselves or their colleagues on the board that a form of compensation is inefficient would require them to confront the knowledge that they have accepted such payments themselves, at the expense of the stakeholders.

The second criterion for a social cascade is that decisions are made sequentially rather than simultaneously.[85] Executive compensation decisions are made at different times by different companies. Chief executive positions become available for a variety of reasons, from planned retirements to sudden terminations. As a result, the CEO's initial hiring, and concomitant compensation negotiations, can take place at any time during the year. Because compensation decisions are not made simultaneously, each board may choose to follow the example of companies that preceded it, rather than follow its own private information about the efficiency of various compensation structures. This is easy to do because of the almost universal use of compensation consultants who provide the board with detailed data on the pay structures and levels of CEOs at 'comparable' corporations.[86]

In addition, if the first few directors to speak on an issue have private information that points in the same direction, the remaining directors may choose to follow their lead, despite possessing some data that point towards a different decision. The first person to speak at a meeting of a compensation consultant is very likely to be the company's compensation consultant.

Reputational concerns may also play a substantial role in a board's compensation decisions. Directors seem unlikely to adopt a compensation mechanism that their peers at other companies may consider to be unorthodox or strange. Such a decision would attract the attention of the financial press and display directors in a poor light, perhaps even damaging their full time careers and reducing their opportunities to serve on additional boards. Once a cascade has taken hold, the resulting decision takes on the legitimacy of the market and any director who wishes to argue for an alternative compensation structure will have to overcome the powerful argument that the market has determined the traditional compensation forms are efficient.

Conclusions

It is difficult to directly observe the operations of boards, mainly due to the company's need for confidentiality, but in considering the psychologists' theories and applying them to the board group dynamics a strong picture emerges as to how the right questions may produce the 'wrong' answers.

Notes

1 Arora, Anu (2011) 'The Corporate Governance Failings in Financial Institutions and Directors' Legal Liability', 32 *Company Lawyer* 1.
2 Posner, Richard A. (2009) *A Failure of Capitalism*, Cambridge, MA: Harvard University Press.

3 Deepwater Horizon Study Group (2011) *Final Report of the Investigation of the Macondo Well Blowout*, Center for Catastrophic Risk Management, California: University of Berkeley.
4 Posner (2009), p. 80.
5 Stout, Lynn (2012) *The Shareholder Value Myth: How Putting Shareholders First Harms Investors, Corporations, and the Public*, San Francisco, CA: Brett-Koehler Publishing.
6 Sunstein, Cass R. (2013) 'Nudges.gov: Behavioral Economics and Regulation', ch. 28 in E. Zamil and D. Teichman (eds), *Oxford Handbook of Behavioural Economics and the Law*, Oxford: Oxford University Press.
7 OECD (2010) *Consumer Policy Toolkit*. http://www.keepeek.com/Digital-Asset-Management/oecd/governance/consumer-policy-toolkit_9789264079663-en.
8 http://dl4a.org/uploads/pdf/1dg-sanco-brochure-consumer-behaviour-final.pdf.
9 http://ec.europa.eu/environment/enveco/economics_policy/pdf/Behaviour%20Policy %20Brief.pdf.
10 Sunstein (2013), p. 2.
11 Based on Sunstein (2013).
12 Levin, Irwin P., Sandra L. Schneider and Gary G. Gaeth (1998) 'All Frames are not Created Equal: A Typology and Critical Analysis of Framing Effects', 76 *Organisational Behaviour and Human Decision Processes*, 2, 149–188.
13 Hirshleifer, D. (1995) 'The Blind Leading the Blind: Social Influence, Fads, and Informational Cascades', in M. Tommasi and K. Ierulle (eds), *The New Economics of Human Behavior*, Cambridge, UK: Cambridge University Press, pp. 188–215; Saez, E. (2003) 'The Role of Information and Social Interactions in Retirement Plan Decisions: Evidence From a Randomised Experiment', 118 *The Quarterly Journal of Economics* 3, 815–942.
14 Sharot, T. (2011) *The Optimism Bias: A Tour of the Irrationally Positive Brain*, New York, NY: Knopf Publishing.
15 Kahneman, D. and S. Frederick (2002) 'Representativeness Revisited: Attribute Substitution in Intuitive Judgment', in T. Gilovich, D. Griffin and D. Kahneman (eds), *Heuristics and Biases: The Psychology of Intuitive Judgement*, Cambridge and New York: Cambridge University Press, pp. 49–81.
16 Lowenstein, G.F. (2001) 'Risks as Feelings', 127 *Psychological Bulletin* 2, 267–286.
17 Thaler, Richard and Cass Sunstein (2008) *Nudge: Improving Decisions About Health, Wealth, and Happiness*, New Haven: Yale University Press, p. 34.
18 Sunstein (2013), p. 31.
19 Epstein, Richard (2006) 'Behavioural Economics: Human Errors and Market Corrections', 73 *University of Chicago Law Review* 111, 125–128.
20 Thaler and Sustein (2008).
21 Kahneman, Daniel (2012) *Thinking, Fast and Slow*, New York: Farrar, Straus and Giroux.
22 Epstein, Richard A. (2007) 'The Neoclassical Economics of Consumer Contracts', 92 *Minnesota Law Review* 803.
23 Gilbert, Daniel (2006) *Stumbling on Happiness*, New York: Vintage Books, pp. 230–32, describing the difficulty people have in assessing the impact of various events on their overall happiness.
24 Ariely, Dan (2010) *Predictably Irrational: The Hidden Forces that Shape our Decisions*, New York: HarperCollins.
25 Epstein (2006).
26 Kahneman and Frederick (2002), pp. 49, 51.
27 Thaler and Sustein (2008), pp. 19–22.
28 Ibid., p. 234.

29 Korobkin, Russell B. and Thomas S. Ulen (2000) 'Law and Behavioral Science: Removing the Rationality Assumption from Law and Economics', 88 *California Law Review* 4, 1070–1074.

30 Colman, Andrew M. (2003) 'Cooperation, Psychological Game Theory, and Limitations of Rationality in Social Interactions', *Behavioral and Brain Sciences* vol. 26(2), pp. 139–153, p. 139.

31 Becker, Gary S. (1976) *The Economic Approach to Human Behaviour*, Chicago and London: University of Chicago Press.

32 Scott, Robert (2000) 'The Limits of Behavioural Theories of Law and Social Norms', *Virginia Law Review*, vol. 86, no. 8, pp. 1603–1647.

33 Dawes, Robyn M. (1980) 'Social Dilemmas', *Annual Review of Psychology* vol. 31, pp. 169–193 at pp. 175–178.

34 Hoch, Stephen J. and George F. Loewenstein (1991) 'Time-inconsistent Preferences and Consumer Self Control', *Journal of Consumer Research* vol. 17, pp. 492–507, p. 497.

35 Stern, Paul C. (2000) 'Towards a Coherent Theory of Environmentally Significant Behaviour', *Journal of Social Issues* vol. 56, no. 3, pp. 407–424 at pp. 419–420.

36 Thaler and Sunstein (2008), pp. 4–6.

37 Ibid., p. 248.

38 Ibid., pp. 7–8, 83.

39 Lobel, Orly (2004) 'The Renew Deal: The Fall of Regulation and the Rise of Governance in Contemporary Legal Thought', 89 *Minnesota Law Review* 342.

40 Simon, W. (2004) 'Solving Problems vs Claiming Rights: the Pragmatist Challenge to Legal Liberalism', *William & Mary Law Review* vol. 46, pp. 177–178 at p. 127.

41 Braithwaite, John and Peter Drahos (2000) *Global Business Regulation*, Cambridge: Cambridge University Press.

42 Lobel, Orly (2005) 'Interlocking Regulatory and Industrial Relations: The Governance of Workplace Safety', vol. 57, issue 4, *Administrative Law Review*, pp. 1071–1151 at p. 1090.

43 Bamberer, Kenneth A. (2006) 'Regulation as Delegation: Private Firms, Decision-making, and Accountability in the Administrative State', *Duke Law Journal* vol. 56, no. 2, pp. 377–468 at p. 380.

44 Anderson, Elizabeth S. and Richard H. Pildes (2000) 'Expressive Theories of Law: A General Restatement', *University of Pennsylvania Law Review* vol. 148, no. 5, pp. 1503–1575 at p. 1513.

45 Sunstein, Cass R. (1996) 'On the Expressive Function of Law', *University of Pennsylvania Law Review* vol. 144, no. 5, pp. 2021–2053 at p. 2022.

46 McMaster, Robert and John W. Sawkins (1996) 'The Contract State, Trust Distortion, and Efficiency', *Review of Social Economy* vol. 52, issue 2, pp. 145–167 at pp. 149–156.

47 Simon, William H. (2006) 'Toyota Jurisprudence: Legal Theory and Rolling Rule Regimes', in G. de Burca and J. Scott (eds), *Law and New Governance in the EU and the US*, Portland, OR: Hart Publishing, p. 37.

48 Arlen, Jennifer and Reiner Kraakman (1997) 'Controlling Corporate Misconduct: An Analysis of Corporate Liability Regimes', 72 *New York University Law Review* 687, 692–693.

49 Donaldson, William (2003) Speech by SEC Chairman: Remarks before the Economic Club of New York, http://www.sec.gov/news/speech/spch050803whd.htm.

50 Lobel, Orly (2009) 'Citizenship, Organizational Citizenship, and the Laws of Overlapping Obligations', *California Law Review*, 31; Sober, Elliott and David Sloan Wilson (1999) *Unto Others: the Evolution and Psychology of Unselfish Behavior*, Cambridge, MA: Harvard University Press, p. 173.

51 Greenspan, Alan (Chairman of the Board of Governors of the Federal Reserve System) (2002) Federal Reserve's Second Monetary Policy Report for 2002:

Hearing Before the Committee on Banking Housing and Urban Affairs, 107th Congress, pp. 7–32. http://papers.ssrn.com/sol3/papers.cfm?abstract_id=266683.

52 Bainbridge, Stephen M. (2002) 'Why a Board? Group Decision Making in Corporate Governance', 55 *Vanderbilt Law Review* 1, 51–54.

53 Hogg, Michael, A. (2005) 'Social Identity and Misuse of Power: The Dark Side of Leadership, 70 *Brooklyn Law Review* 1239.

54 Bainbridge (2002) describes how group thinking is common in board decision making and encourages board members to value conformity over quality decision making.

55 O'Connor, Marleen (2003) 'The Enron Board: The Perils of Groupthink', 71 *University of Cincinnati Law Review* 1233.

56 Hirshleifer, David, Angie Low and Siew Hong Teoh (2012) 'Are Overconfident CEOs Better Innovators?' 67 *Journal of Finance* 4, 1457–1498.

57 Malmendier, Ulrike and Geoffrey Tate (2005) 'CEO Overconfidence and Corporate Investment', *Journal of Finance* 2661–2700.

58 Campbell, David, David Edgar and George Stonehouse (2011) *Business Strategy: An Introduction*, London: Palgrave Macmillan.

59 Banerjee, Suman, Mark Humphrey-Jenner and Vikram Nanda (2014) 'Restraining Overconfident CEOs through Improved Governance: Evidence from the Sarbanes-Oxley Act', Seminar at University of Calgary, 22 December.

60 Nadler, D. (2004) 'Building Better Boards', *Harvard Business Review* vol. 82, no. 5, pp. 102–111, at p. 110.

61 Carter, Colin B. and Jay W. Lorsch, (2013) *Back to the Drawing Board: Designing Corporate Boards for a Complex World*, Harvard Business School Press, pp. 23–24.

62 Nadler (2004), p. 110.

63 Stout, Lynn (2003) 'On the Proper Motives of Corporate Directors', 28 *Delaware Journal of Corporate Law* 1, 2.

64 Sharpe, N. (2012) 'Questioning Authority: Why Boards do not Control Managers and how a Better Board Process can Help', University of Illinois, working paper.

65 *Smith v Van Gorkom*, 488 A 2d 858, 872 (Del. 1985).

66 Dorff, Michael (2007) 'Group Dynamics Theory of Executive Compensation', 28 *Cardozo Law Review.*

67 Janis, Irving (1982) *Groupthink: Psychological Studies of Policy Decisions and Fiascoes*, 2nd edn, Houghton Mifflin Company.

68 O'Connor (2003), p. 1240.

69 Bikhchandani, Sushil, David Hirshleifer and Ivo Welch (1998) 'Learning from the Behaviour of Others: Conformity, Fads, and Informational Cascades', *Journal of Economic Perspectives* vol. 12, no. 3, pp. 151–170 at p. 154.

70 Banerjee, Abhijit V. (1992) 'A Simple Model of Herd Behaviour', *Quarterly Journal of Economics* vol. 107, no. 3, pp. 797–817.

71 Bebchuk, Lucian and Jesse Fried (2004) *Pay without Performance: The Unfulfilled Promise of Executive Compensation*, Cambridge, MA: Harvard University Press.

72 Dorff (2007), p. 256.

73 Bebchuk and Fried (2004), p. 23.

74 Ibid.

75 Price Waterhouse Coopers Survey (2005) *What Directors Think, The Corporate Board Member*, p. 14. https://www.pwc.com/us/en/corporate-governance/assets/what-directors-think-2008.pdf.

76 Janis (1982), pp. 9–10.

77 Ibid.

78 Ibid., p. 247.

79 Ibid., p. 250.

80 Fanto, James A. (2004) 'Whistleblowing and the Public Director: Countering Corporate Inner Circles', *Oregon Law Review* vol. 83, no. 2, pp. 335–540 at pp. 462–466.

81 Sunstein, Cass R. (2000) 'Deliberative Trouble? Why Groups Go to Extremes', *Yale Law Journal* vol. 110, no. 1, pp. 71–118 at p. 82.
82 Ibid., p. 78.
83 Dorff (2007), p. 265.
84 Cognitive dissonance refers to individuals' discomfort when their actions contradict their beliefs. People tend to act to reduce their cognitive dissonance by changing their beliefs to justify their behaviour. Festinger, Leon (1957) *A Theory of Cognitive Dissonance*, Stanford: Stanford University Press, pp. 1–31.
85 Shiller, Robert J. (1995) 'Conversation, Information, and Herd Behaviour', 85 *American Economic Review* 181–183, p. 181.
86 Bebchuk and Fried (2004), p. 37.

10 A number of ways forward

Forward, forward let us range,
 Let the great world spin for ever down the ringing groves of change
                              (Lord Tennyson, *Locksley Hall*, 1842, l. 181)

Introduction

The challenge of controlling directorial behaviour is intrinsic in large public companies characterised by dispersed shareholding. This is prevalent in both the US and the UK tradition and has given rise to a number of legal issues revolving around three main areas. First is the direction of corporate activity and in whose interest it should be pursued to make the company sustainable through both hard and soft law. In other words, does hard law at the state level, which leads to short termism, need changing, or can we rely on soft law in the shape of international principles, codes, and guidance, which encourages a more long term view, to influence senior managers to make decisions regarding sustainability of the company. The second concerns the relationship between shareholders and directors as regards their conflicting interests, in particular their short term and long term interests; in other words can the interests of the directors and those of the shareholders, particularly institutional shareholders, be realigned to be consistent with long term sustainability? And the third area concerns the set of duties that are designed to align the senior managers' interests to those of the company by using tools from social psychology, that is, nudge theory and the use of cultural types in different jurisdictions.

Regulatory initiatives

No one doubts any longer that sustainable development is a normative imperative, and yet there is unmistakably a reluctance to acknowledge any legal basis upon which companies are obliged to forgo 'shareholder value' when such a policy clearly dilutes responsibility for company action in the face of continuing environmental degradation.

This influence of shareholder primacy means that there has been little exploration of how far boards, the strategy setting, supervisory organs of companies, are legally permitted to go in moving towards sustainable business. Boards frequently do not even choose the environmentally friendly, low carbon option where there is an arguable business case, let alone challenge the outer boundaries of the rules by pursuing sustainability where the profitability of a particular decision may be challenged. The practice of companies in the aggregate is therefore detrimental both to those affected by climate change and environmental degradation and to future generations, whose ability to fulfil their own needs is in peril. 'Business as usual' is in fact detrimental both to any shareholder with more than a very short term perspective on their investment, including institutional investors such as pension funds and sovereign wealth funds. At the individual company level shareholder primacy has negative implications for the long term prospects of the company itself.

In the context of corporate groups, shareholder primacy is even more prominent, with the parent company's control of the group going way beyond the scope of company law combined with very limited possibilities for holding the parent company liable for subsidiaries' environmental transgressions.

Whilst company law gives those who control companies ample scope to take account of sustainability, company law has also allowed the social imperative of shareholder primacy to develop to the point that it constitutes the main barrier to more sustainable companies. This has occurred because of what the law regulates and what it does not. Suggestions for legal reform have been put forward by a team working under the auspices of Oslo University, some of which are discussed below.[1]

Companies addressing sustainability issues must have a strategy and policy to manage those issues which affect their stakeholders. Multinational companies recognise that they can play an active role in the forms of engagement through their operations, product and services and public policy engagement. The multinationals and their stakeholders need to understand how they can contribute to the global issues of energy access, energy efficiency and renewable energy use. The multinational company should indicate how they will contribute to innovation and transfer of new technology for the purpose of addressing these global issues.

It is generally understood that for the global issues to be sufficiently addressed, there will need to be a degree of technology transfer from the developed nations to the developing nations and intellectual property rights will play some part in achieving this objective. This technology transfer trend could be business led or legislation led. The majority of the mature national intellectual property legislation has a certain degree of resilience by which access to relevant climate change technology may be facilitated. However, some degree of legal reform could be beneficial to prevent any abuse of the intellectual property rights system and encourage technology transfer. The reforms could be in the areas of compulsory licensing, exclusion from protection, length of protection terms, free movement of trade and anti-competition legislation. Multinationals need to consider how they will manage and disclose their sustainability performance and whether they will commit to transferring their technologies into developing regions in which they operate, in line with the guiding principles of the World Trade Organization's TRIPS[2] agreement and the Guidelines for Multinational Enterprise of the OECD.[3]

Reforming company law

Nordic corporate governance

The suggestion is to redefine the purpose of the company to explicitly state that the purpose is sustainable value within the planetary boundaries as set out by Johan Rockström.[4]

In Nordic company law, as in many other jurisdictions, the highest administrative organ is the board. It has the overall responsibility for the company's activities, including the strategy, organisation, financial planning and management. The board has a unique role and position in balancing the involved interests.[5] Both the Norwegian and Finnish Companies Acts provide that the board shall promote the interests of the company thus making the primary loyalty of the board to the company. Defining the interests of the company is a key issue for the parties involved in the company and the interests affected by its business generally, and notably, the protection of the environment. However, the company interest is an elusive and controversial concept in most company law within the developed world, and it is no less so in the Nordic countries. Reforming company law to expressly set out the role and the duties of the board consistent with the proposed redefined purpose of the company would clarify the existing state of law and expand the competence and the duty of the board to pursue sustainable value within the non-negotiable planetary boundaries.

Beate Sjåfjell and Jukka Mähönen suggest that a specification of the redefined role of the board should be integrated in the Companies Act's stipulation of the duties of the board in sections 6–12 of the Norwegian Acts and section 1:8 of the Finnish Companies Act,[6] to mandate a clear duty to promote the purpose of the company.

This redefined role of the board would promote the purpose of the company to 'sustainable value' and thus effectively restrict the competence of the board to promote sustainability. This new duty would also clarify the 'business judgement rule', emphasising notably that the due care includes a duty to implement a life cycle analysis of the business of the company and an integrated internal control and risk management system. In other words, the board would have a duty to act if the company is unsustainable in the environmental as well as in the economic sense. This would include taking immediate action to rectify the situation to the greatest possible extent, and if this is not possible, Sjåfjell and Mähönen suggest then steps should be taken to dissolve the company, as in the current rule in Norwegian company law if sufficient financial capital cannot be ensured.[7] This duty of the board to ensure that due diligence and risk management systems are in place would also include the supply chain and other contractual parties. This would also include full transparency through reporting and regular auditing.

Norway has a very progressive company law that includes gender equality in the board room; this has sparked an international debate and is inspiring other countries and the EU to make similar efforts. If all of the suggestions of Sjåfjell and Mähönen are taken up (as with the gender equality legislation) there may be unintended consequences; for example, if boards are required to take steps to dissolve the company for environmental transgressions due to third contractual parties.

Reforming English company law

Andrew Johnston, when reviewing English company law,[8] considers that shareholder primacy is so entrenched in English company law that it is most unlikely that any government would consider any changes which would call into question the issue of shareholder primacy. After the major review of company law in England resulting in the 2006 Companies Act there will be little political will to go through the exercise again soon. However, he does go on to make some suggestions for reform, should the impetus come from the EU.

Under the 2006 Act section 172 requires company directors to promote the success of the company for the benefit of its members as a whole, whilst taking account of a number of stakeholder considerations, including the consequences of any decision in the long term.[9] In fact this gives the directors a very broad remit as to how they interpret this when taking business decisions, as long as they can produce a credible argument that any decision would be likely to produce shareholder returns in future. In addition, the business rule means that the English courts do not police that discretion in any meaningful way. As Johnston remarks, the obstacle to directors using their discretion to include environmental sustainability is not found in law but in the broader corporate governance system.

Directors already have a great deal of discretion in English company law to take advantage of sustainability considerations. However, directors are also given strong incentives to maximise short term shareholder value.[10] The result is that directors do not exercise their legal discretion to take account of sustainability nor externalities.

Johnston puts forward two areas of possible reform. Firstly, the takeover regulation in the UK has prohibited boards from taking measures that frustrate takeover bids. The effect of this is to provide for managers to focus on keeping the share price high enough to deter would-be bidders. This prohibition on 'frustrating action' effects on corporate governance inasmuch as it effectively reduces management's discretion to take account of considerations such as sustainability. For any reforms to be effective this prohibition on frustrating action must be removed. This could be done as the EU Takeover Directive *permits* individual member states *not* to impose the prohibition, and some have taken that course of action.

The other main barrier to directors using their discretion to take greater account of sustainability in their decision making is the practice of executive pay, as most executives are remunerated, to some extent, with stock options, with the effect of aligning their interests with those of the shareholders as expressed in the current share price. However, there is little reason to believe that the share price of companies reflects the long term sustainability of the company.

For English law, then, there are serious ideological and political barriers to the reforming of English company law as a method of governing companies so that they take account of sustainability considerations. However, should reforms be introduced they would need to be both at the core company law level and also in the broader governance system.

United States company law

Likewise US company law provides little incentive to include environmental responsibility in managerial decision making and shareholders have little power to alter this state of affairs.[11] Celia Taylor claims that environmental issues at present remain difficult to quantify economically and therefore the harms caused by climate change and other environmental concerns may seem both remote and uncertain. Although US law is becoming more cognisant of the need to account for environmental impacts under the environmental regulations, the law remains focused on the financial impacts of climate change, with disclosure requirements relying on the 'materiality' of the environmental concern on the company's performance.

As in the UK it is unlikely that an obligation to act in a sustainable manner could be imposed under US law, because company law generally does not dictate managerial behaviour. It is more likely that to achieve the desired result action must be taken to focus on how to best quantify the economic impact of environmental concerns. Once quantified, the cost of environmental decisions will then become part of the profit maximising calculations that directors must engage with when making decisions about company actions. If environmental impacts are economically quantified, the disclosure requirements will be more directly applicable.

In respect of shareholder influence, as they continue to be educated about environmental harms, they can put pressure on company management through shareholder proposals and public campaigns. As discussed previously, this is a way to work within the existing legal regime to encourage responsible environmental actions by US corporations.

This Anglo-American model is unlikely to be changed by regulatory action with regard to sustainability. The current regime allows for consideration of sustainability, but it makes it easy for company management to evade the issues. Taylor suggests that methods to quantify the impacts of environmental harms that are more measurable and certain would advance the degree to which such impacts would be required to be addressed under US law.[12]

Chinese company law

When considering Chinese company law with regard to sustainability, again the stated purpose of the company is profit maximisation for the shareholders with many mandatory rules to protect shareholders' interests.[13] However, the company law and other laws and regulations have relevant articles to protect the interests of all other stakeholders. There is a general acceptance in China that a company should not only work for shareholders as an instrument to make profits but also exist as an entity which cares for the common good of other stakeholders.[14] There is an underlying theory of putting shareholders' interests first and simultaneously caring about other stakeholders in a company.[15] In 2005 the Chinese company law was revised and a specific article on corporate social responsibility (CSR) was added,[16] which provided in article 5 that a company shall, when engaging in business activities, undertake social responsibilities.

A unique point in Chinese company law is the system of the legal representative. In 1986, the *General Principles of the Civil Law of the People's Republic of China (GPCL)* founded a system of legal representatives which is still valid. Under this system the legal representative with the company is the personification of the legal personality of the company and acts for the company in all its dealings with others and in relation to internal administrative management, such as signing contracts etc. According to article 43 of *GPCL*, the legal representative acts on behalf of the company and is normally the chairman, executive director or manager, and is registered. The legal representative is also liable for the company's wrongdoings, and in fact in any criminal proceedings it is the legal representative who is imprisoned and fined, with the company also being fined.[17]

A further point in Chinese company law is article 20 of the law which introduces the principle of disregarding the corporate personality, or piercing the corporate veil in order that a parent company might be held liable for the debts or liabilities, including environmental, of its subsidiaries. However, from the cases studied by Jianbo and Lei, it is easier for the courts to agree to pierce the corporate veil in matters related to contract disputes, etc., as compared to environmental torts or human rights violations.[18]

As China is a collectivist state, Chinese company law has travelled further than the other jurisdictions studied towards sustainability within the legal system. Nordic company law reflects the more collaborative approach, and is cognisant of all stakeholders, but the Anglo-American company law system is fundamentally opposed. As the majority of major international companies, including those in the energy sector, are incorporated under the Anglo-American system of company law, then we need to look to other means and structures to encourage senior decision makers to make the right decisions for the sustainability of the company.

The Community Interest Company

Further thoughts on the restructuring of company law in the search for sustainability are put forward by Carol Liao.[19] This hybrid is suggested as a corporate entity that embodies legal tools which require and/or encourage the pursuit of dual economic and social mandates within business.

It is suggested that by converting into a hybrid, former charities and non-profit organisations may attract venture capital and make a profit, thus lessening their dependence on public funds and enabling better use of the market to disseminate social products and services. On the other hand, profit conscious businesses that convert into a hybrid would be better able to integrate stakeholder interests, social mandates, and sustainable practices into their business models well beyond what is permitted under shareholder primacy. This development would provide opportunities for entrepreneurs seeking to house social enterprises in legal structures that can support their needs whilst affirming that 'the independence of social value and commercial revenue creation is a myth'.[20]

The Community Interest Company (CIC) first appeared in the UK in 2005,[21] with similar hybrid models being explored in other jurisdictions. By the end of 2013 there were over 8,700 CICs registered in the UK with many more being reported each month. The most noteworthy features of the CIC are the asset lock and the dividend cap. These prevent the assets and profits from being transferred out of the company unless the transfer is for full fair market value, or is transferred to another CIC subject to an asset lock or charity, or is otherwise made for a community benefit.[22] Dividends on CIC shares and interest on bonds are capped to ensure that profits are either retained by the CIC or used for a community benefit purpose.[23]

These companies are used mainly for local community purposes currently and it is too early to evaluate whether they will become more than an adjunct to the mainstream corporate model. Nevertheless, in respect of corporate social responsibility, it is the core principle for such hybrid companies.

Control by boards

As we have seen, the challenge of controlling directorial behaviour is intrinsic in large public companies characterised by dispersed shareholding. This is particularly prevalent in both the US and the UK tradition and has given rise to a number of legal issues as identified previously. We have also discussed the problem of 'groupthink' within a board of directors which militates against any board control over the CEO. The lack of necessary competence and independence in boards emerged as a central issue, in addition to the intellectual bias of board members who remained driven by shareholder primacy and by short term goals.

The Report of the environmental disaster which followed the BP oil spill uncovered deep seated problems in the supervision of high risk activities and raised questions on the role and goals of corporations. The nature of BP's business and the obvious repercussions of its activities on society prompted reflections on how such corporations balance different interests.[24] It has been observed that BP repeatedly ignored environmental legislation in favour of pursuit of short term profits from oil extraction.[25] This behaviour was the result of flawed decision making by the board whereby the observation of environmental legislation and CSR was seen as subordinate to the pursuit of shareholder value. In other words, the interests of the other stakeholders at BP were not adequately represented nor considered.

A new institutional framework

Vincenzo Bavoso suggests a new model whereby there is an inclusion on the board of directors of major companies of a state member as an equilibrating arbiter of both economic and social interests. Thus a broader concept of corporate law encompassing wider socio-economic interests would rectify the democratic deficit in large public companies.[26] He suggests that the state, because of its democratic underpinning, is envisaged as the natural custodian of different societal interests.

However, it is the state, through legislation, that has brought about the current regulatory system in most jurisdictions. We have seen above that the Anglo-American model as used by the majority of multinational corporations is fundamentally opposed to change to the shareholder primacy principle. Both the USA and the UK have recently enacted legislation which, in principle, encompasses the stakeholder interests, but major companies continue to use it merely to their marketing advantage.

Soft law imperatives

Boards of directors need to be educated in the soft law imperatives in relation to the long term sustainability of the company. The fact is that shareholders do not *own* public companies, which hold legal or juridical personality. This means they cannot be owned by anyone. Shareholders own their own shares, which gives them certain rights in relation to the company. This means that the shareholders' relationship with the company is analogous to the relationship between the company and other stakeholders, including employees, creditors and bondholders.

The OECD Principles note that self regulation should be a complement to, not a replacement of, hard law requirements. For example, in the UK it has been a soft law requirement for institutional investors to publish their policy on shareholder engagement since the adoption of the 2002 Institutional Shareholders' Committee (ISC) Principles. The obligation was endorsed by reference in the UK Corporate Governance Code in 2003, and has been a 'comply or explain' requirement since the introduction of the 2009 ISC Code, which evolved into the Stewardship Code in 2010. The objective of this requirement has been to foster engagement by institutional shareholders, which are considered to have a longer term approach to corporate governance.

The board should be reminded of its fiduciary duty to act in the best interest of the company. International energy companies should recognise the impact on climate change if they emit large amounts of greenhouse gases. That will entail a cost in the future, thus bringing down the sustainability of the company.

In both the Anglo-American company law model and the Nordic company model the laws as they stand are sufficiently resilient to provide for the long term sustainability of companies if the directors and senior decision makers use their discretion positively, under their fiduciary duties, in the interests of all stakeholders and thus sustainability of the company. Of those companies whose senior personnel were interviewed, it was the companies whose home state was within the Nordic countries which embraced the principle of sustainability most positively.[27]

Control by investors

Sovereign funds

An impressive trend in global financial markets is the growth of sovereign wealth funds (SWFs), some of which claim to invest ethically by considering the social and environmental impact of their financing. Yet, like private investors, these funds primarily view themselves as financial institutions interested in enhancing their investment returns. There is, therefore, a significant tension emerging between the ethical and financial expectations of the SWFs.

Both the Norwegian Government Pension Fund and the New Zealand Superannuation Fund have legislative mandates to invest ethically, and have been hailed by some as having among the most progressive approaches in this area.[28] However, neither fund yet manages its entire portfolio comprehensively to promote sustainable development.

Increasingly nation-states are establishing SWFs in a trend that seemingly defies an era in which many governments have sought to deregulate or otherwise limit their control in the market.[29] In their governance SWFs are public institutions but functionally they are generally expected to be private actors. They invest large amounts of state owned assets in the market to meet macro-economic policy objectives,[30] such as to buffer the sponsoring state's budget and economy against swings in international markets, or to build savings to meet future financial burdens such as pension payouts.

Such concentration of wealth has made SWFs an institutional phenomenon and influential actors in the global economy.[31] With SWFs' assets expected to double within the next decade,[32] and growing awareness of their economic influence and capacity to project state political power, international efforts to create voluntary behavioural codes for such funds have grown. The principle achievement to date is the Santiago Principles,[33] which emphasise transparency, clarity, and equivalent treatment with private funds similarly operated.

SWFs share several characteristics which might lead them more than the private sector financiers to invest in sustainable development. Their ownership or control by a state can carry them into the machinery of government, and thereby render them instruments of public policy. Additionally, because of their size and government backing, SWFs tend to have a higher risk tolerance and might therefore bear investment strategies eschewed by private investors. Further, SWFs necessarily have longer term financial considerations than the private sector, which should encourage investing that is mindful of issues such as climate change.

Conceivably, if each SWF made sustainability a priority, they would be justified in divesting from a vast number of companies. However, because so few companies in the world currently meet rigorous sustainability standards,[34] such an approach would probably be unworkable. Therefore, rather than divesting, the SWF should rely upon a mix of corporate engagement and positive investment in environmental programmes. Such strategies would allow the maintenance of a broadly diversified portfolio without compromising any financial returns. If SWFs acted in concert with other institutional investment groupings this would achieve a critical mass of influence.

Institutional investors

Institutional investors play a major role in global companies. They are critical to individuals, equity markets, publicly held companies, the economy, and to the troubling issue of good versus bad short termism in investor and trustee behaviour. In other words, the fundamental issue is whether institutional investors are part of the problem or part of the solution within the current state of market capitalism. By institutional investors we mean pension funds, mutual funds, insurance companies, hedge funds and endowments of non-profit entities like universities and foundations. Recent developments in public policy in the USA treat shareholders as part of the solution under the Dodd–Frank Act 2010.[35] But with these changes in market and legal powers have come questions about institutional investors that are similar to those raised in the recent past about the companies in which they invest.

For large institutional investors, the sustainability imperative has mostly been theorised through the concept of the 'universal owner'. According to Hawley and Williams, institutional investors who invest widely across the market will benefit financially by taking into account the social and environmental externalities in their portfolios.[36] As economy wide investors, they should 'have no interest in abetting behaviour by any one company that yields a short term boost whilst threatening harm to the economic system as a whole'.[37]

In the UK, institutional investors own and manage more than 70 per cent of the stock market, and now politicians and regulators say that such institutions must share the blame for enabling the financial crisis through passive corporate governance and a focus on short term returns. The EU has charged that the financial crisis has shaken the assumption that shareholders can be relied on to act as responsible owners. Indeed, a movement is growing apace across the developed world to encourage institutional investors to become better stewards of the companies they invest in; by adopting a more active and long term stance, and engaging in governance issues such as board effectiveness, executive remuneration, and succession planning, concurrently with matters such as strategy and risk.[38]

In this respect and in response to climate change risk, which has become a major issue for international companies, the Institutional Investors Group on Climate Change (IIGCC) has issued their expectations of companies in regard of best practice.[39] This is in order to fulfil their fiduciary duty to safeguard the long term interests of their clients and beneficiaries, as they believe it is essential to take action now. As part of these expectations under the governance of the company there must be clearly defined board and senior management responsibilities and accountability processes for managing climate change risks and opportunities. The company must also have a committed strategy and targets.

In respect of the energy sector the IIGCC has issued a specific document recognising that climate change will have an impact on their holdings, portfolios and asset values in the short, medium and long term. They are using their influence and concerns to provide a guide for investors to have a constructive engagement with boards and management of oil and gas companies. Because evidence shows that an energy transition towards lower carbon energy sources is occurring, and major macroeconomic and technological trends are shaping a new direction of travel in favour of low carbon systems, the IIGCC recognises both incremental and disruptive changes in policy, technology and demand dynamics presenting material risks and opportunities to the energy sector. This is a critical time for oil and gas and there need to be resilient business strategies that have been sufficiently stress tested.

The energy sector is no stranger to disruptive technology change, and most recently the exploitation of shale oil and gas in North America has changed the international energy market. The IIGCC, therefore, are advising their members to use their influence and control over the boards in order to ensure that the investee company has a robust and resilient business strategy to encourage a smooth transition to a lower carbon energy system. The expectation is that the investee company will engage with public policy makers and other stakeholders in support of cost effective policy measures to mitigate climate change risks and support low carbon investments, such as those advocated for in the 2014 'Global Investor Statement on Climate Change'.[40] If institutional investors exert such long term scenario testing requirements upon the investee company then control by major institutional investors could become part of the solution against the current short termism.

Nudging senior managers to do the right thing

In experiments at Stanford University carried out by Greg Walton[41] discoveries are made every month that attest to how a sense of belonging and purpose can boost performance in astonishing ways. As Professor Jennifer Aaker put it: 'Stories serve as glue to unify communities. Stories spread from employee to employee, from consumer to consumer…strong stories can be told and retold. They become infectious.'[42] The tragedy is that many organisations neglect the power of the narrative. At some companies the culture is largely cynical. There is little about history or tradition. Instead there is a management view that employees, including the board and the CEO, are there only to collect a cheque, with the consequence that employees act as if the pay cheque is the only reason to be there.

Robert Reich, the Secretary of Labor under Bill Clinton and a renowned economist, has noted how language alters when people feel that they are part of an organisation; when they are there for reasons other than money. He called it the 'pronoun test'. He asked frontline workers to tell him about the company: if the answers described the company using the words 'them' or 'they', he knew it was a particular type of place; if the answers included 'we' or 'us' then he knew he was in 'a new world'.[43]

As with frontline workers, so with CEOs and directors of companies; if they can align themselves and their self interest to that of the company and all stakeholders they may make the right decisions to make a more sustainable company.

It is recognised that the most effective and sustainable changes in behaviour will come from the successful integration of cultural, regulatory and individual change. Stiff penalties, good advertising and shifting social norms all combined to change the behaviour of drink drivers over a number of years.[44] To change the decision making behaviour of senior managers will need the same approach. The Law School at Oslo University has considered how the law could change in different jurisdictions to support sustainable companies. Some of these we have considered above. The use of soft law, in forms of international principles, guidelines, and social norms, are already in place. However, the main response that came from all of the interviews conducted by the authors was that 'loss of reputation' for either the individual or the company was the strongest motivation for considering CSR and sustainability.

Drawing on psychology and the behavioural sciences, we have seen that the basic insight of behavioural economics is that our behaviour is guided not by perfect logic and the analysis of the costs and benefits of each action, but it is led by our human, sociable, emotional and sometimes fallible brain. In other words, the sophisticated mental shortcuts that serve decision makers so well in much of life can also lead to making unsustainable decisions in the long term.

How can we use social psychology to nudge those decision makers into recognising that certain activities could lead to the loss of that prized 'reputation'?

Case study of the BP Macondo well blowout disaster

The University of California set up a Study Group to investigate the BP Macondo well blowout and produced a number of reports on their findings.

We have quoted a number of passages from these reports to identify points where the decision making process had been at fault. Based on these quotes we then go on to analyse, through the prism of the UK Government document 'MINDSPACE' checklist of influences on behaviour, the possible reasons for such breakdowns in the decision making process.

> This disaster was preventable had existing progressive guidelines and practices been followed. This catastrophic failure appears to have resulted from multiple violations of laws of public resource development, and its proper regulatory oversight.[45]
>
> ... these failures (to contain, control, mitigate, plan, and clean-up) appear to be deeply rooted in a multi-decade history of organizational malfunction and shortsightedness. There were multiple opportunities to properly assess the likelihoods and consequences of organizational decisions (i.e., Risk Assessment and Management) that were ostensibly driven by the management's desire to 'close the competitive gap' and improve bottom line performance. Consequently, although there were multiple chances to do the right things in the right ways at the right times, management's perspective failed to recognise and accept its own fallibilities despite a record of recent accidents in the U.S. and a series of promises to change BP's safety culture.[46]
>
> As a result of a cascade of deeply flawed failure and signal analysis, decision making, communication, and organizational – managerial processes, safety was compromised to the point that the blowout occurred with catastrophic effects.[47]
>
> At the time of the Macondo blowout, BP's corporate culture remained one that was embedded in risk-taking and cost cutting – it was like that in 2005 (Texas City), in 2006 (Alaska North Slope Spill), and in 2010 ('The Spill'). Perhaps there is no clear cut 'evidence' that someone in BP or in the other organizations in the Macondo well project made a conscious decision to put costs before safety; nevertheless, that misses the point. It is the underlying 'unconscious mind' that governs the actions of an organisation and its personnel. Cultural influences that permeate an organisation and an industry and manifest in actions that can either promote and nurture a high reliability organization with high reliability systems, or actions reflective of complacency, excessive risk taking, and a loss of situational awareness.[48]

MINDSPACE

Influencing behaviour is nothing new to governments in both the USA and the UK as the vast majority of public policy aims to shape our behaviour. The UK has developed a tool called MINDSPACE[49] which here we will use to evaluate the decision making process at the Macondo oil well and suggest some ways forward.

The checklist for policymakers called 'MINDSPACE' was developed by the Institute for Government in the UK after the Cabinet Office commissioned research to explore the application of behavioural theory to public policy. The research showed that there was a real interest in behavioural theory and how to translate the theory into practice. The research group, therefore, developed the checklist as a tool to make sure that policymakers take account of the effects of individuals' behaviour.

The acronym takes the first letter of each area to be considered as follows:[50]

- *'Messenger'*: This identifies the fact that people are influenced by who communicates information to them. The Macondo Report found that decision makers did not follow the rules and procedures laid down. Whilst expertise matters, so do peer effects and so in practice a consensus across the company as to the importance of health and safety regulations, for example, and risk analysis should be embedded into the company culture. There should be face to face instruction. Governments may not be prepared to intervene with new legislation as we have seen, therefore soft law in the form of international groupings' guidelines should be employed by companies to identify the benefits of stakeholder inclusion for the sustainability of the company.
- *'Incentives*: our responses to incentives are shaped by predictable mental shortcuts such as strongly avoiding losses.' As discussed in Chapter 9, CEOs incentives are normally based on financial rewards of some kind. However, as research shows that this has little effect in the long term then the alternative would be a loss or charge to be imposed if boards and CEOs failed to do something. The fear of losing money creates a strong incentive. In extreme cases, the loss of liberty, as under Chinese company law, would be an even stronger incentive. The Report found that there was 'a culture with incentives that provided increases in productivity without commensurate increases in protection'.[51]
- *'Norms'*: Individuals tend to do what those around them are already doing. In Chapter 9 we noted that boards of directors usually included at least one who was a CEO of another company and so in respect of remuneration this influenced the whole board. If institutional and SWF shareholders used their power to change the makeup of the remuneration committee so as not to include any CEO from another company the committee could consider the remuneration packages in another light and change the accepted norm. The Report found that the industrial governance management environments unwittingly acted to facilitate progressive degradation and destruction of the barriers provided to prevent failures. A more visible pro-stakeholder norm should be encouraged and mainstreamed throughout the company.
- *'Defaults*: we normally "go with the flow" of pre-set options.' Many decisions have a default option, which exerts influence as most people will accept the default setting, even if it has consequences. This default

setting is often selected through natural ordering or convenience, rather than to maximise benefits for all stakeholders. Structuring the default option to maximise benefits for all stakeholders can influence behaviour without restricting the individual choice of the board member. The Macondo Report found that although there were meetings held with operations personnel at the same time and place the initial failures were developing, the meetings were intended to congratulate the operating crews and organisations for their excellent records for *worker safety*. This demonstrates that there are important differences between *worker safety* and *system safety*. One does not assure the other. Loss concentrates the mind, and so the media coverage and the loss of both reputation and share value for BP should encourage other multinational oil companies to be more aware of the down side of 'going with the flow', of making macho decisions in a macho industry.

- '*Salience*: our attention is drawn to what is novel and seems relevant to us.' In everyday life individuals are bombarded with stimuli, which are unconsciously filtered out as a coping strategy. In order to stand out, such stimuli must be novel, accessible and simple. For example, how gains and losses are expressed can influence the decision maker. Because individuals find losses more salient than gains, the decision makers will react differently when identical information is framed in terms of one or the other. The Report shows that if existing progressive guidelines and practices had been followed (the Best Available and Safest Technology) the disaster could have been prevented. BP's organisations and operating teams did not possess a functional safety culture.[52] Too many choices can lead to people making poor decisions and may even lead to people refraining from making any choice at all.[53] The design of a simple matrix can help people to make the right decision in a particular circumstance.

- '*Priming*: our acts are often influenced by sub-conscious cues.' Primers are real and robust and have been repeatedly proven in many studies. The Macondo Report states that 'the tradeoffs that were made were perceived as safe in a normalized framework of business as usual'.[54] Companies should consider how the wider visible environment in which people work may prime a safety culture.

- '*Affect*': Emotional responses to words, images and events can be rapid and automatic. 'Risk assessment and management...were ostensibly driven by BP management's desire to "close the competitive gap" and improve the bottom line performance.'[55] A reminder of the major BP incidents at Texas City in 2005, and the Alaska North Slope Spill in 2006, could have been highlighted on notice boards around the installation to remind workers of the possible result of taking short cuts with safety.

- '*Commitment*: we seek to be consistent with our public promises, and reciprocate acts.' Individuals have a very strong incentive to achieve a stated goal. Unfortunately BP was committed to 'close the competitive gap' and improve the bottom line, rather than to a safe working environment.

- '*Ego*: we act in ways that make us feel better about ourselves.' At the time BP was running a marketing campaign of 'Beyond Petroleum' which highlighted the 'green credentials' of the company. In all of our interviews the respondents gave 'loss of reputation' as the main trigger for them to think about making the right decision for the sustainability of the company. This demonstrated a core allegiance with the company and themselves.

Nearly everyone wishes to work for a 'good company', even if different people tend to emphasise different things when defining it. To enable behaviour changes in senior decision makers we need to recognise the practical and structural barriers that people face. Some may be regulatory, some the attitude of the major shareholders, whilst others could be the nature of the business sector in which they operate. Any attempt to encourage new behaviours needs to consider the wider contexts and choices available, but applying such tools as MINDSPACE will handle most of the 'heavy lifting' in behavioural change.

As the Nobel Prize winning psychologist Daniel Kahneman states:

> We tend to believe that somebody is behaving that way because he wants to behave that way, because he tends to behave that way, because that's his nature. It turns out that the environmental effects on behaviour are a lot stronger than most people expect.[56]

Holding senior decision makers responsible for their actions can only be done if they can act rationally, supported by substantive freedom of choice.

Long term value

Larry Fink, the CEO and Chairman of BlackRock,[57] has sent a letter to the chairpersons of more than 200 companies across Britain and the European continent, calling on them to resist the temptation to use bumper payouts and cash returns to win short term popularity with some shareholders. He says that handing back cash to investors risks sending a 'discouraging message' that executives have no credible plan to put money to better use by investing it in development and growth. Fink says that there is 'nothing inherently wrong' with returning capital to shareholders in a 'measured fashion'.

> It is critical, however, to understand that corporate leaders' duty of care and loyalty is not to every investor or trader who owns their companies' shares, but to the company and its long term owners. Successfully fulfilling that duty requires that corporate leaders engage with a company's long term providers of capital; that they resist the pressure of short term shareholders to extract value from the company if it would compromise value creation for long term owners; and most importantly that they clearly and effectively articulate their strategy for sustainable long term growth.[58]

Larry Fink has also written to the chief executives of 500 companies in the USA, making a similar case.

Looking to the future trends

Campaign aims to turn oil companies into climate allies

A new campaign to require fossil fuel companies to disclose any risks to the company created from their dependence on carbon assets has been set up by a group of investors, companies and non-profit organisations. The prime movers are Ceres, based in Boston, USA, and Carbon Tracker, based in London. The campaign issued a letter from 50 major global investors which called upon the U.S. Securities and Exchange Commission (SEC) to improve oil and gas companies' disclosure of any risks of possible reduced demand for their products or risk of lower prices due to climate change. Such risks would affect the oil companies' profitability if they found themselves with 'stranded assets' such as fossil fuel reserves which may lose their value.

The SEC had issued guidance on the need to disclose climate related risks to investors to all publicly traded companies in 2010.

The letter to the SEC highlighted the 'inadequate disclosures' from ExxonMobil, Chevron and Canadian Natural Resources to emphasise the need for the SEC to make its guidance stronger. However, the Cleveland Oil Company said that if the SEC required companies to disclose any reduced demand for oil products, this would affect their business. It is expected that such disclosure will affect investors' decisions. However, if the fossil fuel companies' directors take such risks seriously they should consider new strategies for making the company sustainable in a carbon constrained world.[59]

Influences of social media

Social media is a phenomenon that influences all aspects of society. Not only do political parties, governments and companies, to name but a few, now use social media for real time information giving, but also NGOs. In fact NGOs have long used their worldwide contacts to hold international corporations to account for their environmental and social behaviour and we have considered some famous cases within these chapters.

However, with the advent of instant social media and information going 'viral', what restraints, if any, are there on the users of social media to behave ethically themselves?

NGOs and lobbyists often have large amounts of financial backing, and groups operating in different jurisdictions throughout the world; they have highly trained professionals working for them. They are able to influence government and legislation both at the state and international level, but how are they constrained?

Quis custodiet ipsos custodes?

Who will guard the guards themselves, or in other words who will make sure that the NGOs, in this era of fast social media, will make sure that they get their facts right? We recall the damage caused to both the reputation and financial efficacy of Shell when the activists from Greenpeace boarded the Brent Spar installation in the North Sea. Shell garages were boycotted both in the UK and Germany and people would not buy petrol/gasoline. However, when the facts were published Greenpeace had 'got it wrong'. But Shell had lost both reputation and money.

In an era of fast news do the NGOs have a reciprocal duty to act responsibly?

Conclusions

Perspectives on the long term

As the recession of 2008 recedes in memory, meaningful reforms have yet to be made despite many calls for action.[60] One issue for sustainable companies is shifting markets and companies from quarterly capitalism to a true longer term way of thinking, and thereby renewing the fundamental ways companies are governed, managed, and led. Achieving that change, however, requires wide ranging shifts in both mindset and practice.

Psychology and reframing mindsets and language

CEOs argue that it is meeting quarterly earnings expectations that prevents them from creating long term economic value. However, the structure of incentives for both CEOs and financial market participants makes short term results more alluring than long term gains. However, it is the forces of a cognitive asymmetry between the uncertainty of long term actions and the certainty of short term actions, with the need to maintain ongoing credibility and to continue to enjoy the license to lead, and the desire to leave a legacy, with the knowledge that it is difficult to do so, which influences CEO decision making.[61]

These internal, psychological forces that drive CEOs to favour the short term over the long term are worth keeping in mind as we consider the causes of the growing managerial myopia. As we know, managerial time horizons are influenced by incentives and compensation, but as discussed above, there are more psychological forces at work, and trying to understand them better is the first step towards trying to design smart counterweights.[62]

Within Chinese culture, long termism is a national ethos. A willingness to forgo short term gratification and keep faith with the fundamentals is at the heart of Chinese philosophy and value discipline. Over the years the Chinese have learned that it is not the time horizon that matters most but the mindset and discipline. The Chinese have also learnt that the right word engenders the right attitude and the right behaviour. For example, in their reports the

Chinese use the phrase 'sustainable results' rather than 'consistent results'. This demonstrates thinking long term instead of short term.

Governance and reporting

Unless long term thinking becomes the driving force behind governance activities of boards, no amount of change to management incentives or investor behaviour will be sufficient to ensure a focus on the long term. Although most boards have focused on broadening their diversity of gender and ethnicity, it is the diversity of thought that is at least as important. Board recruitment should be considered as an opportunity to add additional expertise and perspective to the board, so that collectively the directors bring experience, expertise, diversity of perspectives, and wisdom to test strategy and become true advisors to the CEO.

Research shows a link between integrated reporting and long term investment.[63] Not only can it help an organisation to better understand and connect the disparate sources and drivers of long term value to improve the formulation of strategy and decision making, but it also provides a synthesis of how value is created. This helps to win trust and secure a company's reputation by encouraging better relationships with investors, employees, and other stakeholders.[64]

Notes

1 Beate Sjåfjell and Benjamin J. Richardson (eds) (2015) *Company Law and Sustainability: Legal Barriers and Opportunities*, Cambridge: Cambridge University Press.
2 https://www.wto.org/english/docs_e/legal_e/27-trips_03_e.htm.
3 http://www.oecd.org/corporate/mne/.
4 Johan Rockström, Will Steffen, Kevin Noone et al. (2009) 'Planetary Boundaries Exploring the Safe Operating Space for Humanity', 14 *Ecology and Society* 20, 32. www.ecologyandsociety.org/vol14/iss2/art32/.
5 Kraakman, Reiner R., John Armour, Paul Davis et al. (2009) *The Anatomy of Corporate Law: A Comparative and Functional Approach*, 2nd edn, Oxford: Oxford University Press, p. 14.
6 Sjåfjell, Beate and Mähönen, Jukka (2014) *Upgrading the Nordic Corporate Governance Model for Sustainable Companies*, University of Oslo Faculty of Law Legal Studies Research Paper Series no. 2014–18.
7 Norwegian Companies Acts section 3–4.
8 Johnston, Andrew (2014) *Reforming English Company Law to Promote Sustainable Companies*, University of Oslo Faculty of Law Legal Studies Research Paper Series no. 2014–05.
9 In fact the Company Law Reform Cm 6456 at 16 states that 'the success of the company for the benefit of its members…can only be achieved by taking due account of longer term performance and wider interests'.
10 Johnston (2014).
11 Taylor, Celia (2012) *United States Company Law as it Impacts Corporate Environmental Behaviour, with Emphasis on Climate Change*, University of Oslo Faculty of Law Legal Studies Research Paper Series no. 2012–31.

12 Ibid., p. 36.
13 Jianbo, Lou and Lei, Tian (2013) *A Study on Sustainable Companies in the P.R. China*, University of Oslo Faculty of Law Legal Studies Research Paper Series no. 2013–05.
14 Jianbo, Lou (ed.) (2009) *Studies on Corporate Social Responsibility*, Peking University Press.
15 Hansong, M. (2010) 'Financial Enterprises Social Responsibility under the Perspective of Stakeholder Theory', 1 *Morality and Civilisation*, 55.
16 Jianbo, Lou and Xiuhua, Guo (2009) 'The Core Idea of CSR and its Practice in China', in L. Jianbo et al. (eds), *Studies on Corporate Social Responsibility*, Peking University Press, pp. 78, 80.
17 See, *The People's Procurator of Chen XI County v Huai Hua Jinli Chemical Co. Ltd.; The People's Procurator of Jin Jiang District, Chengdu City v Jian; The People's Procuratorate of Pan'an County v Yi Wu Huayi Fine Chemical Co. Ltd.; The People's Procuratorate of Ming Shan County v Ming Shan Hengda Chemical Co. Ltd. Etc.*
18 Jianbo and Lei (2013), p. 62.
19 Liao, Carol (2014) 'Disruptive Innovation and the Global Emergence of Hybrid Corporate Legal Structures', 11 *European Company Law* 2, 67.
20 Julie Battilana, Matthew Lee, John Walker and Cheryl Dorsey (2012) 'In Search of the Hybrid Ideal', 51 *Stanford Social Innovation Review*, 52.
21 UK Companies (Audit, Investigations, and Community Enterprise) Act 2004, c 27, s 172; Community Interest Company Regulations 2005, no.1788.
22 UK Companies Act, sec. 30, 31; CIC Regulations, Part 6.
23 UK Companies Act, sec. 51, 94.
24 Nick Lin-Hi and Igor Blumberg (2011) 'The Relationship between Corporate Governance, Global Governance, and Sustainable Profits: Lessons Learned from BP', 11 *Corporate Governance* 5, 571.
25 Miriam A. Cherry and Judd F. Sneirson (2011) 'Beyond Profit: Rethinking Corporate Social Responsibility and Greenwashing after the BP Oil Disaster', *Tulane Law Review* vol. 85, no. 4, pp. 983–1040 at p. 114.
26 Vincenzo Bavoso (2014) *Sustainable Companies through Enlightened Boards: Combining Private and Public Interest in the Decision-making of Large Public Firms*, University of Oslo Faculty of Law Legal Studies Research Paper Series no. 2014–02.
27 For example Statoil and IKEA.
28 United Nations Environment Programme – Finance Initiative (UNEP-FI) Asset Management Working Group and UK Social Investment Forum (UKIF) (2007) *Responsible Investment in Focus: How Leading Public Pension Funds are Meeting the Challenge*, 7.
29 Ashby Monk (2011) 'Sovereignty in the Era of Global Capitalism: The Rise of Sovereign Wealth Funds and the Power of Finance', 43 *Environment and Planning* 8, 1813–1832.
30 A. Blundell-Wignall, Y. Hu and J. Yermo (2008) 'Sovereign Wealth and Pension Fund Issues', 14 *OECD Working Papers on Insurance and Private Pensions* 4.
31 Rumu Sarker (2010) 'Sovereign Wealth Funds as a Development Tool for ASEAN Nations: From Social Wealth to Social Responsibility'. *Georgetown Journal of International Law* vol. 41, issue 3, pp. 621–623.
32 Sovereign Wealth Fund Institute, http://www.swfinstitute.org.
33 Available at http://www.iwg-swf.org/pubs/eng/santiagoprinciples.pdf //
34 Paul Shrivastava and Stuart Hart (1995) 'Creating Sustainable Corporations', *Business Strategy and the Environment* vol. 4, issue 3, pp. 154–165 at p. 163.
35 Dodd-Frank Wall Street Reform and Consumer Protection Act, Pub. L. 111–203. https://www.sec.gov/about/laws/wallstreetreform-cpa.pdf

36 James P. Hawley and Andrew T. Williams (2000) *The Rise of Fiduciary Capitalism: How Institutional Investors Can Make Corporate America More Democratic*, University of Pennsylvania Press.

37 Stephen Davis, Jon Lukomnik and David Pitt-Watson (2006) *The New Capitalists: How Citizen Investors are Reshaping the Corporate Agenda*, Boston, MA: Harvard Business Press, p. 18.

38 Simon Wong (2010) 'How Institutional Investors Should Step Up as Owners', McKinsey & Company, http://www.mckinsey.com/insights/risk_management/how_institutional_investors_should_step_up_as_owners.

39 http://www.iigcc.org/publications/publication/2014-global-investor-statement-on-climate-change

40 AIGCC, IGCC, IIGCC, INCR, PRI, and UNEP-FI (2014) 'Global Investor Statement on Climate Change', http://investorsonclimatechange.org/wp-content/uploads/2014/09/GlobalinvestoresStatement2014_Final.pdf.

41 Gregory Walton, Department of Psychology, Stanford University.

42 http://universitywebinars.org/university-lecture-on-harnessing-the-power-of-stories-from-jennifer-aaker-at-stanford/

43 Syed, M. (2015) 'Bournemouth a prime example of team who have embraced the club', *The Times*, 27 April, London, p. 20.

44 Itzhak Yanovitzky and Courtney Bennet (1999) 'Media Attention, Institutional Response and Health Behaviour Change: The Case of Drunk Driving 1978–1996', *Communication Research*, 26(4): 429–543.

45 Deepwater Horizon Study Group (2010) *Investigation of the Macondo Well Blowout Disaster*, http://ccrm.berkeley.edu/pdfs_papers/bea_pdfs/dhsgfinalreport-march2011-tag.pdf.

46 Ibid.

47 The Third progress report. P. 4 December 1st 2010. http://ccrm.berkeley.edu/pdfs_papers/bea_pdfs/dhsg_thirdprogressreportfinal.pdf

48 Ibid., p. 4.

49 Cabinet Office (n.d.) 'MINDSPACE: Influencing Behaviour through Public Policy', http://www.instituteforgovernment.org.uk/publications/mindspace.

50 Ibid., p. 18.

51 Deepwater Horizon Study Group (2011) Final Report, p. 10.

52 Ibid., p. 9.

53 Ibid., p. 9.

54 Ibid., note xlvi at p. 9.

55 Ibid., p. 9.

56 Quoted in Cabinet Office (n.d.), p. 71.

57 BlackRock manages about US $4.65 trillion in assets and is an owner of shares in virtually every quoted company in Britain, as well as internationally.

58 Miles Costello (2015) 'Ditch the Dividends, Demands BlackRock', *The Times*, 15 April, London.

59 Marc Gunther (2015) 'Campaign Aims to Turn Oil Companies into Climate Allies, *The Guardian*, 17 April.

60 Dominic Barton and Mark Wiseman (2015) 'Where Boards Fall Short', *Harvard Business Review*, January–February, https://hbr.org/2015/01/where-boards-fall-short; Dominic Barton (2011) 'Capitalism for the Long Term', *Harvard Business Review*, March, https://hbr.org/2011/03/capitalism-for-the-long-term.

61 Dominic Barton and Mark Wiseman (2015) 'Perspectives on the Long Term', *McKinsey Quarterly*, March.

62 Nitin Nohria and Nicholas G. Carr (2015) 'Confronting psychology and technology', in Barton & Wiseman, 'Perspectives on the long term', *McKinsey Quarterly*, March 2015.

63 George Serafeim (2014) 'Integrated Reporting and investor clientele', Harvard working paper, number 14–069, February 2014 revised April 2014, www.hbs.edu.

64 The Chartered Institute of Management Accountants and Tomorrow's Company (a London based international think tank) have produced a tool kit of questions that aims to promote boardroom discussion on integrated reporting and in particular the importance of a thorough understanding of the organisation's business model and how it creates value. See www.tomorrowscompany.com.

Index

For Product Safety Concerns and Information please contact our EU
representative GPSR@taylorandfrancis.com Taylor & Francis Verlag GmbH,
Kaufingerstraße 24, 80331 München, Germany

Printed and bound by CPI Group (UK) Ltd, Croydon, CR0 4YY
08/05/2025
01864343-0001